POPULATION, LABOR FORCE, AND LONG SWINGS IN ECONOMIC GROWTH / THE AMERICAN EXPERIENCE

NATIONAL BUREAU OF ECONOMIC RESEARCH

NUMBER 86, GENERAL SERIES

Population, Labor Force, and Long Swings in Economic Growth

THE AMERICAN EXPERIENCE

RICHARD A. EASTERLIN

UNIVERSITY OF PENNSYLVANIA

NATIONAL BUREAU OF ECONOMIC RESEARCH

New York 1968

Distributed by COLUMBIA UNIVERSITY PRESS

New York and London

TO SIMON KUZNETS WHO TAUGHT ME
THE MEANING OF SOCIAL SCIENCE

RELATION OF THE DIRECTORS TO THE WORK AND PUBLICATIONS OF THE NATIONAL BUREAU OF ECONOMIC RESEARCH

1. The object of the National Bureau of Economic Research is to ascertain and to present to the public important economic facts and their interpretation in a scientific and impartial manner. The Board of Directors is charged with the responsibility of ensuring that the work of the National Bureau is carried on in strict conformity with this object.

2. The President of the National Bureau shall submit to the Board of Directors, or to its Executive Committee, for their formal adoption all specific proposals for research to be instituted.

3. No research report shall be published until the President shall have submitted to each member of the Board the manuscript proposed for publication, and such information as will, in his opinion and in the opinion of the author, serve to determine the suitability of the report for publication in accordance with the principles of the National Bureau. Each manuscript shall contain a summary drawing attention to the nature and treatment of the problem studied, the character of the data and their utilization in the report, and the main conclusions reached.

4. For each manuscript so submitted, a special committee of the Board shall be appointed by majority agreement of the President and Vice Presidents (or by the Executive Committee in case of inability to decide on the part of the President and Vice Presidents), consisting of three directors selected as nearly as may be one from each general division of the Board. The names of the special manuscript committee shall be stated to each Director when the manuscript is submitted to him. It shall be the duty of each member of the special manuscript committee to read the manuscript. If each member of the manuscript committee signifies his approval within thirty days of the transmittal of the manuscript, the report may be published. If at the end of that period any member of the manuscript committee withholds his approval, the President shall then notify each member of the Board, requesting approval or disapproval of publication, and thirty days additional shall be granted for this purpose. The manuscript shall then not be published unless at least a majority of the entire Board who shall have voted on the proposal within the time fixed for the receipt of votes shall have approved.

5. No manuscript may be published, though approved by each member of the special manuscript committee, until forty-five days have elapsed from the transmittal of the report in manuscript form. The interval is allowed for the receipt of any memorandum of dissent or reservation, together with a brief statement of his reasons, that any member may wish to express; and such memorandum of dissent or reservation shall be published with the manuscript if he so desires. Publication does not, however, imply that each member of the Board has read the manuscript, or that either members of the Board in general or the special committee have passed on its validity in every detail.

6. Publications of the National Bureau issued for informational purposes concerning the work of the Bureau and its staff, or issued to inform the public of activities of Bureau staff, and volumes issued as a result of various conferences involving the National Bureau shall contain a specific disclaimer noting that such publication has not passed through the normal review procedures required in this resolution. The Executive Committee of the Board is charged with review of all such publications from time to time to ensure that they do not take on the character of formal research reports of the National Bureau, requiring formal Board approval.

7. Unless otherwise determined by the Board or exempted by the terms of paragraph 6, a copy of this resolution shall be printed in each National Bureau publication.

(*Resolution adopted October 25, 1926, and revised February 6, 1933, February 24, 1941, and April 20, 1968*)

CONTENTS

TABLES

FIGURES

This study builds directly both on some of the oldest and some of the newest National Bureau work. Along with national income and business cycles, international migration was one of the first subjects to which attention was directed at the Bureau. In 1926, this work yielded Harry Jerome's analysis of the relation between international migration and economic activity during the business cycle, probably still the leading work on the subject. Not long thereafter, the monumental two-volume study, *International Migrations,* compiled by Imre Ferenczi and Walter Willcox, was published. On the subject of long swings, Arthur Burns' *Production Trends in the United States since 1870* (1934), closely linked in conception to Simon Kuznets' *Secular Movements in Production and Prices* (1930), contributed important insights into what he termed the "trend cycle."

Since World War II, Kuznets has returned to the subject of long swings and, in particular, examined demographic aspects in the NBER Occasional Paper which he wrote in collaboration with Ernest Rubin (1954) and in his book *Capital in the American Economy: Its Formation and Financing* (1961). In addition to this last, other studies in the series on capital formation and financing devoting special attention to long swings are those by Grebler, Blank, Winnick, and Melville Ulmer. Mention should be made too of G. H. Evans' earlier study, *Business Incorporations in the United States, 1800–1943* (1948). In the field of labor force, the present volume owes a major debt to Clarence Long's *The Labor Force under Changing Income and Employment* (1958).

While Kuznets' work on long swings was only a part of research projects on which he was engaged, in the 1950's Moses Abramovitz initiated a project on long swings as such. NBER publications resulting specifically from this work are *Evidences of Long Swings in Aggregate Construction Since the Civil War* (1964) and Manuel Gottlieb's technical paper, *Estimates of Residential Building, United States, 1840–1939* (1964).

The present study was initiated in late 1958 as part of the Abramovitz project and intended to focus specifically on demographic aspects of the U.S. swings. An initial manuscript, "Long Swings in American Labor Force Growth, 1870–1950," was completed in 1961. The final results of the project are presented in this volume, of which Chapter 2 summarizes the main findings of the earlier manuscript. Chapter 4 has previously appeared as an NBER publication.

Acknowledgments should start first with explicit recognition of the extent to which this study builds on a number of major historical monographs in the field of population and labor force. Without attempting to be exhaustive, mention should be made of contributions by Gertrude Bancroft, Donald Bogue, Carol Brainerd, M. Claire Casey, Daniel Carson, R. O. Carleton, John D. Durand, Alba M. Edwards, Hope T. Eldridge, E. P. Hutchinson, David L. Kaplan, A. J. Jaffe, Stanley Lebergott, Everett S. Lee, Ann R. Miller, Gladys L. Palmer, Dorothy S. Thomas, Warren S. Thompson, Leon E. Truesdell, and P. K. Whelpton. Through careful sifting and testing of the primary data, works such as these have served, among other things, to fill out and clarify the historical record. Without them, the present study would not have been possible.

The intellectual debts accumulated in a project of this duration are numerous. The pervasive influence of Simon Kuznets on this study should be apparent to all. A year at Stanford University in 1960–61 provided me with the opportunity to benefit from personal association with Moses Abramovitz as well as from close contact with his work. The ideas in this study owe so much to Abramovitz and Kuznets that I can lay no claim to any uniquely personal contribution. For my indoctrination in demography, my greatest debt is to Dorothy S. Thomas, whose work has and continues to exemplify that field at its best. I am also grateful in this connection to John D. Durand, Hope T. Eldridge, Everett S. Lee, Ann R. Miller, and my other associates at the University of Pennsylvania Population Studies Center who have patiently endured the often naïve and overconfident assertions of an analytical economist. I have benefited too from frequent discussions with my colleagues in the economics department at that university. In particular the support and encouragement of Irving B. Kravis and Sidney Weintraub during the years this study has evolved have been much appreciated. Acknowledgment should also be made of many stimulating exchanges with my associates in the "new" economic history, among them, Kenneth A. H. Buckley, Dorothy S. Brady, Paul A. David, Lance E. Davis, Albert Fishlow, Robert W. Fogel, Robert E. Gallman, Stanley Lebergott, Duncan McDougall, R. Marvin McInnis, Gordon Marker, Douglass C. North, William N. Parker, Nathan Rosenberg, Matthew Simon, Eugene Smolensky, Peter Temin, William G. Whitney, and Maurice Wilkinson. This was especially facilitated by the annual Purdue University seminars, where some of the ideas in this book were first presented.

For helpful observations relating to particular chapters, I am grateful to Omer Galle (Chapter 2); Arthur I. Bloomfield, Irwin Friend, F. Thomas Juster, Robert E. Lipsey, Marc L. Nerlove, and Almarin Phillips (Chapter 3); Arthur A. Campbell, Joseph S. Davis, and W. Lee Hansen (Chapter 4); Campbell, Ronald Freedman, and Alice M. Rivlin (Chapter 5); Robert Summers and Thomas W. Merrick (Chapter 6); and Dave M. O'Neill (Chapter 7).

At the National Bureau, Gary S. Becker, Solomon Fabricant, Jacob Mincer, Geoffrey H. Moore, and Victor R. Fuchs have often made helpful comments. Becker, Mincer, and Moses Abramovitz, who acted as the staff reading committee, reviewed the final manuscript and their suggestions led to a number of improvements. Abramovitz' lengthy and detailed comments on several occasions during the course of this project call for special thanks. The NBER Directors' review committee consisted of Wallace J. Campbell, Douglass C. North, and T. W. Schultz; North's frank views were especially helpful.

During 1963–64, support for this study was provided by a contract with the Office of Manpower Policy, Evaluation and Research, U.S. Department of Labor, under the authority of Title I of the Manpower Development and Training Act of 1962, as amended. Researchers undertaking such projects under government sponsorship are encouraged to express freely their professional judgment. Therefore, points of view or opinions stated in this document do not necessarily represent the official position or policy of the Department of Labor. Among the benefits arising from this grant were the salient comments provided by Joseph S. Zeisel, Gertrude Bancroft, and Sophia Cooper, as well as special tabulations of data. Thanks are also due to Conrad Taeuber, Henry Shryock, and others at the Bureau of the Census, as well as individuals at other official agencies who generously responded to various requests. I am also grateful to the University of Pennsylvania for a sabbatical leave in the fall of 1964, which helped in completion of the study, as well as for the tolerant and encouraging attitude of the administration throughout the course of the project. In 1965–66, when I held a Ford Foundation Faculty Fellowship, part of the time was devoted to this volume. National Science Foundation grant GS-942 contributed in part to the support of this study between September 1, 1965 and August 31, 1967.

In the execution of this study, I have been singularly blessed with assistants of unusual ability and dedication. Most of all I am indebted to Chantal de Molliens Dubrin, who has loyally suffered through the many false turns this study took and has continued to turn out work of the highest quality. At an earlier stage, Marcel Tenenbaum and Radivoj Ristic made extended contributions of exceptionally high quality. Among others who participated at one point or another are Henry Gemery, John Hagner, S. R. Lewis, Jr., Soren T. Neilsen, Adrian Throop, and Regina Weiss. James F. McRee, Jr., Gerald Paul, and Joan R. Tron edited the manuscript, and despite the obstacles I had created did much toward making it a cohesive whole. I am grateful to Robert Dickler for preparing the index. For the charts, which are the heart of the study, I am grateful to H. Irving Forman.

RICHARD A. EASTERLIN

POPULATION, LABOR FORCE, AND LONG SWINGS IN ECONOMIC GROWTH / THE AMERICAN EXPERIENCE

CHAPTER 1 / INTRODUCTION

AND SUMMARY

Since the late 1930's the American economy has been undergoing an immense wave of population growth. One comprehensive study of the postwar economy has characterized this as "perhaps the most unexpected and remarkable social feature of the time . . ." [88, pp. 161–162].* Yet, while its important economic impact is widely acknowledged, the reasons for it and the likelihood of its continuation are questions almost completely ignored by economists.[1] Now the movement appears to be slackening. Is this indeed the case? If so, why is this change occurring? How long and how much of a decline is in prospect? Why did the earlier upsurge occur? Is a resurgence likely in the more distant future? These are questions of some urgency.

Actually such waves in population growth are not new in American experience. The historical record, at least in so far as it can be reconstructed, suggests that marked longer-term fluctuations have occurred since at least the first half of the nineteenth century. Indeed, the existence of such movements in various series relating to demographic phenomena, particularly international migration, had been a recurrent source of comment by specialists.[2] Is it possible that the current U.S. wave is but the most recent manifestation of a more widespread and persistent phenomenon?

EARLIER STUDIES

Unfortunately there has been relatively little intensive research on these movements, even by demographers, so that answers to questions

* EDITOR'S NOTE: All numbers in brackets refer to works cited in bibliography.
[1] A noteworthy exception is the work of Joseph S. Davis [43–45].
[2] For example, though his concern was with short-term business cycle fluctuations, the first substantive observation made by Harry Jerome in his study of international migration relates to the "violence of the major fluctuations" [96, p. 33]. The survey of international migration experience in the study by Willcox and Ferenczi points out these movements and provides extensive evidence on them [65, Part I]. Cf. Losch [117] regarding swings in other demographic series.

such as these are not easily obtained. Over the past few decades, however, one promising line of work has gradually developed which associates these waves in demographic variables with economic phenomena. In the United States, the first such efforts came in connection with the pioneering investigations of the long building cycle by Riggleman, Newman, and others.[3] A major step forward occurred in the early forties with Walter Isard's formulation of the concept of the "transport-building cycle" [92, 93]. Isard placed particular emphasis on population migration and saw such movements as entering into this cycle as both cause and effect. He attempted to support this view with evidence from American experience going back to the 1830's. At virtually the same time, Norman J. Silberling presented views similar in some respects to Isard's [145].

In the 1950's, analysis of these population movements became increasingly associated with the newly emerging subject of long swings in economic growth. The latter, in the past variously termed "long cycles," "secondary secular movements," and "trend cycles," have in recent years increasingly received the more distinctive designation "Kuznets cycles," in recognition of Simon Kuznets' pioneering work and continuing contributions in this area. Brinley Thomas' wide-ranging *Migration and Economic Growth* [156] in 1954 gave a major impetus to linking demographic movements to long swings in economic growth. In the same year, Margaret Gordon's study of employment and population growth in California provided evidence at the local level [77]. In Canada, Kenneth A. H. Buckley conducted several pioneering investigations in this vein [24–26]. Kuznets, who had himself pointed at an early date to the apparent association between demographic and economic swings, presented important evidence not only on international migration but on other components of population change as well [102, 103, 107]. Dorothy S. Thomas demonstrated that swings existed in *internal* migration and were associated with similar movements in economic activity [160, 163]. Moses Abramovitz presented evidence that the swings in demographic variables formed a fairly systematic part of movements in output, input, and productivity generally [4, 5].

[3] Moses Abramovitz' recent examination of long swings in construction reviews the relevant literature [1].

The work of these scholars has in turn stimulated further research. Important recent contributions emphasizing demographic phenomena include studies of the United Kingdom by J. Parry Lewis [113], Australia by Allen Kelley [98], Sweden by Maurice Wilkinson [215], Canada by Donald Daly [40], and Japan by Morris Silver [146].

PURPOSES

The present volume seeks to supplement this literature with a fuller analysis of United States experience than has heretofore been attempted. Descriptively, it seeks to synthesize and extend existing knowledge of the demographic waves; and at the theoretical level, it aims to clarify some of the channels through which economic forces affect demographic magnitudes and are, in turn, affected by them. Its primary purpose, however, is to seek an explanation of the causes and economic effects of the observed demographic swings and thereby to derive new insights into recent experience as well as possible implications for the future.

SCOPE AND TERMINOLOGY

The period covered extends from the 1820's to the present, though due to data considerations the historical analysis is primarily based on the period since 1870. Recent experience is studied in the light of this longer-term perspective ("recent," unless specifically qualified, refers broadly to the period since 1940). I also attempt to assess implications for the future.

Because the labor force is a central point of contact between economic and demographic factors and because the U.S. Census provides concurrent observations on population and labor force, it has been accorded coordinate stress with population. As the inquiry progressed, it became clear too that there was a need for explicit study of growth in the number of households; however, the fact that this was recognized relatively late, coupled with poorer census coverage for this magnitude, made it impossible to treat it as fully as population and labor force.

These three magnitudes—population, labor force, and households

—and their underlying components are collectively described by the term "demographic variables." Any such designation is largely arbitrary; it is adopted here because it provides a convenient rubric and because such population-related magnitudes have typically fallen outside the purview of traditional economic analysis.

The present study uses the terms "long swing" and "Kuznets cycle" interchangeably. The latter term has the advantage of minimizing any confusion with other concepts of longer-term fluctuation, such as the Kondratieff concept, but has the disadvantage of suggesting substantial periodicity. Abramovitz has suggested in an unpublished manuscript that such movements be defined as "swings in the level or rate of growth of a variable with a duration longer than normal business cycles but shorter than the very long swings with which Kondratieff, Schumpeter, and others have been concerned. To permit ample room to consider all the possibly relevant evidence, we might set the minimum limit at five years and the maximum at thirty."

The concern with such movements throughout this study does not imply any precommitment to the view that the long swing is an independent time-series component or that long swings are self-generating, any more than previous NBER studies, such as those by Burns, Kuznets, and Abramovitz, in which this or an equivalent concept has been employed. Given this interest in demographic waves and the growing tendency in the literature to associate these waves with swings in economic growth, it was clear from the start that the exploration of the long-swings concept would be one promising line of inquiry. As is shown in Part I, certain repetitive features of the swings, together with related theoretical considerations, tentatively supported the economic meaningfulness of the concept. Accordingly, it was employed in the interpretations set forth in Part I and subsequent parts. However, a thorough inquiry into the validity of the concept would lead into theoretical and statistical issues ranging beyond the present study's main concern. Moreover, the validity of much of what is said here concerning these relationships does not depend on whether or not there "really" is a long swing. It is possible to view "long swings" simply as a convenient statistical framework for testing the postulated relationships, a framework whose adoption follows naturally from the intermittent nature of the observations on many of the basic magnitudes.

SOURCES AND METHODS

A scholar interested in quantitative study of an extended historical period is ill-advised to have strong preconceptions about data requirements and statistical methodology. All too soon he will find himself pushed to the brink of despair by the fragmentary nature of the data and by problems of conceptual and statistical comparability. He must be prepared, moreover, to become a producer as well as consumer of historical series.

This study, though plagued with its share of such woes, has been fortunate in a number or respects. With regard to demographic variables, it proved possible to use the historical censuses, especially those since 1870, and the immense wealth of detail contained therein as the principal data base for analysis of the period up to World War II. Use of these materials was greatly facilitated by a number of previous monographs on population and labor force (see the Preface for citation of authors) in which problems of comparability and reliability were carefully investigated and long-term trends analyzed. In the case of economic magnitudes, it was possible to draw extensively on well-known historical studies produced by the National Bureau, such as those by Kuznets, Kendrick, Burns, and Creamer, and to benefit from similar efforts by Gallman, Lebergott, North, and others, which were stimulated by emergence of the "new economic history."

For the recent period, principal reliance for data is shifted to official series produced by the Bureau of the Census, Bureau of Labor Statistics, National Office of Vital Statistics, National Income Division, and other agencies. An especially rich source was the population, labor force, and income data obtained in the Current Population Survey which, since the late forties, has provided information formerly unavailable.

The materials for the recent period were usually combined with the historical data in overlapping fashion in order to piece together the picture for the entire period. The resulting mix of annual, quinquennial, and decennial data, of discontinued and overlapping series, provides a substantial and remarkably consistent basis for reconstruction of historical experience, which in itself is a tribute to the effort and dedication that has gone into the estimation of historical time series. It is, nevertheless, an unwieldy body of data for statistical manipulation, and only the simplest techniques of analysis have been used. More rigorous and sophisticated methods could probably have been profitably employed—especially if the full content of the eventual data base had been adequately foreseen—and it is to be hoped that the present study may encourage efforts along those lines.

ORGANIZATION OF THE VOLUME

Part I presents evidence on the nature of the demographic fluctuations and develops the general conception of their cause-effect connections with swings in economic magnitudes, drawing to some extent on the results of the two subsequent parts. Chapter 2 deals primarily with the historical pattern. With regard to evidence of the swings, it deals chiefly with the period through 1950; with regard to the causal analysis, primarily with the pre-World War I period. Chapter 3 develops further the analytical conception of economic-demographic relationships and following that examines recent experience in the light of the longer-term record as well as the implications of the analysis for future long swings. This chapter contains the fullest discussion of the long-swings issue, both its theoretical aspects and contemporary relevance.

Parts II and III, on population and labor force growth, respectively, go more thoroughly into the causes of the demographic movements, focusing particularly on the nature of, and reasons for, the striking differences between recent and earlier experience. Chapter 4 centers on the reasons why fertility played such an important role in the recent upsurge in population growth, whereas in the pre-World War I period migration was the principal underlying component. Chapter 5 updates and extends this "baby boom" analysis to the recent fertility decline. Chapter 6 seeks to explain the disproportionate part played by participation-rate change in the recent upsurge in labor force growth, and Chapter 7 why this rise was largely concentrated among older women. Chapters 3, 5, 6, and 7 contain sections assessing the bearing of the analysis on official population, labor force, and household projections.

Chapters 2 through 5 have been previously published and are presented here with some style revisions, but virtually no change in substance. Although minor repetition occurs, the chapters are very largely complementary rather than duplicative. The original articles were divided between two journals with quite different professional audiences: economists, on the one hand, and demographers, on the other.[4] In bringing them together here the full picture may perhaps be more readily seen.

Part IV gives the data underlying the text analysis and details on sources and methods.

PRINCIPAL CONCLUSIONS

The following summary focuses on the broad issues of the nature of demographic swings and their interrelations with economic conditions. While it incorporates some of the chief findings of the chapters on fertility and labor force, they are subordinated to this more general theme.

Although summarization offers a fresh chance to state the main results in their most succinct form, it inevitably strips an author's findings of the numerous qualifications and reservations with which he has been at pains to clothe them. Moreover, the scope of the present inquiry is such that the potentials for testing are beyond the capacities and resources of a single investigator. Hence, while what follows may convey an air of definiteness, it should be recognized that the statements are in fact more in the nature of hypotheses. While they seem consistent with the data assembled and the analysis attemped here, they are subject to revision and reconsideration as further research accumulates.

Some Facts on U.S. Experience
Pronounced fluctuations usually of some fifteen to twenty-five years' duration in the growth of population, labor force, and households can be traced back at least to the first half of the nineteenth century—though direct data on these variables become increasingly scarce as one moves back in time. The conviction that these swings are not

merely a product of faulty data or methods is buttressed by several considerations. On the statistical side, they cannot be definitely ascribed to known data deficiencies. Moreover, data on demographic variables from various independent official sources provide complementary support for the swings. On the analytical side, certain repetitive features of successive swings come to light if the data are disaggregated. Thus, in the industrial sphere, the swings appear with high regularity in most of the major subdivisions of the nonagricultural sector, and are especially prominent in construction. Spatially, the swings were centered in nonfarm areas and places undergoing new agricultural settlement. Although not every single city or state necessarily participated in every swing, these swings were widely diffused throughout the nation. Finally, the observations on demographic variables, both with regard to the timing of the swings and certain component characteristics, tend to be reinforced by independent readings on nondemographic magnitudes. Thus, similar swings occurred in the growth of output and capital stock. Likewise, the building cycle, or, more generally, an urban development boom, formed a part of the swings.

In the period since 1940, the demographic movements have exhibited some striking differences from the earlier pattern. Previously the component of change principally responsible for the swings in population, labor force, and households was migration, both external and internal. Recently, the dominant components of change have been, respectively, the birth rate, labor force participation rates (particularly of older women), and household-headship rates,[5] although internal migration too has continued to play a part. Moreover, as long as migration was the dominant component, the three aggregative series moved fairly synchronously. However, since 1940, differences in timing have been emerging, and in the 1960's we seem to be witnessing for the first time an upswing in labor force growth accompanied by a continued downswing in population growth. Clearly, an important question is whether such new developments can be reconciled with past experience.

[5] The household-headship rate is defined, by analogy with the labor force participation rate, as the proportion of the population in a given demographic group (e.g., classified by age and sex) who are household heads.

Analytical Viewpoint

Do the demographic swings initiate swings in economic conditions or vice versa? What are the specific cause-effect mechanisms? The possibilities are clearly varied and a number are considered in the subsequent chapters. The main features of the viewpoint emerging from the study are noted below; I will not, however, attempt to incorporate the detailed mechanisms here but will leave this discussion to the body of the volume.

1. *Causes of demographic swings.* Past swings in immigration and more recent swings in fertility, labor force participation, and household-headship rates appear to have been primarily induced by corresponding variations in economic conditions, that is, in income and employment opportunities in the labor market. This is not to suggest that noneconomic factors have no influence at all on demographic behavior; but when one's purpose is to explain pronounced demographic *fluctuations,* the fact that stands out is that economic conditions also exhibit such movements, whereas noneconomic factors usually change only slowly or irregularly.

At a more fundamental level, the changes in income and employment opportunities and associated responses in demographic variables can be traced back to variations in supply-and-demand conditions. Major surges in the growth of labor demand (especially in the nonfarm sector) are seen as occurring in conjunction with conditions in the growth of labor supply which vary with secular, irregular, and other factors. A swing in the growth rate of aggregate demand is characteristically responsible for initiating the demographic movements, but the nature of the induced response varies with the labor supply conditions under which it occurs.

In analyzing demographic behavior, it is often desirable to focus specifically on the group or groups within the total population responsible for the demographic observations. It is not necessarily true that economic indicators for the population as a whole adequately reflect the circumstances of component groups, and mistaken inferences about economic-demographic relationships have sometimes resulted from failure to take account of this fact. In the present study, special attention is often given to young adults, who make most decisions regarding marriage, family formation, and migration.

2. *Economic effects of demographic swings.* A demographic swing, though initiated by economic conditions, may have important feedback effects on the latter. When household growth in nonfarm areas is noticeably accelerated, this generates new demands, not only for housing but for urban services generally. Conditions are thus created for an urban development boom—new real estate activity and residential construction; new municipal investment in roads, water supply, sewers, and so on; new business investment in electricity, telephones, retailing, and similar activities. The source of accelerated household growth could be a surge in in-migration or a general tendency toward an earlier age of household formation. In either case, there would occur a bunching of commitments by households to new and greater spending, extending over several years as a new home is established and a family started or settled. Thus the rise in household growth would lead to an increase in consumer spending and in private and public investment expenditure. This induced rise in the growth of aggregate demand would help cushion the economy against the usual business cycle and would become exhausted only gradually.[6]

A bunching of long-term spending commitments such as this may be the key to Kuznets cycle phenomena. This applies not only to decisions of households but other spending units as well, though no attempt is made here to examine changes in the population of business or governmental units. The investigation stops short too of exploring financial aspects of the swings as well as possible accelerator-type relationships. Whether Kuznets cycles may be self-generating is left open; no more is claimed than that a plausible mechanism has been identified which once initiated, for whatever reason, might help to sustain the economy over a period longer than the usual business cycle.

3. *Interrelations between long swings and secular development.* This sequence of economic-demographic interactions should be seen in the broader context of long-term economic growth. The secular development process sets the stage for the mechanism's operation, since inherent in it is a major imbalance between the geographic distribution of growth in labor demand and labor supply. The evolution of

[6] An analytical possibility not explored in this study is that higher labor force growth may help sustain high output growth and thereby high induced capital formation.

modern technology and rising per capita income increasingly favors concentration of economic activity in nonfarm areas. At the same time, the initial preponderance of agriculture coupled with relatively high rural natural increase provide a labor supply through natural growth which is disproportionately located in farm areas. In a free market economy the need for population redistribution which results tends to be met by the multiplier-type process described above.

Secular and other changes modify the mechanism's operation over time, with resultant shifts in the characteristics displayed by long swings. The nature of the economic opportunities at an early stage of economic development differs from those at a later stage; hence variations occur over time in the specific industrial and geographic sources of increased labor demand. The potential sources of labor supply shift with the secular decline of agriculture, as well as with developments in transportation and foreign economic conditions which influence the potential responsiveness of domestic and foreign labor sources. Irregular factors, such as educational changes affecting labor quality and immigration restriction, also play a part.

Interpretation of U.S. Experience

The analytical supposition is thus that an economic boom engenders a swing in demographic conditions through its impact on the labor market, but that the demographic swing in turn has a feedback effect on economic events through accelerated household growth and associated expenditure effects. Secular conditions set the stage for operation of this mechanism and modify its characteristics over time.

To explain the demographic waves actually experienced in the United States, one must add to this analytical conception the relevant real-world labor supply conditions within which the mechanism tended to operate. The principal (but not only) relevant circumstances are: (1) largely or wholly free immigration through the mid-1920's; thereafter a ceiling but no floor; (2) a farm population growing in absolute size until the first decade or so of this century, then leveling off, and since 1940 declining rapidly; (3) a contribution to labor force growth from natural increase which declines with fair regularity from the last half of the nineteenth century to an all-time low in 1940–55, followed by a recent upsurge; (4) for nonfarm persons outside the labor force—

comprising largely youths, older persons, and females—a mixture of secularly changing conditions affecting their propensity to join the labor force, some of which, such as compulsory education and OASDI, operate to reduce entry, and others, particularly in the case of adult women, to encourage entry.

Consider now the typical sequence set in motion by an upswing in the growth of aggregate demand under the labor supply conditions prevailing prior to World War I, that is, free immigration and a large reservoir of farm population in older settled areas. An economic boom, once started, led to a rise in the growth rate of hourly wages and a decline in that of unemployment, signifying a gradual tightening of the labor market. As this progressed, it induced an upsurge in migration from older farm areas and abroad, thus raising the growth rate of population, labor force, and households in the centers of opportunity. With spending money provided by the new jobs, the newly established migrant households in turn generated new demands and investment opportunities—for food, clothing, shelter, and a variety of urban services. The growth in output and investment which this induced—typically, an urban development boom—sustained and prolonged the expansion.

Although the interwar period differed in some respects, the above sketch is roughly descriptive of the mechanism in this period too. The most restrictive immigration legislation was not enacted until the mid-twenties, and the period as a whole was marked by an upswing and subsequent decline in both immigration from abroad and out-migration from farm areas.

The economic boom starting with World War II was the first to be initiated under conditions of sharply restrictive immigration legislation and incipient farm population decline. Furthermore, labor force growth due to natural increase of the working-age population was at an all-time low. (The population of persons aged 15–29 actually declined in absolute number from 1940 to the mid-fifties.) Moreover, younger workers enjoyed an exceptional educational advantage over older workers as a result of rapid acceleration of secondary schooling between 1920 and 1940. Under these conditions a major upswing in the growth of aggregate demand created an unusually strong labor market for younger men. The result was a very rapid growth in their relative income, accomplished by unusually high upward mobility on the occupational scale and a more rapid increase in wages for young than old workers in given occupations. In turn, this led to a sharp reduction in the average age at which they married, established separate homes, and started families, and led also to expenditure effects associated with new-household formation of the type previously caused by migration. Thus, as in the past, an economic boom induced a rise in population and household growth and an associated urban development boom, but this time through its income effects in the labor market for young persons rather than through migration. At the same time, the labor market adjustments of younger persons, in conjunction with the high over-all demand situation, left open a number of less skilled jobs of both the service and manual variety, thereby encouraging greater labor force growth. The chief beneficiaries of this, through significantly increased labor force participation rates, were older women whose alternative costs in the form of school or small-child care responsibilities were low, though even persons with such responsibilities showed some positive response to the plentiful job opportunities. As before World War II, internal migration also rose in response to the swing in demand, but its quantitative importance was relatively less because of the secular leveling off and decline of the farm population, the principal reservoir for such migration. In short, an economic boom again induced a rise in population, household, and labor force growth, and an associated urban development boom, but its underlying mechanism and the specific demographic responses were substantially different from the past because of the new labor supply conditions under which the boom occurred.

With the waning of the boom in the 1950's, the labor force and household growth rates declined and the population growth rate leveled off. In the first half of the 1960's, as the economy regained momentum, the growth rate of the labor force swung up again. In contrast to past experience, however, the household growth rate continued to decline, and the population growth rate turned down as the birth rate started to drop. Correspondingly, there was little evidence of sizable feedback effects from the demographic side in the form of an urban boom.

This anomalous situation on the demographic side appears to have arisen, at least in part, from another new development in supply conditions, a sharp upsurge in the growth rate of the young adult population, echoing, with a lag, the baby boom of the forties and early fifties. The surge has pushed up labor force growth, thereby supplying the labor requirements of the new economic boom. It has not, however, raised household growth correspondingly because, compared with labor force entry, household formation tends to occur later and to be spread over a wider age range. Furthermore, this upsurge, by producing a sharp rise in the relative number of young adult workers, has led to a deterioration of their relative income position, and through this to a shift toward deferment of marriage, later household formation, and reduced fertility. A decline in the educational advantage of young over older workers has also contributed to a weakening of the relative labor market position of young adults. Finally, the impact of expanded OASDI coverage in sustaining household growth reached its peak in the fifties and has dropped off since then.

Implications for the Future

Just as the post-World War II baby boom is currently being echoed in a labor force surge, so too the ongoing fertility decline presages an eventual downturn in labor force growth due to natural increase. Thus, some thirty years following the World War II era, labor supply conditions are in prospect which would repeat at least partly those of the earlier period. This observation points up what may be the distinctive feature setting off post-1940 from earlier experience, namely, the emergence on the labor supply side of a built-in swing of about a generation's duration. The discussion of the 1960's has already indicated why such a swing may not itself generate a corresponding economic swing. Nevertheless, the existence of a natural-increase cycle could conceivably give rise to a distinctive new pattern of population booms, of which post-1940 experience may be illustrative. As long as the dominant feature of labor supply conditions was the potential response through immigration, economic booms tended to induce population booms on a one-to-one basis. When, however, the dominant feature on the labor supply side is a built-in swing due to natural increase with a period of some thirty years' duration, then the impact of an economic boom on population growth depends on the stage of the labor supply cycle at which it occurs. An economic boom occurring at the ebb stage, such as that of the post-World War II period, would be accompanied by shifts in the relative numbers and income of young persons favorable to increased fertility, higher population and household growth, and the expenditure feedbacks associated therewith. On the other hand, one occurring at the flood stage would be associated with shifts in the relative numbers and income of young persons unfavorable to fertility and a demographic boom. Such, it would seem, may be the situation in the 1960's.

Thus, the experience since 1940 conceivably could be the precursor of a future in which economic booms at certain times may engender surges in population and household growth and associated expenditure feedbacks, and at other times may not, depending on the stage of the natural-increase cycle. Correspondingly, the underlying mechanism, formerly centering on migration, is replaced by one involving fertility and household-headship rate movements arising from shifts in the numbers and income of younger relative to older adults. While there are elements of continuity with the past, post-1940 experience could mark, in a sense, the beginning of a new era.

The weight one attaches to this possibility depends on the importance attributed to the natural-increase cycle in the explanation of events since 1940. While this development is considered to be important in the present study, a number of other causal factors are suggested too. Some of them are of an irregular character, such as developments in education and OASDI. Also specific problems of the timing and magnitude of relationships are only tentatively explored. There is the question too of the likely strength and duration of economic booms if demographic feedbacks are weak or absent. A conservative position perhaps would be that, while migration-dominated population swings may be largely a thing of the past, it is not unlikely that population swings arising from fertility movements, such as that since 1940, may occur again in the future.

NEEDS FOR FURTHER RESEARCH

A study such as this increasingly unfolds new and enticing lines of inquiry as it progresses. While the present volume is reasonably complete in its own terms, much more might have been done. Note may be taken of some of the possibilities on the pretext that they represent "needs for further research"; in fact, they catalog some of the shortcomings of the study.

1. It would be preferable to take the nonfarm economy as the primary spatial unit rather than the national economy because this would make it possible to incorporate internal migration into the analysis in a more explicit way.

2. With regard to demographic variables, more intensive study of marriage, household formation, and perhaps mortality along the lines attempted here for fertility would be desirable.

3. With regard to labor market variables, fuller attention to hours and wages is needed. In general, more study of price variables would be desirable to complement the study of the quantity variables which are the main basis of the present analysis. The bearing of the study on income distribution, which is only touched on in the present inquiry, merits explicit investigation.

4. The question of whether economic-demographic interactions tend toward self-generating long swings deserves careful investigation.

5. Comparisons should be made between business-cycle and long-swing patterns with a view to clarifying similarities and differences.

6. The geographic scope could usefully be extended to the regional and local level.

7. Whereas time-series analysis is the basis of this study, it should be possible to develop cross-section tests for a number of the hypotheses.

Despite these and other shortcomings, these essays may help clarify in some small measure a few of the tantalizing problems which have arisen in recent years—the slowdown in the economic growth rate in the 1950's, the baby boom and subsequent fertility decline, the sensitivity of labor force participation to changing employment conditions. To the extent they do, they may demonstrate what is by no means universally accepted: that population is a proper subject for economic analysis and that an understanding of the past may shed useful light on the present and future.

PART I / NATURE OF THE

DEMOGRAPHIC SWINGS AND THEIR CAUSAL

INTERRELATIONS WITH ECONOMIC SWINGS

CHAPTER 2 / HISTORICAL PATTERNS
AND PRELIMINARY CAUSAL
ANALYSIS

This chapter summarizes evidence on the historical characteristics of long swings, or Kuznets cycles, in the growth of U.S. population and labor force, chiefly for the period through 1950. It then explores the cause-effect relations between immigration waves, the principal factor in the demographic movements prior to World War I, and similar movements in the rate of economic development, as the basis for developing a fuller analytical model in the next chapter.

As noted in the Preface, most of the results summarized in this chapter are drawn from a larger manuscript prepared at an early stage of the project. While it is not possible to include all of the supporting evidence here, an attempt has been made to present a representative proportion. Many of the findings for population and labor force are based on the decennial population censuses 1870 to 1950. The timing of the censuses during this period (but not before) occurred close enough to turning points in the demographic swings to permit use of such intermittent observations for analysis of the swings. This is illustrated in Figure 1, which shows how observations confined to census dates (the broken line) reproduce in rough form the pattern of fluctuation revealed in fuller detail by annual data.[1] Although analysis of timing and amplitude patterns is not possible with such fragmentary data, the wealth of detail in the census permits an exploration of a number of other characteristics. Among those covered here are color-nativity, place of residence (farm-nonfarm, urban-rural, and standard metropolitan area), geographic division and state, industry, and

[1] A ten-year average of annual data is employed because decade changes in the stock of population or labor force, derived from successive censuses, are equivalent to observations at decade intervals on a ten-year moving average of annual changes.

FIGURE 1

TEN-YEAR MOVING AVERAGE OF NET IMMIGRATION AND OF ANNUAL CHANGE
IN TOTAL POPULATION AND GROSS CONSTRUCTION (KUZNETS), 1869–1950 [a]

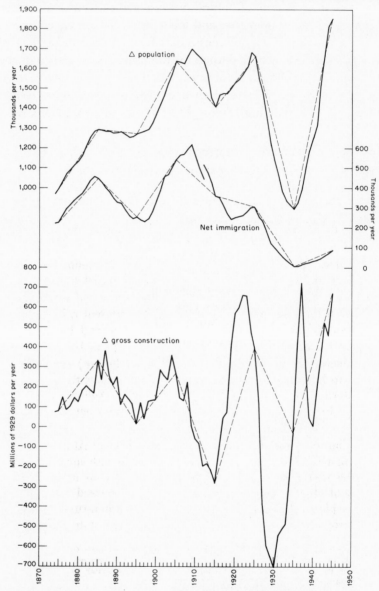

[a] Broken lines connect values for periods corresponding to census intervals.
SOURCE: Table A-1.

occupation. In addition, cross-classifications of age and color-nativity permitted an estimation of natural increase and migration components of change in total population and labor force. Where expert analysis has led to revision of the raw census data for a particular characteristic, use has generally been made here of the refined series, though some discrepancy is consequently introduced between this characteristic and others in their over-all rates of change. Details regarding sources and methods and the data underlying charts are given in Appendix A.

THE NATURE OF LONG SWINGS IN POPULATION AND LABOR FORCE

What is the picture of the demographic swings which emerges when the evidence from this and other studies is pieced together? From data on nationwide swings by component of change and color-nativity, spatial characteristics, and economic aspects, the following generalizations seem warranted for the nation as a whole:

1. The growth of both population and labor force has been characterized by roughly synchronous long swings since at least 1870 and probably since early in the nineteenth century. The swings were typically of substantial amplitude and averaged approximately fifteen to twenty-five years in duration, as shown in Figures 2, 3, and [102, 103, 107, 159, 163].

2. Until 1920, swings in both series arose very largely from corresponding movements in immigration.[2] Recently, however, fertility has assumed a more important role for population swings, and participation-rate change for labor force movements (Figures 2 and 3).

3. The color-nativity components of population and labor force reflect the typically predominant influence of immigration in the swings. Historically the swings are most apparent in the growth of the foreign-born population and labor force. Recently, however, the native-born category has become important—both the native white and nonwhite components [102, 103].

Examination of various spatial components of the national aggregate reveals the following points:

[2] However, evidence of swings is apparent in fertility and mortality [32, 103] (see Chapter 4).

FIGURE 2

AVERAGE GROWTH RATE OF POPULA-
TION BY COMPONENT OF CHANGE,
QUINQUENNIALLY, 1870–1955

FIGURE 3

AVERAGE GROWTH RATE OF
LABOR FORCE BY COMPONENT OF
CHANGE, DECENNIALLY,
1870–1950

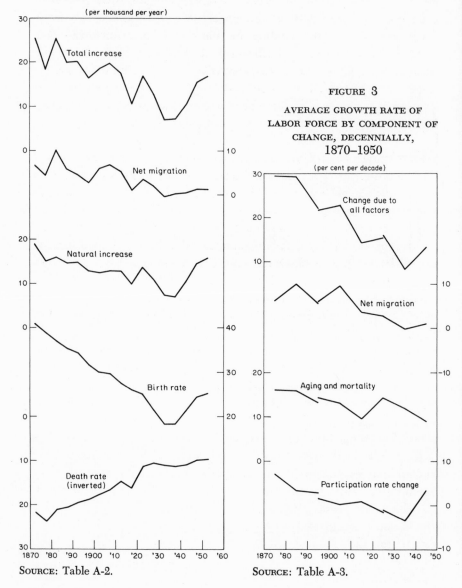

SOURCE: Table A-2.

SOURCE: Table A-3.

1. The swings have typically been a nonfarm, nonagricultural phenomenon. Relatively high positive conformity is apparent in the growth of the total population residing in nonfarm areas, both urban and rural, and in metropolitan areas (SMA's), old and new. Relatively high positive conformity is also apparent in the *number* of urban places and SMA's, and, holding the number of places or SMA's in a given size class constant during each decade, in the growth of the aggregate population in towns and villages and in cities or metropolitan areas of small, medium, and large size. The swings are also evident in the growth of the labor force in nonagricultural industries and in urban areas, see Figures 4, 5, and [59, 119–121].[3]

2. The growth of farm population, of the population in rural areas taken as a whole and in rural territory outside of metropolitan areas, and of the agricultural and rural labor force typically either fails to conform or conforms inversely (Figures 4 and 5). A possible exception, which is of greatest quantitative importance in the pre-Civil War period, is population and labor force growth in new agricultural areas. These magnitudes appear to conform positively while these areas are being settled [176, pp. 1–18 to 1–23; 131].

3. The swings in growth of nonfarm population and nonagricultural labor force are widely diffused geographically, typically occurring at about the same time in the various regions and geographic divisions of the country. When *total* population or labor force in a region or division fails to conform, this is almost always due to the discordant behavior of the farm or agricultural component of the total, as shown in Figures 6 and 7.[4]

The generalizations above regarding positive conformity relate to broad classes of population and labor force. It is less true that any given city or metropolitan area, or even the urban population of a single state, will consistently show every long swing. Thus broad, general stability in the spatial incidence of the swings is accompanied by variability in individual cases.

4. The contrasting behavior of population growth in farm and

---

[3] Unless otherwise specified, nonagricultural labor force is the reference series for statements in this chapter regarding conformity of decennial series to the long swings pattern.

[4] Important contributions at the state and local level have been made by Gordon [77], David [42], and Smolensky and Ratajczak [147a].

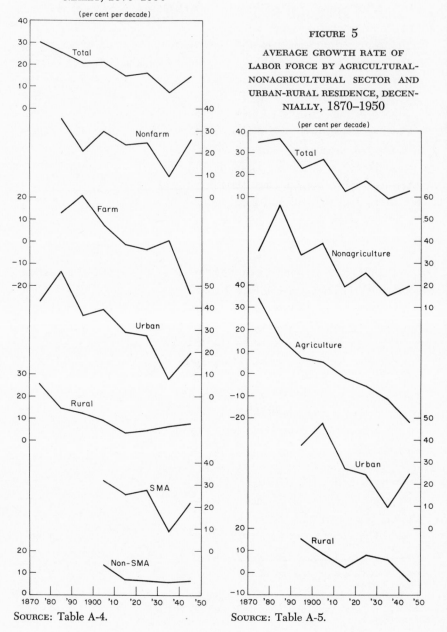

FIGURE 4

AVERAGE GROWTH RATE OF POP-
ULATION BY RESIDENCE, DECEN-
NIALLY, 1870–1950

(per cent per decade)

SOURCE: Table A-4.

FIGURE 5

AVERAGE GROWTH RATE OF
LABOR FORCE BY AGRICULTURAL-
NONAGRICULTURAL SECTOR AND
URBAN-RURAL RESIDENCE, DECEN-
NIALLY, 1870–1950

(per cent per decade)

SOURCE: Table A-5.

FIGURE 6

AVERAGE GROWTH RATE OF
URBAN POPULATION BY GEO-
GRAPHIC DIVISION, DECENNIALLY,
1870–1950

FIGURE 7

AVERAGE GROWTH RATE OF NON-
AGRICULTURAL LABOR FORCE BY
GEOGRAPHIC DIVISION, DECEN-
NIALLY, 1870–1950

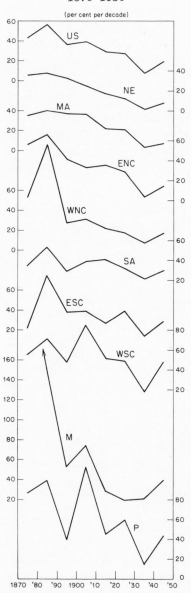

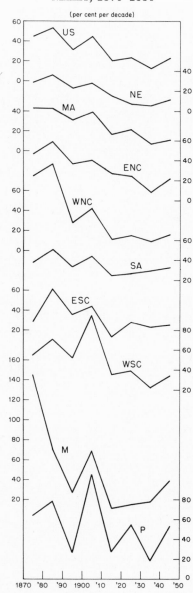

SOURCE: Table A-6.

SOURCE: Table A-7.

nonfarm areas suggests the possibility of long swings in *internal* migration, and this, indeed, is the case. Estimates of the over-all rate of net interstate migration of the native-born population, available by decade since 1870, exhibit high positive conformity to long swings. Much cruder estimates which I have made for rural and urban areas show that rates of rural net out-migration and urban net in-migration of the native-born population also tended to conform positively. When the four major regions are studied separately, one finds that while the secular levels of the rates necessarily differed according to whether the area in question was on balance a supplier or recipient of migrants, the same pattern of decennial fluctuation in native-born net migration rates—interregional, rural, and urban—usually occurred in each. At the level of individual states, however, net migration rates—available for the total population but not rural and urban separately—conformed less consistently [59, 158–160, 163].

5. In both the interstate and rural-urban migration estimates, the white component of the native-born population shows positive conformity to long swings throughout the entire period, and the Negro component, from 1920 on. An interesting feature of the Negro migration before 1910 is that the interstate movement tends if anything to move inversely, but the substantially larger rural-urban flow conforms positively to the swings. On balance, therefore, the evidence at the subnational level indicates that roughly synchronous fluctuations occurred in internal as well as external migration, and that, typically, all three color-nativity classes—foreign-born white, native white, and Negro—participated in migration swings throughout the period since 1870.

The figures for the main industrial and occupational components of the nonagricultural labor force reveal additional economic characteristics of the swings:

As shown in Figure 8, the swings appear with high regularity in the same industrial sectors, namely, construction; transportation; trade; finance, insurance, and real estate; professional services and amusements; domestic service; and personal services. Manufacturing and forestry and fishing show no consistent pattern, and mining tends to move inversely, but the patterns for these particular sectors may be

FIGURE 8

AVERAGE GROWTH RATE OF LABOR FORCE BY INDUSTRY, DECENNIALLY,
1870–1950

(per cent per decade)

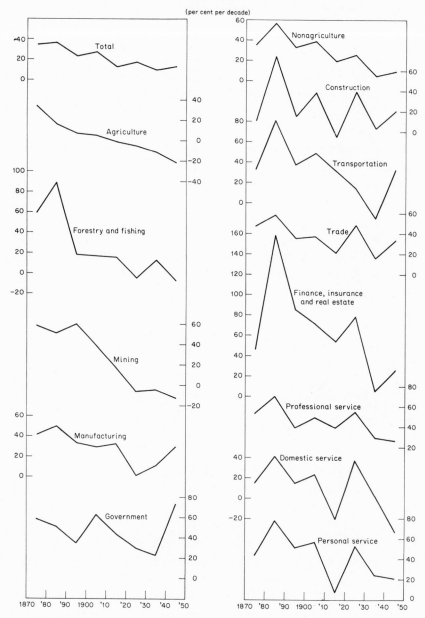

SOURCE: Table A-8.

obscured because of the level of aggregation involved and the intermittent nature of the observations. Finer industrial detail and more frequent observations suggest a more complex pattern for manufacturing (discussed in connection with Figures 10 through 12 below).

The occupational data, which are available only from 1900 on, show quite consistent swings for both the total white collar group and its components, but only for the total of the manual and service workers.[5] The movements shown by a number of major occupational groups appear to be determined by the industrial pattern, specifically, by the relative weight in each occupational class of the nonconforming manufacturing sector, on the one hand, and the positively conforming construction, trade, and service sectors, on the other.

CAUSES OF MIGRATION SWINGS

Since nationwide swings in population and labor force growth before World War I were predominantly due to swings in immigration, a closer look at the immigration waves provides a useful starting point for the more general cause-effect analysis of demographic swings undertaken in Chapter 3.

The flow of migrants between two geographic areas is influenced by a variety of factors at origin and destination, such as current and expected economic opportunity, rates of labor force entry, transfer costs, the volume of previous migration, as well as noneconomic conditions such as language and culture, war, and political revolution. All of these factors and more determine the level of migration at a given time, but they need not all fluctuate in order to generate migration swings over time. What interests us here is whether there is evidence that the observed immigration waves were repeatedly associated with fluctuations in the same factor(s), and particularly whether they were initiated by changing conditions in the United States or in the areas of origin? This question is important in clarifying not only the causes of the waves in demographic growth but also the originating role, if any, of these waves in the swings in economic growth.

The answer appears to be that, typically, the swings in im-

[5] See Kaplan and Casey [97a].

migration were a response to corresponding swings in the demand for labor in the United States.[6] The evidence is as follows:

In the United States, turning points of long swings in output growth typically preceded those in the rate of immigration, suggesting that immigration was responding to changed conditions in the United States rather than abroad (Figure 9, [4]).[7] If new circumstances in the areas of origin were the source of the immigration swing, then, other things remaining unchanged, one would expect immigration to initiate a corresponding movement in the growth rate of GNP, and thus to move concurrently rather than lag behind it.

During long swings in the U.S., a rising immigration rate was typically preceded by a rising rate of growth in hourly wages and, as far as the limited evidence goes, a declining unemployment rate; a falling immigration rate tended to follow a decline in the growth rate of hourly wages and a rising unemployment rate (Figure 9). Since the growth of the U.S. labor force from domestic sources, whether from demographic factors or participation-rate change, showed but slight evidence of long swings before World War I (Figure 3), the implication is that immigration waves were one of several symptoms of common origin, namely, alternating tightness and slack in the labor market associated with swings in the growth of labor demand. The immediate stimulus to migration was probably changes in unemployment conditions (Chapter 6, [96]).

There is a substantial similarity in the timing of out-migration waves from diverse areas of origin—different parts of Europe, Canada, Latin America, Asia, and even the rural sector within the United States [54, 103]. This observation is consistent with the view that these areas were responding to a common external stimulus such as swings in labor demand at destination. It is difficult to explain in terms of conditions in the originating areas, unless these areas were themselves subject to forces generating common swings.

[6] This conclusion differs from that of Brinley Thomas for the period before 1870 [156]. Albert Fishlow [66, pp. 200–203] has also questioned Thomas' analysis, and criticized the reliability of the underlying railroad building series he uses.

[7] Analysis of the pre-Civil War period has been significantly aided by the newly developed estimates of GNP and components by Robert E. Gallman, who has himself commented on the long swings apparent in the series. I am grateful to Professor Gallman for making available his preliminary estimates. See [74a, 74b].

FIGURE 9

AVERAGE ANNUAL RATE OF CHANGE IN AGGREGATE PRODUCTION, AGGREGATE
CONSTRUCTION, AND WAGE RATE; AND AVERAGE LEVEL OF IMMIGRATION RATE
AND UNEMPLOYMENT RATE, NBER REFERENCE CYCLES, 1834–1914

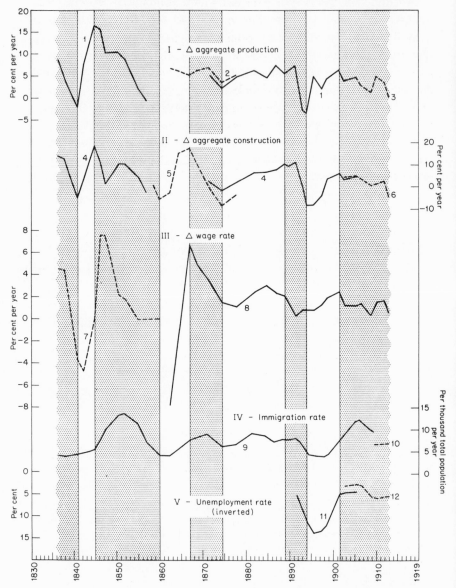

Investigation of the possibility that common forces generated concurrent swings in areas of origin indicates that, within Europe, although there is evidence of a cross-section association among countries between the *secular* rate of overseas emigration and the rate of labor market entry from demographic sources (as reflected in the rate of natural increase twenty years prior to emigration), there is no evidence that the emigration *swings* were responding to similar swings in the rate of labor market entry. Rather, while swings in the latter did occur, countries tended to coincide in their peaks and troughs in emigration rates despite differences in those in their rates of labor market entry. Similarly in the U.S. rural sector, there is no evidence of a systematic fluctuation in rates of labor market entry from demographic sources which could be held responsible for the waves in rural outmigration [54].

Evidence regarding a common movement among European countries in economic opportunity, as measured by agricultural or industrial swings, is mixed [104, 133]. If there was any such movement regularly associated with the U.S. swing, and it should be emphasized that the evidence on this is unclear, it was probably a common swing in industrial conditions, conforming *positively* to the U.S. swing. The U.S.

Legend for Figure 9

  I Rate of change of aggregate production, percentage per year.
    1. Nonperishable commodity output, 1860 dollars (Gallman).
    2. Index of industrial and commercial production, 1899 weights (Frickey).
    3. Gross national product, 1929 dollars (Kendrick).
 II Rate of change of aggregate construction, percentage per year.
    4. Gross new construction, 1860 dollars (Gallman).
    5. Index of physical volume of construction (Abramovitz).
    6. Gross new construction, 1929 dollars (Kuznets).
III Rate of change of wage rate, percentage per year.
    7. Money daily wages, Erie Canal (Smith).
    8. Real hourly wages, manufacturing, 1957 cents (Long).
 IV Alien immigration rate, per thousand total population per year.
    9. Gross immigration.
    10. Net immigration.
  V Unemployment rate, percentage of civilian labor force.
    11. Manufacturing and transportation (Douglas).
    12. Civilian labor force (Lebergott).

NOTE: To facilitate visual comparison of the series, vertical lines have been drawn through the long-swing peaks and troughs of the rate of change in aggregate construction, and the area from peak to trough has been shaded.

SOURCE: Table B-2, except series 10 and 11, Table A-9.

farm sector does clearly show a positively conforming movement in agricultural opportunity (as measured by per capita real farm income), arising from a corresponding swing in farm product prices.[8]

A case might be made that positively conforming movements in economic opportunity in areas of origin could generate common out-migration waves by providing financing for relocation and thus initiate U.S. nonfarm swings. However, a substantial proportion of European emigrants, at least at the end of the nineteenth century, appear not to have financed their own migration, but to have relied on funds provided by relatives or friends who preceded them [169, p. 119; 96, p. 77]. As for the U.S. farm sector, even if the swing in agricultural opportunity did provide financing for migrants, it would seem that this agricultural income swing was itself the result rather than the cause of the nonfarm swing. This is because the swing in farm product prices, which is responsible for the positively conforming movement in agricultural opportunity, is evidently a reflection of a swing in the domestic nonfarm demand for food and materials. In other words, the nonfarm economic boom generated a swing in the demand, not only for labor (with a resulting migration wave) but also for U.S. farm products (with a corresponding movement in farm prices and income).

In the U.S., the influence of fluctuations in demand conditions is apparent too in the age data on interstate migration. For every cohort, the migration rate at ages 25–29 exceeded that at ages 35–39. However, a cohort going through the peak migration ages, 25–29, during a long-swing depression showed a substantially lower migration rate than one reaching these ages during a long-swing boom. Ten years later, at ages 35–39, when the long-swing stage encountered by each cohort tended to be reversed, their order with regard to migration rates was likewise reversed. This suggests that a cohort's

[8] This statement is based on an analysis of the conformity with the aggregate output series in Figure 14 of indexes for the following three series: real farm income, 1869–1929; farm prices, 1834–1929; and farm output, 1834–59 and 1869–1929. The first was derived in the same way as the series in Appendix C, Table C-9, column 2. For the other two indexes, the source from 1869 on was [151]. Prior to 1869 [187, series E-2] was used for price; for output, Gallman's unpublished annual estimates of the output of perishable commodities was used.

migration propensity at ages 25–29 was sometimes significantly deferred until demand conditions became more favorable [59].

It is sometimes claimed that the waves of immigration to the U.S. originated in catastrophic events in Europe, such as famines, revolutions, pogroms, etc. Thus the surge in emigration from Ireland and Germany in the late 1840's and early 1850's has been attributed to famine and political events. Doubtless, it is sometimes possible to identify such occurrences in connection with high or rising emigration. But to establish the argument, it is necessary to show that when emigration was low or falling, events such as these were *not* occuring, and therefore that pressure for emigration was less. As a crude test of this, I drew on Thorp's business annals for each of eight countries: England, 1820–1914; France, 1840–1914; Germany, 1853–1914; Austria, 1867–1914; and Russia, Sweden, Netherlands, and Italy, 1890–1914. In the fifth paragraph of the yearly entry for a country, Thorp lists "various non-economic phenomena which may have exerted influence upon the conditions of business. Political events, epidemics, and natural catastrophes are the chief subjects of note" [164a, p. 105]. I counted first the *total* number of entries under this head falling in periods of high versus low migration (also rising versus falling migration was used), and then repeated the procedure, counting only obviously "push" entries, such as riots, famines, "distress," "anxiety," war, and mobilization. In both cases the results were the same—if anything, more entries for catastrophic events occurred in periods when emigration was low or falling than when it was high or rising. Thus it seems doubtful that the recurrent migration waves originated in the intermittent occurrence of such events.

This is not to say that such events had no influence on the migration pattern if demand conditions in the United States were favorable. On the contrary, as between two long swings characterized by a similar movement in the demand for labor, the response induced would vary from one country to another (as well as between Europe and the U.S. farm sector), not only because of irregular events such as these, but also because of secular developments with regard to transport costs, the geographic diffusion of economic growth, and so on. The point is that labor demand conditions in the United States were the systematic factor initiating an upsurge, though the amplitude and composition of the response depended upon the particular supply conditions prevailing at the time.

EFFECTS OF MIGRATION

While surges in population and labor force growth associated with immigration appear to have been the result rather than the cause of swings in the rate of economic growth, this does not mean that the demographic movement did not play an important functional role in such swings. Rather, the evidence since at least 1870 suggests that the flow of foreign and internal migrants responding to an upswing in labor demand itself generated a wave of urban development.[9] The rise in aggregate demand associated with the population movement sustained the long upswing and may have been an important factor accounting for its prolonged duration.

Since the data supporting this view relate largely to industrial structure, it is pertinent first to identify those industries most dependent on final urban consumer demand. A clue to their identity is provided by ranking the industries in the fifty-sector input-output table for 1947 [61] according to the percentage of gross output flowing directly to households.[10] The highest one-third are as follows:

Food and kindred products	Trade
Tobacco manufactures	Communications
Apparel	Finance and insurance
Furniture and fixtures	Rental
Leather and leather products	Personal and repair services
Radios	Medical, education, and nonprofit
Miscellaneous manufacturing	organizations
Transportation other than rail	Amusements
and ocean	Eating and drinking places
	Government

To these should be added residential construction, not separately distinguished in the table, and industries in the manufacturing sector

[9] Isard's early work emphasized this effect of the demographic movement during long swings [92, 93].

[10] A preliminary estimate by William G. Whitney of a similar table for 1899 yields virtually the same list of industries at that date.

closely related to it such as lumber products; stone, clay, and glass products; and plumbing and heating supplies. In the absence of special constraints this group of industries would be expected to respond most sensitively to changes in demand caused by swings in the urban consuming population arising from migration. Is this the case?

It has already been noted that the nationwide data show positively conforming swings both in urban population growth and the *non*-manufacturing sectors listed above (cf. Figures 4 and 8). Further evidence of this association was found in data for the individual geographic divisions as well. Thus, approximate estimates of the construction and trade labor force in each division, 1870–1950 (derived from the census reports on the principal occupations in these industrial activities), show fluctuations conforming closely to those of the urban and SMA populations.

What of the subsectors of *manufacturing* listed above? In order to get at a level of industrial detail more comparable to that of the input-output study, I used Alba Edwards' 100 or so industry-occupation series on labor force covering the period 1870–1930 [173, pp. 104–112]. Classifying these series according to conformity of movement with the nonagricultural total reveals that a group of industry titles much like those listed above from the input-output table conform positively. Although in Edwards' data the manufacturing labor force as a whole does not show conformity, the subsectors dependent on construction and urban consumer demand do. One activity prominent in Edwards' data, printing and publishing, though missing from the input-output list, ranks only slightly below the industries listed there. Industries appearing in the input-output list but which do not show up particularly in Edwards' detailed labor force data are typically those with special output constraints such as government or industries relying substantially on extractive activity, e.g., manufacture of food products.

These findings are in line with what we would expect about the nature of the industrial response if swings in migration to urban areas generated concurrent movements in product demand. In the preceding section we found that immigration swings typically lagged behind swings in the growth rate of nonagricultural output as a whole. Together, these findings suggest a more elaborate pattern in the industrial

FIGURE 10

AVERAGE RATE OF CHANGE OF BURNS' CONSTANT-PRICE-BUILDING PERMITS AND
STANDARD-TREND CYCLE,[a] KUZNETS' GROSS CONSTRUCTION IN 1929 PRICES, AND
MALE POPULATION OF WORKING AGE, DECADES ENDING IN 0 AND 5, 1870–1950

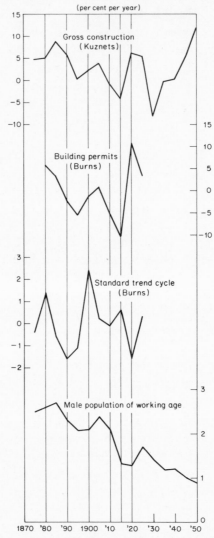

NOTE: To facilitate visual comparison of the series, vertical lines have been
drawn through peaks and troughs of the rate of change in the standard trend cycle.
SOURCE: Table A-10.
[a] Both of Burns' series are trend-adjusted.

FIGURE 11

AVERAGE TREND-ADJUSTED RATE OF CHANGE OF SELECTED BASIC COMMODITY
SERIES, DECADES ENDING IN 0 AND 5,[a] 1870–1930

(per cent per year)

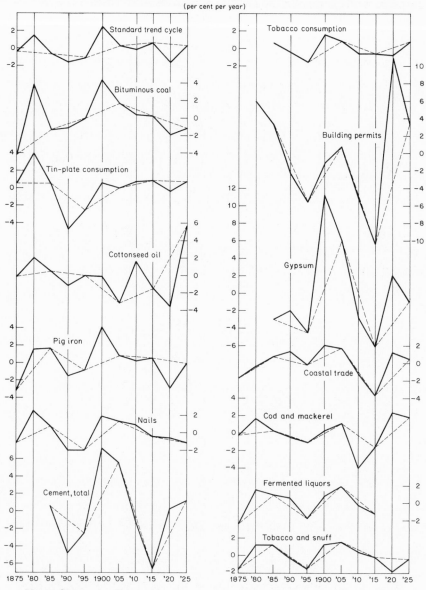

NOTE: See note to Figure 10.
SOURCE: Table A-11.
[a] Broken lines connect values for decades ending in 0 (i.e., census intervals).

FIGURE 12

AVERAGE RATE OF CHANGE OF TOTAL MANUFACTURING CAPITAL IN 1929
PRICES, BY SELECTED MAJOR MANUFACTURING INDUSTRIES, 1880–1961

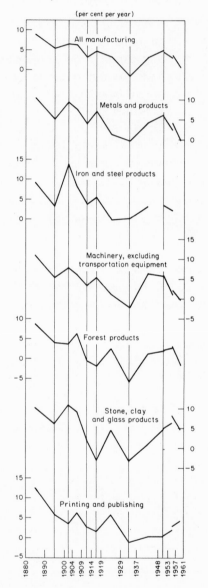

(per cent per year)

NOTE: To facilitate visual comparison of the series, vertical lines have been
drawn through peaks and troughs of the rate of change in all manufacturing.
SOURCE: Table A-12.

structure of long swings than that revealed by the decennial census data in Figure 8. Among the positively conforming industries, some are moving with the growth rate of nonagricultural output, but others, more closely dependent on construction and urban household demand, either lag or, if turning concurrently, do so sluggishly. Although observations on labor force are too infrequent to discern this finer pattern, evidence of it is apparent in output and capital data, as follows:

1. The turning points in Burns' series on building permits coincide almost perfectly with those in Kuznets' series for gross construction and male population of working age. However, they lag behind those in Burns' "standard trend cycle," a series which reflects the consensus of movement of basic unfinished industrial commodities (Figure 10).

2. This lag characterizes a number of Burns' individual commodity series other than building permits, series closely related to construction or final urban consumer demand (Figure 11, right panel). Even among the industrial commodity series conforming to the standard-trend cycle there are several in which construction demand figures more prominently, and these tend to turn sluggishly reflecting the imprint of that demand (Figure 11, left panel, see pig iron, rails, cement).

3. In Creamer's data on growth of real capital stock in manufacturing, long-swing turning points in forest products; stone, clay, and glass products; and printing and publishing tend to lag behind those in the metals industries and in manufacturing as a whole (Figure 12). The identity of the *leading* manufacturing industries indicated by Creamer's capital data is the same as that suggested by Burns' commodity series, namely, the "capital goods" industries. All in all, the data suggest, then, that an upswing in the capital goods industries and industries closely related to them is followed by a surge in industries depending on construction and urban household demand as a gradually tightening labor market induces migration to urban centers.

CHAPTER 3 / THE ANALYTICAL

MODEL: RECENT AND

PROSPECTIVE EXPERIENCE

The foregoing analysis of immigration waves suggests that, typically, demographic swings are induced by changes in economic conditions but, in turn, have important feedback effects on the economy. This chapter builds on this to develop a fuller analytical conception of economic-demographic relations during long swings. It also considers whether recent experience is consistent with this viewpoint and discusses implications for the future. To start with, however, attention is focussed on a methodological issue.

ARE KUZNETS CYCLES A STATISTICAL ILLUSION?

Two arguments in the affirmative should be distinguished. The first is that long swings may be artificially produced by certain defects in the raw data. For example, if the population is underenumerated at one census date, but correctly counted at the preceding and following dates, this single error will bias the growth rate in the second period upward relative to that in the first period. However, while such bias is possible with regard to any single series, it seems highly implausible that a large number of series from widely differing sources would share a common bias creating the illusion of long swings with similar timing. To the variety of series and sources relating to output, capital, and demographic variables already covered in Chapter 2, one may, if necessary, add still more that show roughly conforming long swings: patents [140], land sales and prices [17, 33, 131], financial series [102], transportation and other public utilities [76, 168], incorporations [60], and international trade and payments [216].

The second argument is that long swings may be an artifact due to the particular statistical method used in smoothing the raw data.

Bird and others have shown that a moving average technique, especially of the type employed by Kuznets may "create" long cycles where only short cycles exist [18]. Adelman, using the new technique of spectral analysis, finds, for the series she analyzes, "no evidence for the existence of a long-cycle component in the business fluctuations of the U.S. economy since 1890," and suggests "it is likely that the long swings which have been observed in the U.S. economy since 1890 are due in part to the introduction of spurious long cycles by the smoothing process, and in part to the necessity for averaging over a statistically small number of random shocks" [10, p. 459].

Such arguments obviously do not apply to those series in which long swings are observed in the raw data. Several of these are assembled in Figure 13—residential construction, incorporations, immigration, and capital imports. The large fluctuations in these series are so manifest, particularly prior to World War I, that they impressed themselves on analysts who were not looking for long swings and who were often not even aware of the idea. Moreover, the series show similar, though not identical, timing. Clearly there is no statistical illusion here. It is true that long swings are not readily apparent in the raw data on aggregate output in Figure 13; indeed, most output series, in which processes of inventory change play an important role, exhibit such high annual variability that the longer term movement, if it exists, is far from obvious. However, since swings in the raw data are shown by one group of series, and since these series relate to important aspects of resource growth, the question naturally arises whether processing other series so as to reduce short-term variability may reveal corresponding long-term movements in them too. Leaving aside for the moment the Adelman results, the answer to this question is yes, the movements appear in a number of other series, although differences in statistical method yield varying conclusions on more demanding issues such as frequency, timing, and amplitude. It seems reasonable to conclude that since roughly synchronous fluctuations are observed in the raw data for series reflecting capital formation and growth of the labor supply, that similar movements obtained in processed data for other series have a basis in reality also.[1]

[1] Clearly, this statement does not mean that these fluctuations are necessarily self-generating—a matter taken up in the next section. The issue at stake here is simply the reality of the fluctuations.

FIGURE 13

UNPROCESSED ANNUAL DATA ON OUTPUT, INCORPORATIONS, RESIDENTIAL CON-
STRUCTION, IMMIGRATION, AND NET CAPITAL IMPORTS, 1820–1964

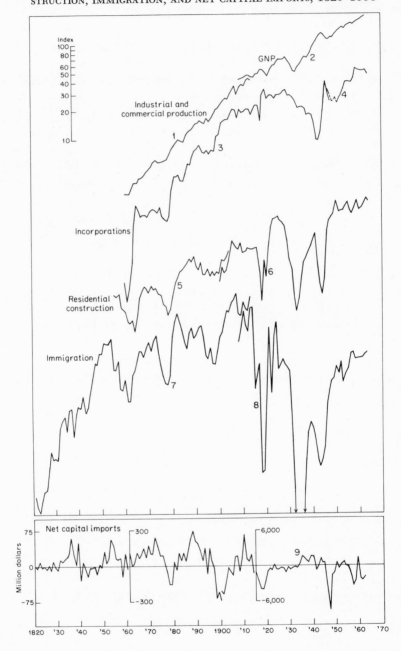

On first glance, the Adelman analysis is disturbing, since here is a method that appears to yield negative results. True, spectral analysis is a new technique, and there is as yet so little experience with it in the analysis of annual economic time series that it is hard to judge how much the results may depend on the particular assumptions made in applying it. But a closer look at the study suggests more concrete reasons for reservations about the findings. First, construction was omitted from her analysis because its spectrum "showed an unusually large amount of distortion at the higher frequencies due to the filtering process" [10, p. 459]. The need to omit this series is especially troubling because, if there is any economic sector on which some professional consensus exists as to the reality of fluctuations of the Kuznets cycle variety, it is this one. Second, only one demographic series was included, total population, and it too was omitted in arriving at her final conclusion because its spectrum "suggests that any genuine cyclical phenomena which may exist in population are longer in duration than 15 years. More work is required on this series before any more detailed conclusions can be drawn" [10, p. 459]. Again, the analysis excludes a series important for the long-swings hypothesis. Not that it much matters in this case; in the population series used, which is not the annual series used by Kuznets or me, the estimates for about two-thirds of the years, 1790–1957, are obtained by linear interpolation between decennial census figures [187, p. 1]. Finally, those series on which the results of the study actually rest start only in 1890, and thus relate chiefly to a period in which statistical analysis of time series for evidence of long swings is seriously handicapped by the occurrence of two world wars. The immense expansion and sub-

---

Legend for Figure 13
1. Index of industrial and commercial production, 1899 weights (Frickey).
2. Gross national product, billions of 1954 dollars (Commerce).
3. Aggregate index of incorporations (Evans).
4. Number of incorporations (Dun and Bradstreet).
5. Production of nonfarm housekeeping dwelling units (Gottlieb).
6. Number of nonfarm dwelling units started (Blank).
7. Gross alien immigration per thousand total population per year.
8. Net alien immigration per thousand total population per year.
9. Net capital imports, millions of current dollars.

SOURCE: Table B-1.

sequent contraction of government expenditure associated with the wars resulted in a major departure from the historical long-swing pattern.[2] A central feature of this pattern (one reason for this is suggested in the next section) was concurrent swings in the growth rates of GNP and aggregate construction. However, the two wars, with their attendant restrictions on construction, forced a break in the pattern, with GNP moving in positive conformity to the expansion and subsequent contraction of government expenditure, and construction in inverse conformity. The result is to interject an additional fluctuation into the usual long-swing relation, differing in timing between the two series, as illustrated by the broken line in idealized fashion below.

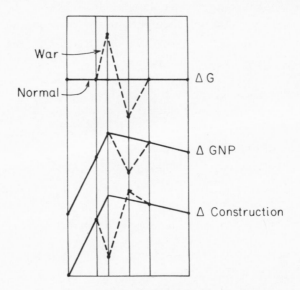

This additional fluctuation appears, of course, not only in these two series but in others as well. While it is eliminated by a statistical procedure averaging the intervals both of expansion and contraction in government expenditure, such as Kuznets' decade averages, it would clearly influence the results of spectral analysis, the more so, the more the period studied is dominated by major wars.[3]

[2] It is possible that the Civil War is another case of this sort, but the data are not now sufficiently complete to determine this.

[3] This paragraph perhaps answers the question posed by several discussants of Hickman's paper [47, 63, 78], namely, whether experience since the 1930's is to

An implication of these observations is that the issue of the "reality" of long swings is unlikely to be resolved, pro or con, by purely statistical studies, valuable and necessary though these are. To the extent one concentrates on output series relating primarily to the war-torn twentieth century, as is true of the Adelman study, the more one is likely to be unconvinced. On the other hand, by emphasizing periods less disturbed by war, as well as series in which the swings are prominent in unprocessed data, a stronger case can be built, though this inevitably leaves doubt as to current relevance. In any case, it is clear that statistical analysis needs to be complemented by economic analysis: Are the observations on long swings consistent with a model of relationships based on economic theory? This is the question I seek to contribute to solving in this chapter.

THE ANALYTICAL MODEL

Although the intellectual progenitors of the model suggested here are numerous, particular acknowledgement is due contributions by Kuznets [102–105, 107], Abramovitz [4–6], Isard [92, 93], Hickman [90], and Burnham Campbell [29, 30]. The model proceeds in three steps: (1) the impact of aggregate demand on labor market conditions, (2) the effect of labor market conditions on the number and spending behavior of households, and (3) the reaction of the latter on aggregate demand.

Aggregate Demand and the Labor Market

Assume, to start with, that growth of GNP in the last business cycle or two occurred at less than the full-employment growth rate and that the economy has accumulated excess capacity with regard to labor. One manifestation of this would be a tendency toward a rising unemployment rate at successive business cycle peaks (or troughs). Assume, next, that for some reason the rate of growth of private investment rises, producing a corresponding upsurge in the growth of aggregate demand, and that the higher level is sustained for some

be interpreted as one long swing or two shorter swings. The additional fluctuation is directly due to the movement in government spending (cf. [90, p. 493]), and is thus an interruption in the basic long swing.

time. The spatial distribution of this increased demand and the employment opportunities thus created would not necessarily conform to that of the existing labor supply. On the contrary, in a developing economy the locus of investment opportunities tends to be predominantly nonfarm, whereas the increase of the labor force through natural growth of the working-age population is disproportionately large in the farm sector.

The increased growth in aggregate product demand would have a corresponding effect on the demand for labor in the favorably affected centers of economic activity. Initially, one would expect the increased labor input requirements thus created to be met locally through an appropriate movement in the rate of change of the unemployment rate, and perhaps via a rise in the growth rate of hours. Increasing tightness of the labor market would tend to be reflected too in an increase in the rate of change of wage rates. The longer this process continues, the more likely it becomes that labor force growth in the favored areas will be enhanced by migration in response to the new employment opportunities. The origins of the migration would be lower wage areas elsewhere in the country (notably the older farm areas) and/or abroad. Labor force growth might also be raised by an increase in labor force participation rates of reserve labor groups such as females, youths, and older persons. The relative role of the several possible sources of increased labor input in satisfying the new demand would depend on the supply elasticities of the groups involved.

Reaction on Household Growth in Centers of Increased Demand

To the extent that increased labor-input requirements are met via unemployment or hours changes, one would usually expect the stimulus to household growth to be relatively mild, since the beneficiaries of the increased income are most likely to be members of established households in the area. To be sure, the slackened growth rate in the immediately preceding cycle(s) and the resulting higher average unemployment rate may have led some young persons to defer marriage or those already married and living with their parents to postpone establishing a separate household. For these, the progressive improvement of labor market conditions would lead to implementing previously deferred decisions. The longer the foregoing slack period, the more sizable the quantitative effect of this would probably be. Moreover, if the labor market impact were for some reason particularly favorable for those in the household-forming ages, plans might be advanced and household growth accelerated through a general reduction in the average age of marriage and of household formation.

Typically, however, one would expect a more immediate and sizable effect on household growth in the centers of increased demand if the increased labor input requirements were met via migration flows, because migration flows add directly to the number of households at the point of destination. In this case the growth in persons employed is more nearly matched by corresponding growth in the number of households. This is the special significance of the migration response: it has a much greater impact than other sources of labor input on household growth in the areas of increased labor demand.

Effect of Household Growth on Aggregate Spending

Households newly established in an area generate demands, not only for housing but for urban services generally, as well as for the furnishing of new homes. They thereby tend to create an urban development boom—new residential construction and new municipal investment in services associated with it, as well as new business investment in retailing and similar activities. (The mechanism might of course involve an intermediate stage in which new migrants displace previous residents in established areas and the latter are those immediately involved in new real estate development.) Thus the increase in households, typically associated with the migration flow, leads to further growth not only in consumer spending but in private and public investment as well, and it is this induced rise in the growth of aggregate demand which tends to sustain and prolong the expansion.

Why Kuznets Cycles Rather than Business Cycles?

Established households whose head or members have profited from new employment and income opportunities would generate a multiplier effect via new consumer spending; possibly, new business investment would also be induced. A reaction of this type figures frequently in theoretical discussion of the regular business cycle.

Why should the present chain of events, operating through household growth result in a more protracted boom? [4] One possible answer lies in the composition of the induced demand which results when household growth intervenes between the labor market response and the increased spending this response produces. This view would emphasize the central importance of housing and real estate development and the associated stimulus to local government spending on municipal services and to business spending on retail services, many of which require a long gestation period to bring to fulfillment. This argument rests essentially on the special characteristics of the industries benefitting from the induced demand—on product supply conditions.

A second, and perhaps more compelling answer, is based on demand considerations. Marriage, household formation, and migration are points of critical decision in the life cycle of an individual. Typically, they involve commitment to new and increased spending over several years as a new home is established and a family started or settled, a commitment reflected in the substantial indebtedness to relatives and financial institutions regularly incurred during this period of the life cycle.[5] On this basis, one might reason that in a population experiencing a substantial rise in the growth of households there will not only be a shift in the composition of consumption but a rise in the propensity to consume as well. This would be sustained over several years, carrying over from one business cycle to the next, and would only gradually become exhausted. In effect, such long-term spending commitments are geared to a notion of permanent income, and tend to be rather insensitive to short-term income changes.

It is this feature of longer-term spending commitments which may constitute the analytical key to Kuznets-cycle phenomena. The frequent association of such commitments with series most noticeably marked by long swings has been pointed out particularly by Abramovitz. Because this feature has so far received insufficient attention, his statement merits repetition in full:

[4] Charles Tiebout [165] has drawn a similar distinction between a long-run and short-run multiplier, with population growth playing a central role in the former.
[5] The most thorough study I have encountered of spending behavior in relation to life-cycle stage (which is not synonymous with age) is that by Lansing and Morgan [108], though even in this the stages are very broad. Consumer panel studies should generate still more pertinent data. Ferber's article [64] provides a valuable survey.

One common attribute of all these processes of resource development involving the movement of people from country to country and place to place, the formation of households and the birth of children, the foundations of business, and the investment of capital in highly durable forms is that they involve long-term decisions and commitments. Hence they pick up speed and come to fruition slowly and when they slow down, they are not easily or quickly set in motion again. They give rise, therefore, to long waves of resource development and output growth. These processes involving long-term decisions, on the other hand, respond only sluggishly to the impact of the ordinary short and mild business contractions. By contrast, the most prominent feature of short business cycles is a fluctuation in shorter term investment, particularly inventory investment [5, p. 414].

While our concern here is with household behavior, it is worthwhile to underscore Abramovitz's point that various types of private business investment also involve longer-term commitments. Perhaps the most notable of these arise in connection with the establishment of new businesses, a phenomenon which, judging from the long-term series on new incorporations (Figure 13) exhibits long swings in the unprocessed annual data.[6] (As for the future, the growth in importance as spending units of various government bodies and private nonprofit institutions, both potentially significant sources of long-term commitments, suggests the need to study them as well.) This line of reasoning obviously leads to the general view that Kuznets cycles may arise from mechanisms, such as that discussed here, which result in a bunching of long-term spending commitments.[7]

The Effect of Major Wars on Kuznets Cycles

The analytical model sketched above starts with a private investment boom, but any source of sustained increase in the growth of aggregate demand, including government expenditure, could initiate

[6] Research on investment spending by new firms (or, more generally, in relation to the "life cycle" of business units) is scarce. One valuable study is that by Bridge [23; cf. also 60, 219].

[7] A discussion of spending behavior inevitably leads on to the question of financing, and thus to the role of monetary and financial variables in long swings. While this subject is clearly "off-bounds," it may be noted that money supply, interest rates, prices, capital imports (Figure 13), and similar variables do show long swings [cf. 4, 22b, 41, 102, 113, 128a, 146a, and 216]. This subject, among others, is treated in the forthcoming NBER study of trends in money, income, and prices by Milton Friedman and Anna J. Schwartz.

the process. In the case of major wars, however, the process is interrupted, because the war itself places constraints on new household formation and construction. At the same time, a protracted war sets the stage for a postwar Kuznets-cycle boom, by building up substantial backlogs not only for private and public investment but household formation and consumer spending as well. Thus, a major war would tend, on the one hand, to interpose an additional fluctuation during which the growth of GNP and aggregate construction pursue divergent paths; on the other hand, if one smooths this fluctuation statistically, a major war would tend to yield a Kuznets-cycle movement of more extended duration.

Are Kuznets Cycles Self-Generating?

While the interaction between economic and demographic phenomena emphasized here is chiefly of a multiplier type, there are clearly elements of induced investment on the basis of which one might postulate a self-generating model of the multiplier-accelerator variety. Also, the positive association between labor market tightness and growth of aggregate demand implies the possibility of labor-cost changes which may react on investment spending in an adverse manner, tending to reverse the movement. On the other hand, irregular events such as wars, legislative acts (e.g., regarding immigration and wages), and speculative capital movements have affected observed long swings. The relative weight of endogenous vs. exogenous factors in initiating the swings is in my view an open question requiring further research.

But the value of the present model does not hinge on resolution of the self-generating issue. As Irma Adelman [8] and others have shown, the Klein-Goldberger model of the regular business cycle is so highly damped that it requires stochastic shocks to produce oscillations of the business cycle variety. The principal value of that model lies in suggesting mechanisms which tend to produce oscillatory movements in response to such shocks. Similarly, while the present analytical scheme leaves open the question whether Kuznets cycles may be wholly self-generating or require either small or strong shocks, it does suggest a mechanism that tends to produce cumulative upward or downward movements over periods longer than the ordinary business cycle.[8]

Long Swings and Secular Growth

How, if at all, are Kuznets cycles related to the primary trend? Is the primary trend itself merely the path traced out by averages of successive Kuznets cycles? The answer suggested here is no. The primary trend reflects processes of technological change and of human resource and institutional development which lie outside the long-swing mechanism itself. However, in an economy where the free market system plays an important role in resource allocation, the pace at which new technology is adopted and diffused tends to be modified by a Kuznets-cycle mechanism. This is because efficient use of the new techniques flowing from the Industrial Revolution and its sequel has required increased geographic concentration of productive resources. This has created an imbalance between the geographic distribution of the growth of labor demand, arising from the industrialization process, and that of labor supply, which typically reflects the widespread population-dispersion characteristic of an agricultural society. Successful adoption of modern industrial technology has required, therefore, redistribution of the population in conformity with the needs of the new technological basis of production, and the provision of the requisite goods and services for this relocated population. The induced stage of the Kuznets-cycle mechanism, an urban development boom, is essentially the accomplishment of this requirement in a free market economy by a multiplier-type process.[9]

[8] Clearly, the present analysis does not agree with the view proposed in a subsequent paper [9] by Mrs. Adelman that a shocked Klein-Goldberger *business cycle* model may be sufficient to account for observed long swings. In this connection, it is worth noting that the simulated long swings that she obtained were of smaller amplitude than those actually observed, and that the Klein-Goldberger model does not incorporate economic-demographic interactions of the type described here.

[9] The long swings in patent data, noted by Kuznets and Schmookler and analyzed by the latter [103, 140], demonstrate that adoption of new techniques is related to Kuznets cycles.

The above aims to identify those conditions which characteristically underlie the observed association between modern economic growth and population redistribution. In certain cases, of which the United States is one, modern economic growth may, in addition, involve the opening up and settlement of new territory, and thus a further stimulus to population redistribution.

For contrast, this formulation may be compared with that of Isard [92, 93; see also 145]. He sees the swings as arising from successive transport innovations, and the urbanization facet as a consequence of the impact of such innovations on the location of economic activity. The present view rests basically on the geographic imbalance between labor demands and supplies created by modern technology generally, and does not require a new transport innovation either to initiate the swing or to account for urbanization, though such innovations may, of course, play a part in particular times and places.

An implication of the present view is that various characteristics of long swings tend to change secularly. The growth opportunities constituting the investment focus at an early stage of development will differ from those at a later stage; hence variations will tend to occur over time in the industrial characteristics and geographical distribution of the swing. For example, agricultural settlement or exports might loom large among the investment opportunities in the early growth stages; at a later time, domestic manufacturing may predominate. Similarly the potential sources of labor supply tend to change secularly. Immigrants may move more readily from one country at one time; from another, at a different time. The reservoir afforded by the farm population in older agricultural areas grows to a point but eventually begins to be depleted, and is perhaps increasingly replaced as a source of labor reserves by some of the nonfarm centers gradually being bypassed in the development process. Secular growth in family income and the appearance of innovations such as the automobile will alter the composition of induced household consumption spending—recent suburban as compared with earlier urban residential development is an illustration of this.

The analytical scheme suggested here bears a superficial resemblance to Schumpeter's [141], for it implies that growth in a free market economy tends to proceed in irregular surges. However, the duration of the movement differs from any contemplated by Schumpeter, as does the underlying mechanism of economic-demographic interactions. Moreover, with regard to secular growth, I would emphasize the independent significance of processes such as technological change and human-resource development. However, Alvin Hansen, in modifying Schumpeter's conception to incorporate the building cycle [87] moved in the Kuznets-cycle direction. This step was carried forward logically by Isard, who arrived at a view similar in a number of respects to that advanced here. In so doing, Isard explicitly rejected Hansen's secular-stagnation thesis, which, one suspects, could be shown to run, in one form or another, a conforming Kuznets cycle of its own in economic discussion. Indeed, in striking contrast to the contemporary professional consensus, Isard, writing in 1942, predicted a postwar boom. His reasoning, however, gave undue weight to transport innovation which, as has been noted, is not an essential ingredient of my analysis.

The analysis here may also bear on the problem of defining a single given phase in the emergence of modern economic growth as an "industrial revolution," "take-off" [139] or "great spurt of industrialization" [75]. Attempts to apply such concepts to actual experience have frequently come up against the difficulty of deciding which among competing periods to so designate. And, where identified, the duration and other characteristics of the period sometimes correspond to those of Kuznets cycles. It is at least a plausible hypothesis that such an interval, seized upon as a unique phase, may be an early and particularly prominent long swing.

RECENT EXPERIENCE IN THE LIGHT OF THE MODEL

Viewed in historical perspective, there are a number of similarities between recent and longer-term experience which are broadly consistent with the crude analytical model sketched above. There are differences, too, however, and on the demographic side these are so serious as to raise doubts about the model's validity. In this section, after noting some of these similarities, I focus on recent dissimilarities with regard to demographic aspects and attempt to reconcile them with the model.[10]

[10] The slackened growth rate of the economy in the cycles of 1953–57 and 1957–60 led several writers to point out similarities between recent experience and earlier lapses from full employment growth [5, 6, 16, 30, 40, 57, 78, 79, 89, 90, 217]. Others, however, have taken sharp issue with such views [47, 63, 129].

FIGURE 14

AVERAGE ANNUAL RATE OF CHANGE IN AGGREGATE PRODUCTION, AGGREGATE
CONSTRUCTION, WAGE RATE, AND HOURS; AND AVERAGE LEVEL OF IMMIGRA-
TION RATE, NONFARM HOUSEHOLD GROWTH RATE, AND UNEMPLOYMENT RATE,
NBER REFERENCE CYCLES, 1830–1964

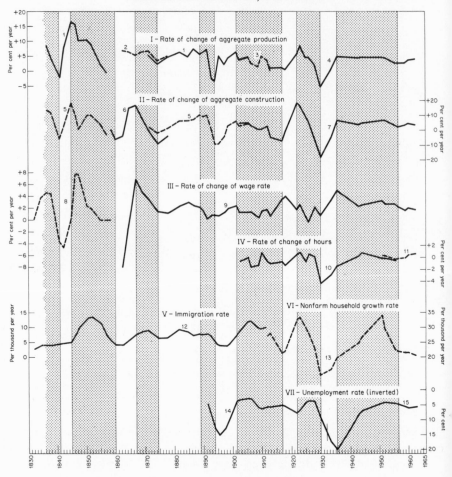

Legend for Figure 14

I. Rate of change of aggregate production, percentage per year.
    1. Nonperishable commodity output, 1860 dollars (Gallman).
    2. Index of industrial and commercial production, 1899 weights (Frickey).
    3. Gross national product, 1929 dollars (Kendrick).
    4. Gross national product, 1954 dollars (Commerce).

(*continued*)

Parallels Between Recent and Earlier Experience

The analytical framework suggests the likelihood of longer-term fluctuations with roughly similar timing in output growth, labor market conditions, and household growth, particularly in the nonagricultural sector. For various reasons, other, perhaps independent, movements might occur in these series, but one would expect as a minimum that there would be some semblance of a common longer-term ryhthm. Is this the case?

Figure 14 assembles series relating to a century or more of U.S. experience on growth of aggregate output and construction, and indicators of changes in labor market conditions (pre-1914 immigration, hours, unemployment, wages), and in household growth (pre-1914 immigration and nonfarm households). A relatively moderate smoothing technique has been employed. The values are averages for successive business cycles as identified by the NBER reference cycle chronology, computed both for trough-to-trough and peak-to-peak cycles and plotted at the cycle midpoints. Only one departure was made from this procedure; it was warranted by the analytical considerations previously presented. The special fluctuations associated

---

Legend for Figure 14 (concluded)

II. Rate of change of aggregate construction, percentage per year.
    5. Gross new construction, 1860 dollars (Gallman).
    6. Index of physical volume of construction (Abramovitz).
    7. Gross new construction, 1929 dollars (Kuznets).
III. Rate of change of wage rate, percentage per year.
    8. Money daily wages, Erie Canal (Smith).
    9. Real hourly wages, manufacturing, 1957 cents (Long).
IV. Rate of change of average hours of work per week in manufacturing, percentage per year.
    10. Jones.
    11. Bureau of Labor Statistics.
V. Gross alien immigration rate per thousand total population per year.
    12. Immigration and Naturalization Service.
VI. Rate of change of nonfarm households per thousand nonfarm households per year.
    13. Bureau of the Census.
VII. Unemployment rate, percentage of civilian labor force.
    14. Lebergott.
    15. Bureau of Labor Statistics.

NOTE: To facilitate visual comparison of the series, vertical lines have been drawn through the long-swing peaks and troughs of the rate of change in aggregate construction, and the area from peak to trough has been shaded.

SOURCE: Table B-2.

with World Wars I and II have been smoothed by ignoring the war-time business cycle peak and first postwar trough.[11] In this way, the cycle average counterbalances the rise in government expenditure and the subsequent decline to a more nearly postwar "normal."

Although certain variations in timing exist, it is possible, as suggested by the shading in the figure, to identify swings in the growth rate of aggregate output and construction, labor market conditions, and household formation, on a roughly one-to-one basis, thus lending some empirical plausibility to the model sketched above.[12] Some of the swings are quite pronounced, such as those terminating in the 1890's and 1930's; others are milder, such as those ending around World War I and the late 1950's. (The parallel between the recent period and experience in the first part of this century was previously pointed out by Hickman [90].) There is an apparent tendency for the swings in the immigration rate, nonfarm household growth rate, and level of the unemployment rate to lag behind the swing in the growth in aggregate output, though not without exception.

Several other similarities between recent experience and previous long swings may be mentioned. The growth rate of manufacturing capital shows a swing, with the capital goods industries tending to precede those oriented toward construction and urban development, as in the pre-1914 period (Figure 12). Spatially, the swing continues to center in nonfarm areas, appearing even more pronounced when more up-to-date census definitions are employed (e.g., metropolitan area rather than urban) and to exhibit wide diffusion among the different geographic divisions of the country. The postwar period has been characterized by an urban and suburban development boom. A swing in internal migration has also occurred [59, 158–160, 163].

Differences in Demographic Aspects

There have, of course, been differences between recent and previous characteristics of long swings.[13] As indicated in Chapter 2, on

---

[11] Thus, in the case of World War II the peak-to-peak average is for 1937–48 rather than for 1937–44 and 1944–48; and the trough-to-trough average is for 1938–49 rather than 1938–46 and 1946–49.

[12] The existence of long swings in the rate of change of wages has been pointed out and analyzed by Clarence Long [115]. A statistically significant association between the annual rate of change of wages and that of unemployment was found by Bowen and Berry [21] in a study covering 1900–58.

[13] For a more general discussion, see [5, 6, 90].

the demographic side, these relate not so much to movements in the aggregate variables, that is, growth of total population, total labor force, and total households, as to the underlying components of change. For the present purpose, it is convenient to group these components of change as follows:

Population	Labor Force	Households [14]
1. Mortality rate	Mortality and aging	Mortality and aging
2. Net immigration rate	Net immigration	Net immigration
3. Fertility rate	Labor force participation rate	Household headship rate

All three of the aggregative demographic variables share in common mortality and migration components. (The addition of the aging component to mortality in both labor force and households is necessary because these variables are defined with reference to a population above some minimum age, and thus receive additions as those initially below the limit grow older.) Each aggregative variable also has its distinctive component: fertility rates in the case of population change, labor force participation rates for labor force, and headship rates for households. If one were dealing with a geographic subdivision of the national total—for example, the nonfarm sector—internal migration would of course be included with international migration as a component of change.

The alignment of the components in the tabulation is designed to facilitate the subsequent discussion. From the viewpoint of demography as such, the components of labor force and household growth on line 1 are analogous to natural increase of the population, i.e., the difference between components 1 and 3 of population growth.[15] This grouping, however, is used to bring out parallel features for long-swings analysis. Thus, the components on line 1 are largely exogenous

[14] I am in debt to Burnham Campbell for recognizing the possibility of the present partition scheme for household growth [30, see also 62]. A "headship rate" is defined, along lines identical with that for a labor force participation rate, as the proportion of the population in a given demographic group (e.g., classified by age and sex) who are household heads.

[15] A more elaborate analysis would, in fact, further subdivide the components of labor force and household growth on line 1 into, respectively, entries versus exits and formations versus dissolutions. A brief investigation, chiefly for 1930 onward, suggests that the movements shown here in the net balance are overwhelmingly due to the positive elements (entries and formations), just as those in natural increase are typically a reflection of births.

to a given long swing; those on lines 2 and 3 are responsive, with line 2 representing a component common to all three variables (migration), and line 3, components which are distinctive. Moreover, since in the subsequent discussion the components on line 3 are frequently referred to collectively, it is convenient to designate each as the "rate" component of its respective aggregate, though this terminology is imprecise.

Figures 15 to 17 show for the nationwide values of each of the aggregative variables, the relevant components of change for the period since 1870 or 1880.[16] The basic data—chiefly the decennial censuses—are too crude to permit a highly refined analysis relating to such questions as timing and amplitude; on the other hand, they clearly show the swings, and permit certain broad inferences pertinent to the comparison between recent and earlier experience. All three figures show the predominant role of net immigration in the swing in the aggregate throughout most of the period covered, but for the swing from the 1930's through the late 1950's, the distinctive "rate" component for each variable becomes paramount. Indeed, the movement since 1940—up and then down—of the "rate" component in the three figures is startlingly similar. Clearly this raises a question whether the analytical model suggested in the previous section is indeed relevant to current experience. In that model, migration played a key part, filling the dual role of labor market response and source of household growth. What happens to the model when migration no longer enters into the swing in substantial magnitude?

In part, the answer to this is that migration in the form of *internal* migration still enters in, and to this extent the model is pertinent in its typical form. As noted, recent experience shows a continuation of the historical swings in internal migration [59, 158–160, 163]. On the other hand, although it is difficult to make temporal comparisons of the amplitude of internal migration, there seems to be little evidence that the current swing in the rate of internal migration reached greater dimensions than previously, as would be necessary if it were to compensate for the damped movement in international migration. More-

---

[16] An alternative, or at least complementary, disaggregation would have been desirable for the nonfarm sector alone, but was not feasible with the time and resources available.

FIGURE 15

AVERAGE GROWTH RATE OF POPULA-
TION BY COMPONENT OF CHANGE,
QUINQUENNIALLY, 1870–1964

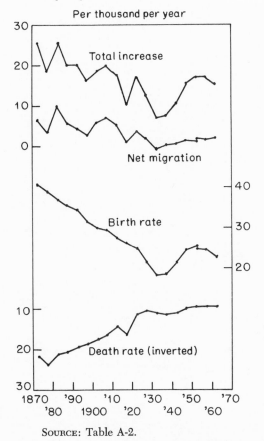

SOURCE: Table A-2.

over, the actual swings in population, labor force, and household
growth, even at the nonfarm level, were undoubtedly due in substantial part to the unprecedented movements in the distinctive "rate"
components, as well as to internal migration. Reconciliation of these
"rate" movements with the analytical model is therefore essential in
accounting for the quantitative features of the current swing. Since
these "rate" movements are, in fact, the main subjects of Parts II and
III, it will suffice here to summarize the pertinent findings.

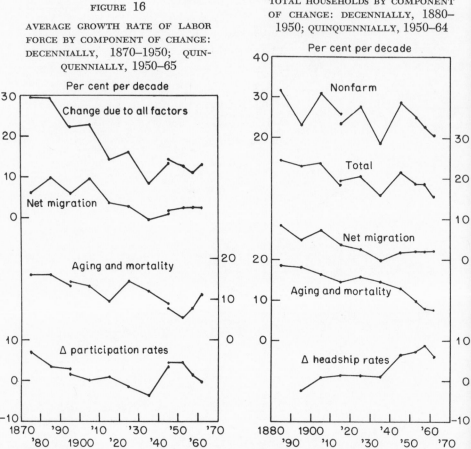

FIGURE 16

AVERAGE GROWTH RATE OF LABOR
FORCE BY COMPONENT OF CHANGE:
DECENNIALLY, 1870–1950; QUIN-
QUENNIALLY, 1950–65

SOURCE: Table A-3.

FIGURE 17

AVERAGE GROWTH RATE OF TOTAL
AND NONFARM HOUSEHOLDS, AND OF
TOTAL HOUSEHOLDS BY COMPONENT
OF CHANGE: DECENNIALLY, 1880–
1950; QUINQUENNIALLY, 1950–64

SOURCE: Table B-3.

Reasons for Recent Demographic Differences

The nature of the reconciliation is suggested by the model itself. It turns on the suggestion that the character of the labor market response to a Kuznets cycle in the growth of aggregate demand depends on the nature of labor supply conditions. In the recent swing these conditions were unique in several respects. First, the historical response through immigration was severely curtailed by restrictions imposed since the mid-1920's as well as by World War II itself. Second, the contribution to labor force growth of the aging and mortality component reached an unprecedented low (Figure 16). This was an echo effect of the exceptionally rapid decline of the birth rate in the twenties and early thirties, and was particularly concentrated in the younger working ages, where, so far as one can judge, for the first time in recorded experience the absolute number of persons aged 15–29 leveled off and actually declined slightly (Figure 18). This number showed a substantial decline in relation to those aged 30–64 (Figure 18, lower panel). Finally, the educational level of younger persons compared with older was dis-

FIGURE 18

MALE POPULATION AGED 15–29 AND
30–64; ACTUAL AND PROJECTED,
1920–85

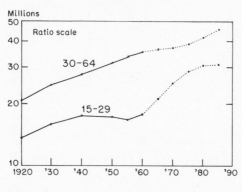

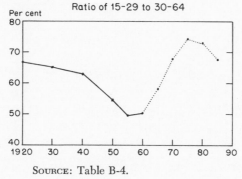

SOURCE: Table B-4.

proportionately higher than usual in the recent period (Figure 19). This arose from the rapid expansion of secondary education in the 1920's and 1930's, which temporarily enlarged the educational gap between young and old. Though there is now no historical evidence on this, I suspect that it would be necessary to go fairly far back in the nineteenth century to find a comparable period of rapid acceleration in universal schooling.

FIGURE 19

PERCENTAGE OF POPULATION AGED 25–29
AND 30–64 WITH 9–12 AND 13 OR MORE
YEARS OF SCHOOL COMPLETED; ACTUAL AND
PROJECTED, 1920–85

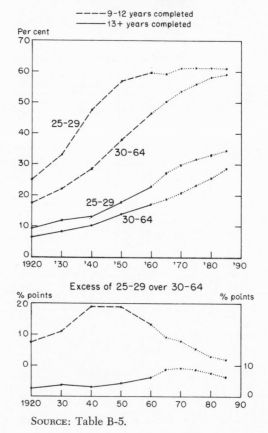

SOURCE: Table B-5.

In short, in the most recent Kuznets-cycle upswing, the relative number of those in young working ages was unusually low, and the relative quality (so far as this depends on formal schooling) was unusually high. These young adults are precisely the ones who in the past played an important part in the quantitative adjustment of labor to the swing in the growth of aggregate demand, as is evidenced by their predominance in migration flows, whether internal or international. The unique labor supply conditions in the recent swing, however, resulted in an exceptionally tight labor market for those in the younger age groups, and gave rise to unusually favorable income growth (and, one suspects, to expectations of such growth as those involved, learned by experience of the tightness of the labor market). In other words, for younger persons, the labor market response took the form predominantly of a price adjustment rather than a quantity adjustment. This unusually favorable income situation for younger persons, in turn, induced a sharp reduction in age at the time of marriage and household formation, and a sharp upswing in fertility. This accounts for the abrupt upsurge in the headship and fertility rates. At the same time, the shortage of younger persons redounded to the benefit of the only labor reserve group available in substantial numbers—older married women who were unencumbered by child-dependency responsibilities. As a result, a substantial increase in the total labor force occurred through participation-rate change for the first time. Thus, as in the past, an upswing in the growth of aggregate demand was accompanied by labor market changes and an associated rise in the growth rate of households which tended to sustain and prolong the boom. Because of the unique labor supply conditions, however, the mechanism of the association was substantially altered, with migration playing a less important role and the "rate" components of change in the demographic variables playing a leading one.

THE FUTURE: IMPLICATIONS OF AN ECHO EFFECT

One of the intriguing features of population growth is that it contains within itself a mechanism capable of generating longer-term swings.

Thus, writing in 1937 about German experience, August Losch states [118, p. 650]:

While the movement of population shows unimportant and irregular [short term] fluctuations which seem to be mere reflections of economic, sanitary and other conditions, we find quite clearly great waves, the main cause of which are the great wars. The deficit of births during a war and the surplus of births in the immediate postwar period repeat themselves about thirty-three years later, when the new generations are at their time of highest fertility. For the same reason thirty-three years later a third wave occurs.

Recognition of this leads naturally to the thought that long swings in economic activity may have their origins in the peculiar structural mechanism of population growth. My analysis of past U.S. experience, however, does not support this view. Fluctuations in demographic variables have typically arisen from movements in immigration or the "rate" components of change rather than from an echo effect of a surge in births, operating through the aging and mortality component.[17] Such demographic fluctuations were induced rather than initiated by changes in economic activity, although they had important feedback effects. This is not to say that no echo effects at all existed. One can, in fact, trace them in detailed data, but in the past they have been mild, reflecting the fact that before 1940 long swings in fertility were confined to the rate of change rather than the level of that variable.

Now, however, things have changed. The new demographic developments accompanying the most recent upswing—notably, the dramatic baby boom—have, in turn, set up an echo effect currently being felt in the form of a sharp upsurge in the young adult population. What, if any, are the implications of this echo effect for future long swings? Has the economy, perhaps, shifted to a new situation in which long swings are at least partly built in through a natural demographic cycle, even though this was not the case in the past?

---

[17] The rise between 1910–20 and 1920–30 in the aging and mortality component, which contributed to a corresponding movement in labor force and household growth, appears to contradict this observation (Figures 16 and 17). This is primarily due, however, not to an earlier upsurge in the birth rate, but to the fact that the 1910–20 level of this component was depressed sharply below normal by high mortality among young persons resulting from the flu epidemic of 1918. Thus, with reference to Figure 15, the movement is chiefly a reflection, not of a prior fluctuation in the fertility curve, but of a concurrent dip in the mortality curve (inverted), centering on 1910–20.

A satisfactory analysis of this question, as of so many this chapter has touched on, calls for a more complete model of long swings. Nevertheless, a few tentative impressions may be gained by looking in some detail at the impact of the echo effect on labor force and household growth now and in the coming decade. Moreover, this is of interest in its own right because of its possible bearing on attempts to assess more generally the outlook for the next decade.[18]

The Next Decade

To start with labor supply conditions, the echo effect of the baby boom is currently yielding its fruits in the form of an unprecedented growth in the labor force from the aging and mortality component. Since the first half of the 1950's, the rate at which this source has been contributing to labor force growth has risen from around 5 to 11 per cent per decade, and the projected figure for the last half of the 1960's is almost 14 per cent. This means that the aging and mortality component alone in the late 1960's will yield a rate of growth in the total labor force as high as that *due to all components* in the 1940's, and higher than that in the 1950's. The impact of this is concentrated among the younger age groups, with the result that the relative number of those aged 15–29 to 30–64 is now increasing more and faster than in the preceding decline (Figure 18). Moreover, an independent but significant development is that the advantage of young over old in high school education has declined sharply in the last decade and will decline somewhat further in the next (Figure 19). With regard to college education, the advantage of the young rose somewhat through 1965, but shows little prospect of further increase. On the whole, therefore, a substantial reversal of the situation in the preceding period as to relative quantity and quality of younger versus older persons is now in progress.

The marked impact of the aging and mortality component on labor force growth suggests that the labor requirements of an upswing in the growth of aggregate demand might for the first time be met very largely from this component rather than from either increased

---

[18] Cf. for example [148]. Interestingly, this NICB study, while not adopting a long-swings framework as such, looks at the next decade on the basis of experience in the past two, viewed not as a succession of short cycles, but as a major boom and ensuing retardation.

immigration or participation-rate change. (One would expect also, of course, a response through internal migration, perhaps taking more the form of a movement among nonfarm centers as the farm reservoir becomes even further depleted.) Would this rather different labor market response be accompanied by an upsurge in household growth as in the past?

One's initial reaction is to say, "of course," for the same demographic echo effect that is operating to raise labor force growth is also acting to increase household growth. On investigation, however, several mitigating circumstances come to light.

First, there is a difference in the timing and shape of the impact of the demographic movement on labor force versus household growth. The average age at labor force entry is lower than that of household formation, so that an echo effect tends to raise labor force growth in advance of household growth. This is illustrated in Figure 20, where the contributions of population change to labor force and household

FIGURE 20

CONTRIBUTION OF POPULATION CHANGE TO LABOR FORCE AND HOUSEHOLD GROWTH: ACTUAL, DECENNIALLY, 1930–50, QUINQUENNIALLY, 1950–60; AND PROJECTED, QUINQUENNIALLY, 1960–80

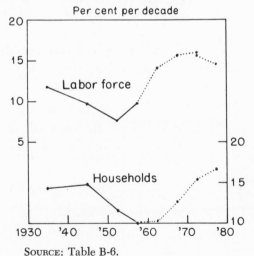

SOURCE: Table B-6.

growth since the 1930's are compared.[19] Note that the movement in household growth tends to lag behind that in labor force growth, reaching its trough and then its peak roughly five years later. Moreover, the rise in household growth is somewhat smaller in amplitude and less precipitous than that in labor force growth. This is because among young males the rise in rates of household headship not only centers at a later age than that in labor force participation, but is also less abrupt. As a result, the temporal distribution of an echo effect on household growth is more attenuated than it is on labor force growth. Thus, while the baby boom does produce an echo effect tending to raise household as well as labor force growth, the former tends to lag behind the latter and be slightly more spread out over time.

Second, in order for an echo effect in the population component of change to raise the *total* growth rate of households—that due to all sources—it is necessary that the headship-rate component not decline in compensating fashion. Since the analysis for 1940–55 has already suggested the possibility of a mechanism causing the population and "rate" components to move in at least partly offsetting fashion, it is essential to appraise the outlook for the rate component as well as that for the population one. This is facilitated by Figure 21, which repeats the curves of Figure 20 for labor force and households and adds the curves showing growth due to all sources (actual through 1960–64 and projected through 1975–80).[20] For each variable, the vertical difference between the two curves represents the contribution of the rate component.

The startling feature of Figure 21 is that while the echo effect is currently producing and, according to the projection, is to produce a sharp rise in the growth rate of labor force, an upsurge of comparable magnitude in that of households, even with a lag, is not foreseen. In the case of labor force, in order to offset the echo effect completely,

[19] For convenience of exposition, immigration has been combined here with the aging and mortality effect. The point remains valid if confined to aging and mortality alone, since the movements during the period shown are due almost entirely to this component.

[20] For households, Series B projections are used, but the use of Series A would not alter the present conclusions, since from 1965 on the growth rates implied by the two projections differ very little.

FIGURE 21

AVERAGE GROWTH RATE OF LABOR FORCE AND
HOUSEHOLDS DUE TO ALL SOURCES AND THAT
DUE TO POPULATION GROWTH ALONE: AC-
TUAL, DECENNIALLY, 1930–50, QUINQUEN-
NIALLY, 1950–64; PROJECTED, QUINQUEN-
NIALLY, 1960–80

————— Growth due to all sources
— — — — Growth due to population change

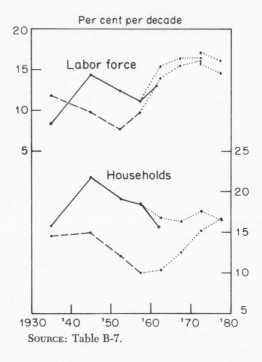

SOURCE: Table B-7.

the contribution of the "rate" component would have to drop to a negative value, that is, participation rates would, on the average, have to decline. This is not the case with regard to households, however. The contribution of the "rate" component has been so high in the past, that a drop to a lower positive value, implying merely a retardation in the average rise of headship rates, is sufficient to almost wholly offset the echo effect.

Is a slowing of the rise in headship rates, such as that implied by the projection, likely? Actual experience in the first half of this decade compared with 1955–60 does show such a tendency. Although further study is needed, two considerations suggesting the likelihood of its continuation may be noted, one endogenous and one exogenous. First, even under relatively high employment conditions, the change in relative quality and quantity of young workers which is now taking place means that they are unlikely to enjoy an excess demand situation comparable to that of 1940–55. Hence, it seems doubtful that a significant contribution to household growth through increases in headship rates will occur among this group. Second, an important factor raising household growth in the past fifteen years has been the noticeable rise in headship rates among the older population, aged 55 and over, and it is questionable that this will continue at the same pace. A principal factor in this has been the rapid extension of social security coverage. The percentage receiving OASDI benefits in the relevant population groups provides a rough though imperfect indication: [21]

	1950	1963	1975 (projected)
Males aged 60–64	0	16	22
Males aged 65 and over	25	78	89
Females aged 60–64	0	29	29
Females aged 65 and over	17	72	90

Although projections relating to such politically sensitive areas are patently hazardous, the figures provide some justification for the view that the economy has largely passed through the period when the adoption of social security would have its largest impact on headship rates among the older population. Though some additional growth from this source is probable, its quantitative importance seems likely to be less than in the immediate past.[22]

[21] I am grateful to Francisco Bayo, of the Social Security Administration, for the absolute data on beneficiaries, on the basis of which these percentages were computed.

[22] This discussion bears on Edward F. Denison's criticism [47, p. 531] that ". . . the long-wave background gets [Burnham] Campbell no farther than others who have based forecasts of housing starts on the normal increase in households that would result from population changes in relevant age-sex groups. . . ." The present analysis suggests that not only the population component of household change should be studied, but also the "rate" component, and that the long-swing

To sum up, although a more thorough investigation is needed, this analysis makes clear that in the current and coming decade, contrary to what one might expect, an upswing in household growth is neither a simultaneous nor automatic accompaniment of a surge in labor force growth arising from the echo effect of the baby boom. True, there is an echo effect exerting an upward pressure on household growth, but it lags behind that in labor force growth and is more attenuated. In addition, there are circumstances, partly endogenous and partly exogenous, which may dampen this upward pressure by slowing the rise in headship rates among young and old, thereby reducing the contribution to household growth from the "rate" component source. Therefore, under such new circumstances of labor supply, in which an echo effect supplies the labor requirements arising from an upswing in the growth of aggregate demand, it is far from clear that a substantial reinforcing stimulus to the boom from an upsurge in household growth will occur as it did in the past.

Longer-Term Future

Though at first glance it is tempting to pronounce that the emergence of an echo effect has created a new "built-in" long-swing mechanism, a more careful look at current changes and those in prospect over the next decade creates doubt that any such simple generalization is warranted. However, more study of the determinants of household growth by age group is needed, including attention to "gross" changes (formations and dissolutions) and their implications for spending. (Clearly, implications for spending when social security forestalls dissolution of a home are likely to be quite different from those arising from accelerated household formation among young persons.) The relative weight of endogenous vs. exogenous elements in labor force and household growth needs clarification too. For example, while the present analytical scheme suggests that there is

approach may be of value in clarifying the movements in the "rate" component. The reference to OASDI, however, shows clearly that other factors are pertinent and that more intensive study is needed of the determinants of headship rate changes, including factors such as school enrollment and marital status. Clearly, throughout this analysis, no attempt has been made to consider the possible bearing of the Vietnam War.

a tendency for movements in the "rate" and population components to be at least partly offsetting for both labor force and household growth, the dampening at present appears to be greater for household growth. Is this attributable wholly to exogenous circumstances or is it partly inherent in the mechanism? Moreover, perhaps undue attention has been given here to demographic reactions from the household growth side. In commenting on this chapter, Abramovitz pointed out that, in addition to such considerations, accelerated growth in labor force, for whatever reason, may at least permit a protracted boom to be sustained by keeping the "natural rate" of output growth above the "warranted rate" for a longer period, thus postponing the time when an output ceiling may act as a brake on long-term capital investment.

Certainly the emergence of demographic echo effects is a new phenomenon which must be reckoned with in assessing the longer-term future. For example, another possibility, though not the only one, is that an echo effect creates a tendency toward waves in labor force growth with a duration longer than Kuznets cycles and, at the same time, upswings in the growth of aggregate demand initiated by nondemographic factors occur with the frequency of past Kuznets cycles. Under such circumstances, the impact of the demand movement on the labor market and the reactions stemming therefrom could be highly variable, depending on whether the flood, ebb, or some intermediate stage of labor force growth prevailed at the time. In this connection, it should be noted that the current decline in the crude birth rate has, in only eight years, wiped out the increase since 1940. (This is not true, however, of age-adjusted fertility measures.) Beyond 1975, this will produce a shift in relative numbers of young and old in a direction similar to that of the 1940's and early 1950's (cf. Figure 18). If aggregate demand conditions are favorable, this creates the possibility of economic-demographic interactions at that time like those of the post-World War II era.

Finally, there is nothing in this analysis which implies that Kuznets cycles in the economy's growth rate are not susceptible to elimination through appropriate policy measures. If the emphasis on the central role of aggregate demand is correct, then, as Abramovitz and Hickman have also suggested, manipulation of effective demand should make it possible largely to eliminate discernible long swings. But the analysis does imply that determination of the appropriate policy measures may call for more attention to variables and relationships of the type suggested here than has been customary in the past.

PART II / FERTILITY ANALYSES

CHAPTER 4 / THE AMERICAN BABY

BOOM IN HISTORICAL PERSPECTIVE

This chapter focuses on the recent baby boom, particularly on the extent to which this represents an abrupt break with past experience. The next chapter extends the analysis to the current fertility decline.

We first take a fresh look at the historical record in the light of the Kuznets-cycle conception of economic change, taking care to discuss separately the experience of three population groups with significantly different patterns—foreign-born, native-born urban, and native-born rural. After a brief retracing of several earlier findings, the analysis quickly moves onto new ground, exploring some possible reasons for the pattern observed.

The analysis is confined to the white population because of the greater reliability of the data for this group and its predominant influence in determining the pattern for the total.

KUZNETS CYCLES IN U.S. POPULATION
GROWTH AND FERTILITY

The Rate of Total Increase

We start with the rate of population growth. Since we are interested in focusing on major movements, we employ five-year averages of the basic data,[1] a choice governed partly by preference—to eliminate or at least reduce the shorter-term changes associated with the ordinary business cycle—and partly by necessity—because of the initial mold in which some of the basic data are cast, particularly those relating to fertility.

NOTE: An earlier version of this chapter was published in December 1961 in the *American Economic Review*, and was reprinted by the National Bureau as its Occasional Paper 79.

[1] For the rate of total increase, the average is implicit. The rate, which is actually calculated from observations on the population stock separated by five years, yields a time pattern equivalent to that of a geometric average of the annual rates of change within the successive quinquennia.

Figure 22 shows the average rate of increase of the U.S. white population in successive quinquennia from 1870 to 1955. The familiar downward drift through the 1930's and the recent increase are immediately apparent. Less familiar, but equally obtrusive, are significant fluctuations in the rate of change. The duration of the fluctuations has run from ten to thirty-five years and their average magnitude has amounted to about one-quarter of the mean rate of change over the period as a whole. In Chapter 2, the components of population growth responsible for these fluctuations were identified (Figure 2). It was noted that, while immigration was typically the principal factor in the past, the recent population upsurge has been due to fertility.

Since 1870, then (and indeed even before [103, p. 36; 107]), the

FIGURE 22

AVERAGE GROWTH RATE OF TOTAL WHITE POPULATION, 1870–1959

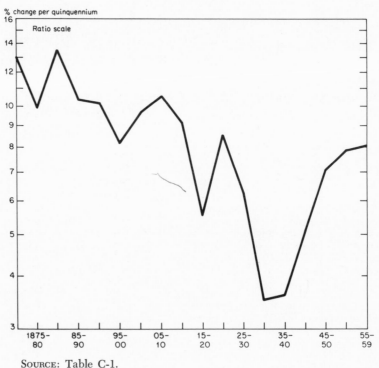

SOURCE: Table C-1.

historical record has consistently been marked by major swings in the rate of population growth. But since the source of the recent upsurge in the rate of population growth has been a rise in the birth rate rather than in immigration, one might maintain that this recent increase bears only a surface resemblance to prior swings and that, given the new immigration restrictions of the 1920's, recovery in the rate of growth was hardly to be expected. Whether this view is correct or whether the recent movement does bear a logical relation to its forebears is a question to which I return toward the end of the chapter.

The Birth Rate of the Total White Population

Let us turn to the component of population change that constitutes the center of our interest, the birth rate. Recent work has made it possible to reconstruct a full century of fertility experience for the white population of the United States.[2] The annual birth rate estimates have been averaged here for successive quinquennia, in keeping with our interest in discerning Kuznets cycles.

The upper panel of Figure 23 brings out clearly the long-term decline in the level of the birth rate and its recent recovery. It also shows that the movement of the birth rate—even when smoothed by a five-year average—has been far from regular. For the period through the secular trough of the 1930's, intervals of rapid decline alternated with intervals of slower decline or even absolute increase. These are the long swings in fertility which Kuznets found in a somewhat different set of figures. They are apparent throughout the entire eighty-year period of fertility decline covered here.

[2] Economists are perhaps not generally aware of the scarcity of historical data on population change. When Kuznets made his study in 1958 [103], there were no annual data on the crude birth rate before 1909. The new series, extending our perspective to the years before the Civil War, is the product of a doctoral dissertation by Melvin Zelnik, carried on at the Office of Population Research, Princeton University, under the supervision of Ansley Coale [220]. The estimates were derived by applying appropriate mortality rates to the decennial census single-year-of-age distributions adjusted for "age heaping" (excessive reporting of certain ages, primarily those ending in 0 and 5). As the upper panel of Figure 23 shows, the patterns traced by these and the official estimates in the overlap period are virtually the same; for earlier dates, however, the Zelnik figures are somewhat less reliable because of the lesser accuracy or availability of data needed for the estimates. The dissertation has now been published [32], but my analysis above uses the figures in the thesis.

FIGURE 23

LEVEL AND RATE OF CHANGE OF CRUDE BIRTH RATE OF TOTAL WHITE
POPULATION, 1855–1959

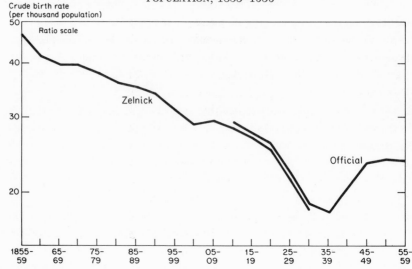

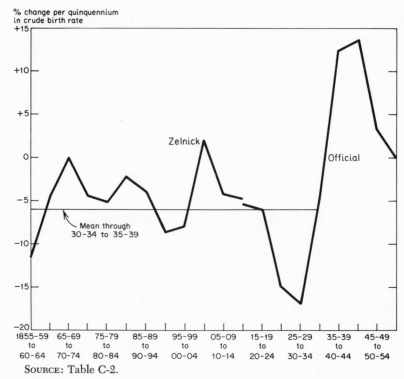

SOURCE: Table C-2.

The lower panel of Figure 23 presents the quinquennial percentage rate of change of the birth rate, computed directly from the data plotted in the upper panel.[3] The average rate of decline per quinquennium through the secular trough in 1935–39 was about 6 per cent. If this rate had prevailed uniformly throughout the entire period, the individual observations would have formed the horizontal line shown in the figure. The movement in the actual observations about the line makes clear that the variations in the rate of change were of substantial magnitude; in fact, the average value of the deviations from the mean amounts to six-tenths of the mean rate of decline itself. The duration of the two swings through the first decade of this century was fifteen to twenty years, whether measured peak to peak or trough to trough. The movements since then have been of much longer duration, on the order of thirty-five to forty years.

But of what interest, it may be asked, is this exercise in quantitative history for analysis of the baby boom? In reply, one might suggest that it leads to revising one's conception of the historical record, which has significant implications for interpreting recent experience. Typically, the historical movement which has been emphasized is the long-term secular decline.[4] To this I would now add the observation that this decline has been far from regular; that, in fact, it has been repeatedly characterized by fluctuations of noticeable amplitude and substantial duration. The customary interpretation of the past leads naturally to the view that recent experience constitutes an abrupt break—a reversal in primary trend. In contrast, the conception of historical change employed here suggests that recent experience *might* be conceived as the latest in a succession of major movements around the trend—a Kuznets cycle which, for some reason, is of much greater amplitude and duration than its predecessors. Clearly this view implies less of a break with historical experience and at least raises the possibility of more easily reconciling the present with the

[3] To avoid confusion, it should be noted that (1) it is the birth rate itself and not the rate of change therein that is the component of the rate of total population change shown in Figure 22, and (2) swings in annual birth or fertility rates do not necessarily imply swings in the completed fertility of successive population cohorts (see the concluding section of Chapter 5).

[4] For examples of this see [86, 185, 206] and more recently [69; 82, Chs. 2, 11; 153, Ch. 13].

past—a *sine qua non* of any attempted explanation of the baby boom. Moreover, it suggests a new research strategy with regard to the baby boom, namely, that one focus on explaining Kuznets cycles, past and present, in an effort to determine whether the underlying causes of these movements may have operated with exceptional force in recent decades. It is in terms of this conception that the subsequent analysis is organized.

Before proceeding to this analysis, there is one more feature of Figure 23 that deserves attention. This is the precipitous decline in the birth rate during the 1920's. A trend line fitted to the pre-1920 data in the upper panel and extended through the next two decades would lie not only above the observations for the 1930's, but above that for 1925–29 as well. From the lower panel, one finds that the rate of decline between the first and second halves of the 1920's was the second highest in the one hundred-year record, falling only slightly below that in the next overlapping decade. This drastic decline during a period of high prosperity has been cited by demographers as grounds for discounting efforts to explain the baby boom on the basis of economic factors. For example: ". . . the interpretation of the baby boom as the natural consequence of prolonged prosperity is hardly more tenable than the earlier interpretation of the reversal in the 1930's as momentary. The next earlier period of notable prosperity in the United States—the 1920's—was a period of sharply falling fertility. In fact, as Dudley Kirk points out, the depressed 1930's produced *more* births by far than one would expect on the basis of an extrapolation of the trend of the prosperous 1920's." [5]

[5] Ansley J. Coale, Introduction [170, pp. 5–6]. The reference is to Dudley Kirk, "The Influence of Business Cycles on Marriage and Birth Rates" [170, pp. 241–260]. The method followed by Kirk in his analysis is to correlate "trend deviations of economic measures (as independent variables) to measures of nuptiality and natality (as dependent variables)" [170, p. 242], using fertility data for the total population for the period 1920–58. While the results are relevant to analysis of fertility variations within the ordinary business cycle, in my view they cannot be used to draw inferences about the baby boom. The "trend" lines fitted for the period 1920–58 largely reproduce the Kuznets cycle which constitutes the baby boom. By concentrating on explaining deviations from "trend," Kirk in effect eliminates from his analysis the baby boom itself. Moreover, even with regard to business cycle analysis, it would be of interest to distinguish components of the total population whose fertility was subject to substantially different influences, as is done below for Kuznets cycles.

TABLE 1. PERCENTAGE DISTRIBUTION OF WHITE FEMALES,
20–44, BY NATIVITY, AND OF NATIVE WHITE FEMALES, 20–44,
BY RURAL–URBAN RESIDENCE, 1890–1950

	1890	1910	1930	1950
Total white	100.0	100.0	100.0	100.0
Foreign-born white	20.9	19.9	14.7	4.6
Native white	79.1	80.1	85.3	95.4
Urban	30.2	39.6	51.5	64.7 [a]
Rural	48.8	40.5	33.8	30.7

SOURCE: Table C-5 and census reports.
[a] Based on 1950 census definition of "urban."

Clearly, an attempt to reconcile present with past experience must devote special attention to the record for the 1920's.

The Fertility of the Native and Foreign-Born White Populations
The fertility of the total white population is a composite of that of a number of subgroups, each subject in part to distinctive, in part to common, influences. We can gain further perspective on the baby boom if we consider separately the experience of the native and foreign-born white populations, and, within the former, the urban and rural components. Table 1 indicates the proportion of total white females of reproductive age accounted for by each of these groups at various dates. In the present section, we consider fertility patterns for the foreign-born and *total* native white populations.

For the dependent variable, instead of the crude birth rate I now use the fertility ratio, the number of children under 5 years old to the number of women 20 to 44 years old, a choice necessitated by the available data.[6] As the following figures suggest, the fertility ratio typically exceeds the crude birth rate by a factor in the neighborhood of twenty to twenty-five:

Total White Population	1885–89	1905–9	1925–29
Crude birth rate (annual average)	35.3	29.4	22.4
Fertility ratio (next census date)	744	632	505

[6] A good discussion of the conceptual and statistical problems relating to the fertility ratio is given in [82, p. 13 and Appendix A].

Analytically, this reflects the fact that the fertility ratio is computed from (a) a denominator about one-fifth as large as that for the crude birth rate (females aged 20–44 instead of the total population), and (b) a numerator four to five times as large. (Implicitly, birth experience over a five-year period is totaled rather than averaged, and is multiplied by a survival rate on the order of .85 to .95 to exclude those dying before the end of the period.) Thus the time patterns traced by the two measures may differ somewhat because of variations in the ratio of women aged 20–44 to the total population and in the mortality of children under 5 years, particularly in infant mortality.[7]

Figure 24 presents fertility ratios for the total white population by nativity from 1875–79 to 1925–29, and, supplemented by general fertility rates, for the native and total white populations to 1954–58.[8] The observations on fertility ratios are at census and mid-census dates, but since they reflect fertility behavior over the preceding five years, we have dated them according to the quinquennia to which they refer. The lower panel shows the percentage rate of change per quinquennium in each series, computed in the same fashion as for the preceding figure.

Several points deserve mention. First, Kuznets cycles are evident in the series for both the native- and foreign-born groups. Through 1925–29, the timing of the swings appears to be usually the same, but the amplitude is substantially greater for the foreign-born white. There is some suggestion of increasing amplitude, particularly for the native white, and in the most recent period the magnitude of the swing for this group is strikingly greater than previous ones. Arithmetic

[7] For the total white population, the only one for which comparison is possible, the directions of change in the rate of change of the crude birth rate and of the fertility ratio are identical from 1885–89 on, the principal period of the analysis, with one exception. This exception is primarily due to an understatement of the fertility ratio for 1910–14, because no adjustment was made for the exceptional effect of the influenza epidemic of 1918.

[8] The fertility ratio estimates, prepared in connection with the present study, are based in large part on a valuable unpublished memorandum prepared by Everett S. Lee providing age and parentage detail underlying the quinquennial estimates of native white population published by Kuznets [103]. Because of omissions or defects in the recent reporting of parentage and nativity, it was not possible to continue these estimates beyond 1925–29. However, to provide some idea of the pattern after 1925–29, use has been made of the official estimates of the closely comparable general fertility rate (live births per 1,000 females aged 15–44) for the total and native white populations.

FIGURE 24

LEVEL AND RATE OF CHANGE OF FERTILITY RATIO, 1865–1929, AND OF GEN-
ERAL FERTILITY RATE, 1920–58: TOTAL WHITE POPULATION, BY NATIVITY

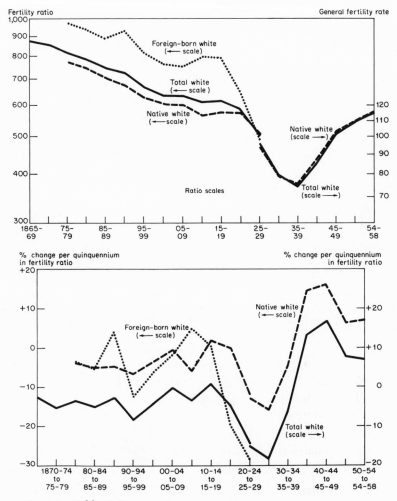

SOURCE: Table C-3.

analysis of the swings in the total white group shows that they are
caused in important measure by the fertility movements of both the
native and foreign-born components, and that the contribution of
shifts in the relative importance of the two groups has been negligible.

The native-born white group, despite the smaller amplitude of its swings, typically accounted for the dominant part of the movement in the total because of its much greater share (Table C-12).

Some light is also cast on the precipitous rate of decline in total white fertility in the 1920's. For both the foreign- and native-born populations there is a substantial drop in the fertility ratio between the first and second halves of the decade. However, the decline for the foreign-born is more than double that for the native—29 against 12 per cent. Hence, a significant part of the decline in total white fertility in the 1920's—to be precise, about one-third (Table C-12)—was owing to the drastic reduction in the fertility of the foreign-born white population.[9] Indeed, for this group, if one adds the movement between the two preceding quinquennia, the drop in fertility was nothing short of spectacular. Between 1915–19 and 1925–29 the foreign-born white fertility ratio dropped by about four-tenths, more than double the decline during the preceding forty years.

The Fertility of the Urban and Rural Native White Populations

Our data now become even more limited, relating only to the latter half of each decade from 1885–89 on. Estimates published by the National Resources Committee [204] for 1905–9 through 1925–29 have been carried back two additional decades. A constant 5 per cent adjustment by the NRC for underenumeration of children under five years has been accepted here, in part because no basis for a differential rural-urban adjustment was readily available, and in part because the analysis rests primarily on the figures for the more reliable censuses from 1900 on. Our immediate interest is in the pattern through 1925–29, and estimates for the native white population by rural-urban residence are only available to this point. To fill out the picture since then, however, we have added overlap figures for the total white population for 1925–29 on, an approximation which seems reasonable in view of the much diminished importance of the foreign-born in recent years.

As is clear from the curve for the total native white group in Figure 25, compared with that in Figure 24, the timing of the Kuznets cycles before 1925–29 is such that omission of the observations for

---

[9] "The decrease in fertility of foreign-born white women was perhaps the outstanding feature of the decline in the birth rate during the twenties" [205, p. 127].

FIGURE 25

LEVEL AND RATE OF CHANGE OF FERTILITY RATIO BY RURAL-URBAN RESI-
DENCE: NATIVE WHITE POPULATION, 1885–1929; TOTAL WHITE POPULATION,
1925–58

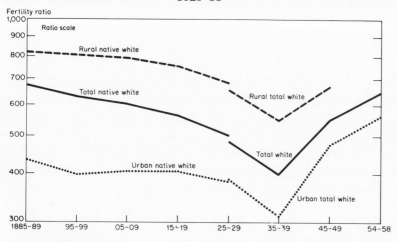

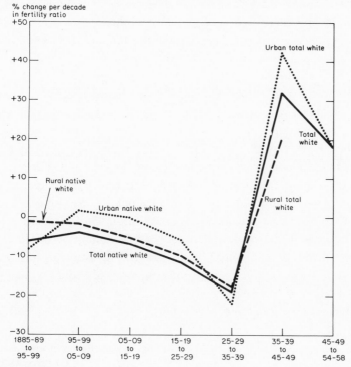

SOURCE: Table C-6.

the first half of each decade tends to conceal the long swings. Nevertheless, some significant points stand out. As the upper panel shows, the decline from 1885–89 to 1925–29 in fertility of the total native white population was significantly greater than that for either of the components. This was caused by the depressing influence on total native white fertility of the continuous redistribution of population from high-fertility rural to low-fertility urban areas. Quantitatively this rural-urban shift accounted for about one-half of the total decline over the forty-year period (Table C-13). The depressing effect on fertility was about the same in each successive decade.

A second point of interest is the greater decline in rural than urban fertility through 1925–29. The rural decline is about half again as great as the urban—18 as opposed to 12 per cent. Indeed, if one considers the estimates for urban fertility from only 1895–99 to 1925–29, there is little evidence at all of a declining trend. The over-all reduction in these three decades is only 4 per cent, and the impression created by the curve is one of general stability.

This observation of substantial stability for a group accounting in this period for a third to a half of white females of reproductive age runs so counter to the common impression of a general and persistent secular decline that it deserves further consideration. This is particularly true since this group has tended to assume an increasingly dominant role in determining the pattern for the total white population and thus is of central significance for consideration of recent and prospective experience of the white population as a whole.[10] Could the finding be a statistical artifact resulting from deficiencies in our estimating procedure? The possibility cannot be discounted—I have attempted to make a reasonable estimate for 1895–99, but with more time and larger resources it undoubtedly could be improved. However, even if we take only the more firmly based NRC estimates for 1905–9 through 1925–29—at the expense unfortunately of reducing our span of observation to two decades—there is still little evidence of a significant decline. In presenting these data the NRC does not call into

[10] Readers may be reminded in this connection of the finding in Dorothy S. Thomas' pioneering study of Sweden [162] that during the nineteenth century *short-term* fluctuations in fertility of the total population were initially dominated by fluctuations in agriculture, but subsequently by those in industry.

question the figures for urban native white population, though they are accorded hardly any attention [205, p. 127]. With regard to regional fertility patterns of the *total* white population, however, the NRC does note that "these data show clearly a tendency toward the leveling off of birth rates in areas long influenced by the lower birth rate pattern" [205, p. 123].

Some additional historical evidence consistent with the finding of stability is perhaps worth citing. In 1930, Joseph J. Spengler published a study of the fertility of native- and foreign-born women in New England, in which he concluded that "during the period between 1860 and 1915 no definite trend appeared in the native fertility rates" [149, p. 34]. For the period from 1915 through 1925 (the last year of the study), he found an upward tendency in fertility. Here, then, is an area in the forefront of the process of urbanization and industrialization in which native white fertility did not significantly decline over a long period stretching well back into the nineteenth century.[11] The appearance of a similar pattern for the nation as a whole at a later date would clearly be consistent with this earlier New England experience.

One final point should be noted regarding Figure 25. The decline of total native white fertility in the 1920's is now seen to be owing more to a decrease in rural than urban fertility. Between 1915–19 and 1925–29, the reduction in rural fertility was close to 10 per cent, while that for urban fertility was under 6 per cent. Thus further understanding of this period calls particularly for an explanation of the rural decline.

Summary

While the fertility of the total white population declined substantially from the latter part of the nineteenth century to the mid-1930's, there was significant variation in the rate of change over time and among component population groups. Even after averaging data so as to eliminate or substantially reduce variability due to the business cycle, marked fluctuations—Kuznets cycles of fifteen or more years

[11] A reexamination by Robert Gutman [83] of the reliability of the Massachusetts birth registration data used by Spengler, while arriving at a somewhat different evaluation from Spengler, does not upset this finding.

duration—stand out in the patterns for the total, native, and foreign-born white populations. Moreover, in the first three decades of this century the over-all decline in total white fertility was owing almost exclusively to declines for the foreign-born white and rural native white populations and to the shift from rural to urban areas; the fertility of the urban native white population, the group of central importance in understanding recent and prospective movements in the aggregate, remained virtually unchanged. Considerations such as these raise the question whether the baby boom, rather than an abrupt reversal in a long-term downtrend, might not be at least in part a Kuznets cycle of much larger magnitude than heretofore. To answer this, it is necessary to look into possible reasons for these movements.

REASONS FOR KUZNETS CYCLES IN FERTILITY OF DIFFERENT POPULATION GROUPS

Briefly stated, the analytical viewpoint underlying the subsequent discussion is this: variations in the fertility of a given population group are caused primarily by changes in two classes of factors—economic condition and demographic composition. The "group" for which these factors should be studied comprises those in the family-building ages. Broadly, this embraces those aged 15–44 years, but for some purposes particular attention should be paid to the younger members, those aged, say 20–29, where so many decisions regarding marriage and childbearing are concentrated. "Economic condition" refers to the employment and income experience of the group. Ideally, "income" here would embrace all sources, including even interpersonal transfers from other age groups, though in the following discussion attention is concentrated on the chief source, labor income. "Demographic composition" refers to the distribution of the group according to characteristics such as age, sex, nationality, and parentage. A change in demographic composition may itself stem basically from economic forces, for example, a change in age composition of the foreign-born due to a rise in immigration, but it is nevertheless useful to distinguish the different channels through which these forces operate. Both economic condition and demographic composition may affect the over-all fertility of a population group by influencing either marriage behavior, marital fertility, or both. No consistent effort is made here to distinguish the role of these two components in over-all fertility change, though it would be of interest in a fuller treatment.[12]

The analysis below for the foreign-born takes up only compositional factors, while those for the two native-born groups concentrate on economic condition. It would have been of interest to examine, where possible, the influence of economic factors on foreign-born fertility in so far as they exert effects other than through compositional change, and of changes in demographic composition on native-born fertility, especially those associated with rural-urban migration.[13] In this discussion, however, I have not attempted an exhaustive analysis, but have singled out those factors which seemed on the basis of my initial investigation to throw significant light on the Kuznets cycles shown by each group.

Foreign-Born White Fertility

As populations go, the foreign-born is an unusual one—primarily because the source of its growth is immigration rather than births.[14] One result of this is a very atypical age distribution. Unlike the usual age distribution of a growing population, where the numbers tend to fall progressively with each older age group, that of the foreign born shows a concentration in the middle age groups with relatively small numbers at the extremes, at least as long as immigration remains high [164, p. 144]. Moreover, not only are the additions to this population fed in at relatively advanced ages—the "prime" working ages—but there is a significant disproportion between the sexes, with males

---

[12] This brief statement of analytical viewpoint is intended merely to highlight the determinants studied here. Among other possibly important factors are variations in the competitive situation of children in the consumers' scale of preference associated, e.g., with the introduction of new consumer durables, or a change in the net income which children add to the family (see Joseph S. Davis [45, pp. 56–58] and Gary S. Becker [170, pp. 209–231]); changes in the availability of credit resources; and shifts in techniques and knowledge of birth control. For other contributions by economists, see [2, 7, 84, 112, 132, 134, 214 and 145a]. See also my recent paper cited in Chapter 5, footnote 5.

[13] A cursory look at the available data on compositional aspects of the native white rural and urban populations suggests that they exhibit much less decade-to-decade variability than the foreign-born white. See the 1890–1930 figures in Thompson and Whelpton [164, Tables 41 and 56, and Appendix Tables 17, 23, and 27]. While there are some excellent recent general studies on U.S. population [19, 153], it is unfortunate that there is nothing that continues this remarkable study to the present in its full analytical depth.

[14] Children born to foreign-born women after immigration are, of course, classified as native-born.

noticeably predominating. Finally, given wide swings in immigration, such as have occurred in this country, the relative size even of adjoining age-sex groups can fluctuate widely in as short a period as a decade.

These considerations explain my starting with demographic composition in seeking clues to the variations in the rate of change of foreign-born fertility. My immediate point of departure in studying these movements, particularly the very steep decline in the 1920's was the observation that the proportion of young foreign-born women who were married dropped sharply from 1920 to 1930, as is shown by the following figures:

Age at Specified Date	Percentage Married	
	1920	1930
20–24	61.6	47.5
25–29	81.6	75.9

Why, one may ask, should such an abrupt decline occur? The chance that a foreign-born white woman aged 20–24 by 1920 was married was almost two in three, but if she reached this age group only one decade later, the likelihood had declined to less than one in two.

An obvious hypothesis, stemming from the observation that the proportion of young foreign-born *men* married remained almost constant over the decade, is that the demand for women to marry dropped off because of a decline in the relative number of males in the market [101, 166]. In testing this, however, one must recognize that the relevant ratio is not that of males to females in a given age group, the standard sex ratio, since, as is well known, men typically marry at a later age than women. For example, in the period 1890–1930, at least 45 per cent of foreign-born white women were married by the time they were 20–24, but for foreign-born white men this proportion was not attained until ages 25–29 had been reached [164, p. 395]. In attempting to explain the marriage proportion for foreign-born white women aged 20–29, therefore, the ratio of foreign-born white males aged 25–34 to females aged 20–29 was computed.[15]

[15] The analysis implies of course that native-born men did not constitute a particularly important source of demand for foreign-born women. This assumption seems consistent with the facts; in 1920 the proportion of foreign-born mothers whose husbands were native-born was less than one in six [188, p. 232].

FIGURE 26

RATIO OF MALES AGED 25–34 TO FEMALES AGED
20–29, AND PERCENTAGE OF LATTER MARRIED: FOR-
EIGN-BORN WHITE POPULATION, 1890–1930

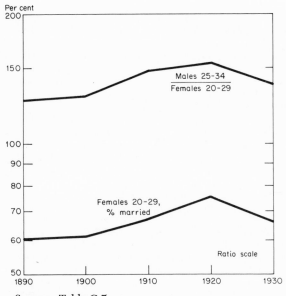

SOURCE: Table C-7.

The relevant series are plotted in Figure 26 for the decennial
census dates 1890–1930. The close similarity between the patterns
traced by the two curves—a similarity which would not appear if
the standard sex ratio for those aged 20–29 were used—is impressive.
Apparently, the marital experience of young foreign-born white females
did depend very considerably on the gyrations of our rather un-
orthodox sex ratio, which in turn arose from the impact of both earlier
and current immigration on the age-sex structure of the foreign-born
population.[16]

In Figure 27, this line of reasoning is pushed a step further.
Here, at five-year intervals, the series for foreign-born white fertility

[16] An interesting by-product of the sharp decline in the marriage-relevant sex
ratio during the 1920's, and the corresponding reduction in the proportion of
foreign-born white females aged 20–24 who were married, was an abrupt rise in
the labor-force participation of this group from 37.6 to 50.1 per cent [116, Table
A-4].

FIGURE 27

LEVEL AND RATE OF CHANGE OF FERTILITY RATIO; AND OF RATIO OF MALES
AGED 25–34 TO FEMALES 20–29, AND OF FEMALES AGED 20–34 TO FEMALES
20–44: FOREIGN-BORN WHITE POPULATION, 1875–1930

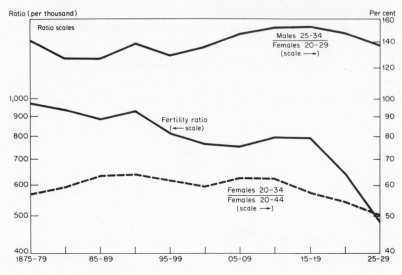

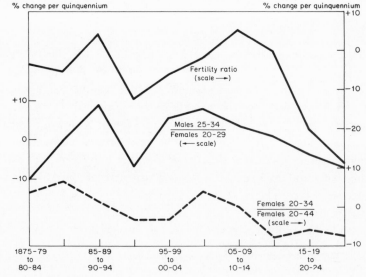

SOURCE: Table C-8.

and our marriage-relevant sex ratio (the two solid lines) are compared, the latter being used in the absence of direct observations on the marriage proportion at mid-census dates. As the lower panel shows, while the movements in the rates of change of the two series are not perfectly consistent, there is a noticeable similarity. Both series show two trough-to-trough swings with the dates of peaks and troughs close, if not identical. This suggests that at least one element responsible for Kuznets cycles in the rate of change of foreign-born fertility was the changing proportion of males aged 25–34 to females aged 20–29 and the consequent effect of this on the marriage proportion.

The broken line in the figure brings out a second demographic feature of the foreign-born population that may have contributed to the fertility swings, namely, the proportion of women aged 20–44 in prime reproductive ages, conceived here as encompassing ages 20–34. Here too there is a suggestion of two trough-to-trough swings with reasonably consistent timing, though the amplitude of the movements is somewhat smaller for this series. However, in the beginning of the period (for which the estimates are probably less reliable), the timing relationships are somewhat off.

This brief discussion of Kuznets cycles in the rate of change of foreign-born white fertility is designed to be exploratory rather than definitive, and enough has perhaps been said to provide some support for the view that shifts in demographic composition of the foreign born associated with the changing impact of immigration were at least in part responsible for these movements. Even if one accepts this suggestion, however, there remain some troublesome discrepancies. One—of particular interest in this analysis—is that in the latter part of the period considered here, the decline in the rate of change of fertility was somewhat greater than one would have expected on the basis of the two factors so far discussed. One possible explanation, suggested in several sources and consistent with the emphasis here on compositional changes in the population, is an abrupt decline in the proportion of foreign-born women in the prime reproductive ages who came from the high-fertility countries of southern and eastern Europe. There is substantial evidence that female immigrants from this area typically had significantly higher fertility than contemporaneous immigrants from northern and western Europe [82, p. 108; 189, pp. 4, 10; 211]. Clearly, a sudden drop in the share of young foreign-born women from this source would tend to depress fertility.

Direct evidence to test this proposition is not available since during the period concerned the census did not regularly publish age detail for the foreign born by country of origin. However, it seems possible to form a rough impression of the validity of the argument. In the period 1890–1915, about two-thirds of all female immigrants came from southern and eastern Europe; in 1915–30, about one-third. I have attempted to estimate, therefore, for foreign-born women aged 20–34 at each of several dates, the proportion who had immigrated between 1890 and 1915, the peak period of the "new immigration." [17] The results are as follows: 1900 = 45, 1910 = 82, 1920 = 86, 1930 = 48. The figures clearly suggest a drastic decline during the 1920's in the share of young foreign-born women accounted for by the new immigration,[18] and thus appear consistent with the suggestion that the decline in the rate of change of foreign-born fertility during this decade, attributable in part to the demographic shifts previously noted, was aggravated by this factor.

Rural White Fertility

The explanation investigated here for Kuznets cycles in rural fertility is a simple one; namely, that the rate of change of rural fertility varies directly with that in the economic condition of the farm population in family-building ages, approximated here by real farm income per head of the farm population (or labor force) as a whole. If the rate of growth of real farm income per head drops off, the rate of change of farm fertility would be expected to decline (algebraically). The converse is true if the rate of farm income growth increases.

[17] The technique for 1930, for example, was to compare the number of survivors from the group of foreign-born women aged 5–19 in 1915, estimated by appropriate survival rates from [111, p. 23], with the number aged 20–34 enumerated in 1930.

[18] Thompson and Whelpton draw an opposite conclusion, namely, that the share accounted for by the new immigration rose slightly during the decade and thus could not have contributed to the fertility decline [164, pp. 271–272]. The procedure they use to infer the share of the new immigration, however, rests primarily on figures for foreign-born women of all ages, and fails to take account of the fact that the major shift in national origins of immigration in the 1920's particularly affected the younger foreign-born age groups, those central to the explanation of fertility.

The analysis comprises two parts, one for 1885–89 through 1925–29 based on observations at decennial intervals; and one, employing averages at quinquennial intervals, for 1920–24 through 1954–58. In the first part of the analysis, I use fertility data for the total rural white rather than native rural white population, since the earlier estimates for the former are probably somewhat more reliable for the present purpose and the bias introduced by the inclusion of the relatively unimportant foreign-born group in the rural total is probably fairly small. This series is compared with five-year averages of real gross farm income per person engaged in farming. The dates chosen for the latter allow for a lead of one to one and a half years over the fertility series. In the second part of the analysis, annual estimates of the birth rate for the total farm population (white plus nonwhite), converted to five-year averages for the first and second half of each decade, are compared with real net farm income per head of farm population, again with allowance for a lead of the latter over the former.[19] Both the quinquennial and decennial farm income series are deflated by an index chosen to approximate the cost of living to farmers. The series are plotted in the upper panel of Figure 28, and the percentage change, our particular interest, in the lower.

By and large, as the lower panel shows, the data seem reasonably consistent with the hypothesis—at least as consistent as one might hope given the shortcomings of the data and the inevitable limitations of any monocausal explanation. Swings in the rate of growth of real farm income per head or per worker appear to be matched fairly closely by swings in the rate of growth of rural fertility. Reference to the adjoining scales will show that the magnitude of the income swings is substantially greater than that of fertility. This might be interpreted as suggesting an elasticity noticeably under one, a result which seems consistent with the findings of similar business cycle analyses.[20]

If this reasoning is accepted, then the historical course of rural fertility change in this century would be conceived as reflecting in

[19] The shift to the farm birth rate series is due in part to statistical convenience, but more fundamentally to the fact that the connection between "rural" fertility and farm income becomes progressively more tenuous as the rural nonfarm population grows.
[20] Cf. the studies of Gary S. Becker [170, pp. 209–231], Dorothy S. Thomas [73, 161], Dudley Kirk [169, pp. 84–85; 170, pp. 241–257], and Morris Silver [145a, pp. 237–255].

FIGURE 28

LEVEL AND RATE OF CHANGE OF RURAL WHITE FERTILITY RATIO (R.F.R.) AND
REAL GROSS FARM INCOME PER ENGAGED (Yw), 1885–1929; AND OF FARM
BIRTH RATE (F.B.R.) AND REAL NET FARM INCOME PER HEAD (Yp), 1920–58

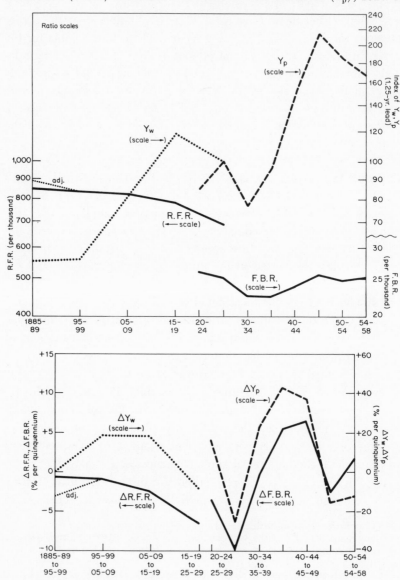

SOURCE: Tables C-9 and C-10.

significant measure the pattern of major surge and relapse which has characterized farm income growth. The accelerated rate of decline of farm fertility in the 1920's and early 1930's would be attributed to the drastic setback to the growth of farm income in the period following World War I, a decline so great that the absolute level itself was substantially reduced. The subsequent baby boom in rural areas would be explained by the corresponding resurgence in farm income growth in the late 1930's and 1940's associated particularly with the war and postwar booms. And finally, the decline in the rate of growth of fertility in the 1950's, which in terms of absolute level meant a leveling off, would be explained by the tapering off of the farm boom and substantial drop in farm-income growth. The data suggest that the adverse effect on fertility in this most recent period has been somewhat less than might have been expected. A number of possible reasons for this come to mind, such as compositional changes, the increased significance of nonfarm sources in the total income of farm families [152, pp. 48–49], and the progressive rise in the proportion of the "farm" population (1950 census definition) not engaged in agriculture [198]; but it is not possible to pursue these questions here.

From what has been said, it should be clear that the fertility trend for the *total* white population has been subject to substantial variation as a result of major fluctuations in the fertility of the foreign-born and rural white components. The fluctuations for these groups in turn appear to have been caused by the impact of the rise and fall of immigration on the age, sex, and nationality composition of the foreign-born, and of major swings in agricultural conditions on the economic condition of the farm population. It would seem to follow that generalizations based on the fertility record of the total white population (or of the entire population, whose behavior is of course dominated by the total white) would be extremely hazardous.

Consider, for example, the experience of the 1920's. If the foregoing analysis is correct, the striking decline in total white fertility that occurred in this decade was caused largely by the conjuncture of two exceptional circumstances—namely, major shifts in the demographic composition of the foreign-born population arising from the effect on immigration of World War I and the subsequent imposition of restrictions, and, second, a major slump in agricultural conditions. When added to the continuous depressing influence of the rural-urban shift, these circumstances created a decline in white fertility noticeably out of line with previous experience. Knowing this, one is inclined to view with some reserve statements such as that quoted previously, which cites the sharp fertility decline for the *total* population in the prosperous 1920's as a reason for discounting the effect of economic conditions on fertility.

It is nevertheless true that even urban native white fertility declined in this decade, though the decline of under 6 per cent for this group is rather less impressive than the almost 20 per cent decline for the white population as a whole. It is time, therefore, to see what might explain the fertility pattern for this group.

Urban Native White Fertility

As in the rural analysis, the aim here is to explore the relation between Kuznets cycles in fertility and in the economic condition of the population of family-building ages. For the rural population, it seemed reasonable to assume that the economic experience of those in family-building ages could be inferred from the income experience of the farm population as a whole. Such an assumption, however, does not seem plausible for the urban group, with its much more varied distribution of industrial and occupational attachments. In the absence of direct information on the situation of those in family-building ages, therefore, I have attempted to infer the state of the labor market for young persons from two indicators, conceived as reflecting respectively the demand and supply sides of the market. The first is the unemployment rate for the labor force as a whole. A low rate is taken as reflecting a generally favorable state of demand for labor, young and old; a high rate, an unfavorable situation. The second is the rate of change of the total white male population, aged 20–29, taken as a crude index of the rate of entry of young persons into the labor market. Other things equal, a decrease in the rate of entry would make for a favorable labor market for young persons because of their scarcity; an increase, an unfavorable market. Thus the hypothesis is that the rate of change of urban native white fertility varies directly with that of aggregate labor demand (read "inverted unemployment rate") and inversely with that of the rate of labor market entry of young persons (read "rate of change of white male population, aged 20–29").[21]

An example may clarify the reasoning. If the economy is experiencing a Kuznets-cycle expansion, the rate of growth of labor demand would increase and, other things remaining unchanged, one would expect this to lead, through its effect on income and employment conditions, to a favorable response in fertility of the native population by encouraging marriage and childbearing. However, under conditions of free immigration, the increased rate of growth of labor demand would also provoke an influx of immigrants. The resulting rise in the rate of additions to the labor market would tend to counteract the tendency toward tightening and thus offset in some measure the stimulus to fertility of the native born. Note, in this connection, that immigrants are typically concentrated in exactly those age groups in which we are interested for the analysis of fertility. Conversely the tendency toward an adverse impact on native-born fertility of a decreased rate of growth of labor demand during a Kuznets-cycle contraction would be moderated by a decrease in the rate of immigration. Thus Kuznets cycles in the rate of change of labor demand would tend to be compensated by swings in the rate of entry into the labor market owing to immigration, and the consequent impact on native-born fertility would be counteracted in some degree.[22]

Figure 29 presents the relevant series; as before, the upper panel shows the levels of the variables, the lower, their rates of change. To facilitate inferences from the graph, the curve for each of the explana-

[21] Although the view that variations in the general unemployment rate primarily reflect changes in aggregate demand seems most consistent with formal theory, it is not essential to the analysis. Alternatively, one might think of movements in the general unemployment rate as indicating the average course of employment conditions, i.e., the net outcome of aggregate demand and supply, and changes in the rate of entry as indicating variations in the deviation from the average of the situation for young persons. However, the fact that for most of the period covered here a rise in the rate of entry accompanied a reduction in unemployment seems consistent with the emphasis on aggregate demand (Table C-11, cols. 2, 3).

[22] Some may note a similarity between this reasoning and Francis Walker's analysis emphasizing the adverse influence of immigration on the fertility of the native population [212, 213]. Walker, however, was concerned with the primary trend, whereas the present analysis refers only to Kuznets cycles, and in addition takes account of the stimulating influence to native fertility of the very conditions which encourage a rise in immigration.

FIGURE 29

LEVEL AND RATE OF CHANGE OF URBAN NATIVE WHITE FERTILITY RATIO
(U.F.R.),[a] UNEMPLOYMENT RATE OF CIVILIAN LABOR FORCE (U), AND RATE
OF CHANGE OF TOTAL WHITE MALE POPULATION AGED 20–29 (S), 1885–1958

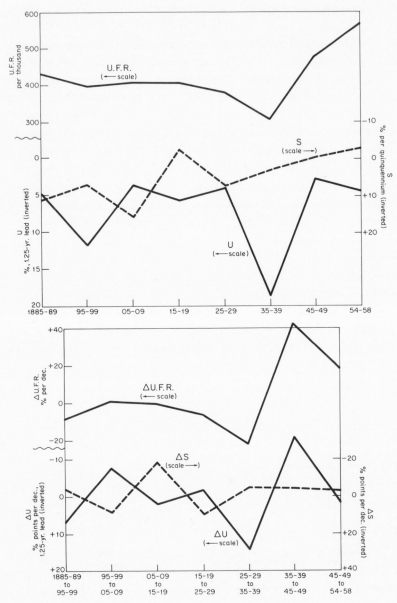

SOURCE: Table C-11.   [a] Total white, 1925–29 on.

tory variables has been plotted inverted so that an upward movement would be expected to cause an upward movement in the fertility curve, other things remaining unchanged.

If we first consider variations in the decade rates of change through 1935–39, the most interesting feature is the inverse movements of the two explanatory series. As the lower panel shows, whenever the rate of growth of aggregate labor demand (the lower solid line) moves in a way favorable to fertility, the change in the rate of entry of young persons into the labor market (the broken line) moves adversely, and vice versa. In the early part of the period the swing in supply conditions reflects chiefly movements in immigration—exactly the situation described in the example above. Later, the supply movement reflects primarily variations arising from demographic sources. For example, the increase in the decade from 1915–19 to 1925–29 compared with that in the decade preceding reflects an exceptional rise in the rate of increase of native white males aged 20–29, which traces in turn to a corresponding movement in the total white birth rate earlier in the century.

So far as directions of movement of the explanatory series during this period are concerned, therefore, they carry no clear implication regarding the expected behavior of the rate of change of fertility—a plus in one is accompanied by a minus in the other. And, indeed, the fertility curve fails to exhibit the fluctuations of either of the two explanatory series. Rather, one finds simply one extended swing from the beginning through the period 1925–29 to 1935–39. The 1920's, with a relatively small decline in the rate of change of fertility, form a consistent part of this picture, a favorable movement in demand conditions being offset by an adverse one in supply. Interestingly, if one were to smooth out fluctuations in the two explanatory curves by, say, a simple two-item moving average, both, and particularly the unemployment rate, would show an extended swing rather similar to that of the fertility curve. An average of the two explanatory curves would produce the same effect.

Still more intriguing is the behavior of the three series after 1935–39. In this period, the rate of change of labor demand continues its pattern of rise and fall, with a swing of noticeably greater amplitude than previously. In striking contrast to the preceding pattern, however, the change in the rate of entry into the labor market levels off instead of fluctuating inversely. And, for the first time, the rate of change of fertility exhibits a Kuznets-cycle movement, reproducing with remarkable similarity the fluctuation in the rate of change of labor demand. The inference suggested by these movements seems clear. With immigration restricted and without a surge in the rate of labor market entry from the native-born population caused by demographic processes, the favorable impact of a swing in the rate of growth of demand—itself much larger than heretofore—was felt with much greater force by the young native whites in the labor market. As a result, the rate of change of fertility of this group reproduced the swing in labor demand in significant measure for the first time.

If one considers magnitudes of the variables rather than simply rates of change, the argument seems reasonably well borne out, though the correlation is not perfect. In Table 2, each of the seven observations on the rate of change in fertility is classified according to the accompanying values of the rate of change in the unemployment rate and in the percentage change in white males aged 20–29. One finds that, holding the change in rate of entry into the labor market constant (that is, examining each row in the table separately), the rate of change of fertility varies directly with the rate of change in demand (inversely with the rate of change in the unemployment rate). Conversely, holding demand conditions constant (examining each column

TABLE 2. OBSERVATIONS ON PERCENTAGE RATE OF CHANGE PER DECADE IN URBAN NATIVE WHITE FERTILITY, CLASSIFIED BY CONCURRENT CHANGE PER DECADE IN PERCENTAGE OF LABOR FORCE UNEMPLOYED AND IN PERCENTAGE RATE OF CHANGE OF TOTAL WHITE MALES, AGED 20–29, 1885–1958

Change per Decade in Percentage Rate of Change of Total White Males, Aged 20–29 (percentage points)	Change per Decade in Percentage Unemployed (percentage points)				
	−16	−8	−2 to +2	+7	+14
+8 to +10		+2	−6		
−2 to −5	+42		+18	−8	−22
−18			0		

SOURCE: Table C-11.

separately), there is a tendency for the rate of change of fertility to vary inversely with the change in the rate of entry into the labor market, though in this case there is one inconsistency (the +18 and 0 entries being out of order vertically). Whether this discrepancy primarily reflects a fundamental deficiency in the analytical scheme or an inadequate approximation to the economic condition of those of family-building age provided by the explanatory series used here, it is not possible to say.

A comprehensive measure of the income and employment experience of young persons for the period covered here remains tantalizingly out of reach. Yet such additional evidence as I have been able to assemble supports the view that the income experience and labor market situation of young persons were exceptionally favorable in recent years. Consider the following: [23]

1. In the 1940's, earnings in the lower-income occupations rose much more rapidly than those in the higher, and then, in the 1950's, at about the same or a slightly lower rate [180, No. 33, Jan. 15, 1960, pp. 6–7, and No. 35, Jan. 5, 1961, p. 52]. Since young people are more highly concentrated in lower-income occupations than older people, they must have particularly benefited from the movement of the 1940's. The very fragmentary evidence available suggests no corresponding development in the 1920's.

2. The shift of young persons into higher-earning occupations proceeded at a much greater rate in the 1940's than in the two preceding decades. In 1940, 17 per cent of males aged 15–24 in nonfarm occupations were in the three highest income classes (professional, technical, and kindred workers; managers, officials, and proprietors, except farm; and craftsmen, foremen, and kindred workers). By 1950, 41 per cent of this same group of males (now aged 25–34) were in these classes, an improvement of 24 percentage points. From 1920 to 1930, the improvement for the cohort moving through the same ages was 17 points,

[23] In the examples cited, the typical movement from the 1930's through the 1950's is consistent with the pattern shown by the rate of change of fertility—that is, the abrupt break with past experience, in a direction reflecting a particularly favorable situation for young persons, occurs between the 1930's and the 1940's. The movement from the 1940's to the 1950's suggests a slowing or even reversal of the process. It is likely that between the first and second halves of the 1950's this pattern would be still more apparent (cf. Chapter 5).

and from 1930 to 1940 it was 12 points. Corresponding figures for the cohorts aging 25–34 to 35–44 in the three successive decades are 7, 4, and 14 points. Other things being equal, this more rapid shift to higher-income occupations points to a significantly higher rate of income growth for young persons in the 1940's than in the two preceding decades.[24]

3. Expansion of government transfer payments provided a new bulwark to income in the 1940's and 1950's, especially in the form of veterans benefits and unemployment compensation for younger persons.

4. Labor force participation rates in the 1940's showed a marked break with previous trends in a manner strongly suggesting a shortage of young workers. The sharp downtrend in participation of white males aged 14–19 which had prevailed since 1900 was completely reversed. A similar movement appears even to have characterized those aged 10–13 [111, pp. 364–367]. The long-term rise in labor force participation of older women was greatly accelerated because jobs that would ordinarily have been filled by young persons were left open. And while, for young women as a whole, labor force participation declined slightly as a larger proportion married and had children, the rates for wives, even those with preschool-age children, rose substantially. Finally, while it is not possible to cite figures on the long-term trend, part-time employment rose substantially after 1940, and it seems likely that this too stemmed at least in part from a shortage of young workers. In the 1950's the rise in labor force participation of older women continued virtually unabated, but the rate for those aged 14–19 resumed its long-term decline.[25]

5. Since 1940, home ownership among young persons has risen to levels markedly higher than had previously prevailed. The following figures for nonfarm household heads show, for each age group, the percentage of dwelling units which were owner-occupied at each date: [26]

[24] The figures for 1930–50 are computed from [94, Appendix Table 1]; for 1920, from unpublished estimates comparable to [94] kindly provided by W. Lee Hansen. Data for armed forces as reported in the census were included with the 1940 and 1950 figures.

[25] The evidence cited in this paragraph is from the excellent census monograph by Gertrude Bancroft [12, pp. 29–31, 58, 77–82, and Ch. 4]. See also Part III below.

[26] The data through 1940 are from the census reports; for 1949 and 1959, from

Age	1890	1900	1930	1940	1949	1959
15–24	14	10	11	12	21	16
25–34	24	21	26	22	35	42
35–44	35	34	44	37	53	63

There is a marked advance in the situation of young persons after 1940, part of which must be due not only to a great increase in credit availability but to a substantially improved income position as well which encouraged taking on long-term commitments.

6. Finally, there are the characteristics of the baby boom itself. A recent study [82] has shown that a major factor in the boom has been the significant decline since 1940 in age at marriage. From 1890 to 1940, age at marriage drifted irregularly downward, the decline in the median for all females amounting to only one-half year. In the next decade, a period one-fifth as long, the reduction was twice as great [186, Series A-229]. In addition, wives have had children much sooner after marriage. These two factors, earlier marriage and earlier child-bearing, rather than mothers having substantially more children, accounted for most of the rise in the fertility rate through 1954 [82, pp. 365–371].[27] The central role of young families in the baby boom is obvious. It would be difficult indeed to account for this unless their income and employment experience had been exceptionally good.

CONCLUSIONS AND POSSIBLE IMPLICATIONS

The most striking feature of the baby boom—and thus the one calling most urgently for explanation—is the apparent abrupt break with historical experience. However, reconciliation of present and past becomes

[91, p. 1107, Suppl. Table 1]. (Data for those aged 18–24 from the latter source were adjusted to 15–24 on the assumption that no heads of households under 18 own their own homes.) The 1930 and 1940 estimates are for male heads of household only, which biases them slightly upward compared to the figures for the other dates.

[27] The draft law policy of deferring fathers doubtless encouraged earlier marriage and childbearing, but without an income situation that favored expansion of the family beyond the first child, it is doubtful that it could have produced a baby boom of the type experienced. There is now reliable evidence that the average number of children per mother has also risen in the postwar period. This development is of course consistent with the analysis presented here. The longer the exceptional labor market situation prevails, the more likely the fertility response will take this form in addition to earlier marriage and earlier childbearing.

easier when one recognizes that even before the 1940's the historical record was characterized by fluctuations of significant magnitude and duration, and that the record for the total white population is a composite of the varying experience of several component groups, subject in part to quite different influences. Major swings in agricultural conditions, on the one hand, and Kuznets cycles in nonagricultural activity with accompanying immigration fluctuations, on the other—each with their peculiar historical timing—gave rise to distinctive fertility responses on the part of the rural white, foreign-born white, and urban native white populations. When one unravels these differing strands of experience and considers their underlying influences, the impression emerges that the recent fertility behavior of the urban native white population, the group of central significance for explanation of the baby boom, is not as inconsistent with its earlier character as was heretofore believed. In the first three decades of the century, the fertility of this group, instead of exhibiting a declining trend, showed reasonable stability. And in the recent period the effect on the labor market of a Kuznets-cycle expansion—an expansion stronger, according to our data, than any preceding ones considered here—was for the first time not accompanied by an offsetting rise in the rate of labor-market entry due to a significant increase in either immigration or the native-born population in young working ages. The unprecedented concurrence of these three circumstances—a Kuznets-cycle expansion in the economy, restricted immigration, and a low rate of labor force entry from the native population resulting from demographic processes —created an exceptional job market for those in family-building ages and as a result drastically accelerated the founding of families.[28] This

---

[28] With regard to the causes of the exceptional labor market for young persons in the 1940's and 1950's, the present chapter emphasizes quantitative scarcity to the exclusion of relative quality. The following figures on median school years completed by young and middle-aged males at various dates may partially right the balance (see also Figure 19):

Age at Specified Date	1920	1930	1940	1950	1960	1970 (projected)
(1) 25–29	8.4	8.7	10.1	12.0	12.3	12.5
(2) 45–54	8.1	8.2	8.4	8.7	10.0	12.0
(3) (1)–(2)	0.3	0.5	1.7	3.3	2.3	0.5

Note the immense gain in the educational advantage of young over middle-aged workers in the 1940's, a change which sharply improved their competitive position

process was further abetted by a concurrent boom in agricultural conditions, which evoked a similar fertility response on the part of the rural white population.

In conclusion, some of the implications of the preceding analysis for the past and future may be set forth.

With regard to the past, it was noted earlier in the discussion that while Kuznets cycles in the rate of population growth are not a new phenomenon in our history, the shift in the source of these movements from immigration to fertility raises a question whether the recent cycle bears any logical connection to its predecessors. The implication of the present analysis is that indeed such a connection does exist. As long as we permitted free immigration, the rise and fall of immigration in response to swings in labor demand associated with Kuznets cycles in this country acted as a buffer to moderate the impact on the urban native white population. With the restriction of immigration, however, the urban native white population felt the impact of a Kuznets-cycle swing in labor demand with unprecedented force, and the result was an unparalleled response in fertility and thus again in the rate of population growth.

The implications of the present analysis for the longer-term future of fertility change are in contrast with that likely to be suggested by the typical demographic discussion of our fertility history. The customary emphasis of demographers on the long-term secular decline in the past would suggest a view of the current fertility decline as a resumption of the primary trend.[29] The interpretation suggested by the present analysis, however, would be that for the group whose

at just the time that labor demand was booming. The timing is fortuitous, stemming from the abrupt advance in the diffusion of high-school education that occurred in the 1920's and especially the 1930's. (The figures are from [176, pp. 236, 238] and [182, pp. 6–7]. The 1920 and 1930 values were assumed the same as those reported by the corresponding cohorts in 1940, the first time that data on educational attainment were collected.)

The sequence of change in the educational differentials calls to mind the recent pronounced convergence in income distribution by size. One wonders to what extent the change in the size distribution in the past forty years may reflect changing income differentials by age associated with variations in both the relative number and quality of young workers.

[29] Clearly the present analysis suggests that a reexamination of the primary trend itself in terms of the differing patterns of the groups distinguished here might prove fruitful.

experience is of central significance for the future, the urban native white population, the nature of the primary trend in this century—whether upward or downward—is not readily apparent, and the recent behavior of this group may be largely explained as a Kuznets-cycle phenomenon. If this is correct, then substantial fertility variation, up or down, may occur again over the longer run.

CHAPTER 5 / THE CURRENT

FERTILITY DECLINE AND

PROJECTED FERTILITY CHANGES

The postwar peak of fertility was reached in 1957. Since that date, the total fertility rate has declined, at first only gradually, but in the past few years quite substantially. At the same time, per capita real disposable income, a commonly used index of economic conditions in correlations with fertility, has continued to rise at an average rate only slightly lower than previously. Does this mean that economic factors have had little to do with the recent fertility decline? Does it raise doubts about the explanation offered in Chapter 4 for the baby boom? While a thorough investigation of these questions is not attempted here, it is possible to determine whether in recent years economic factors have changed in at least a direction conducive to fertility decline, and to consider the implications for recent fertility projections. As in Chapter 4, the focus is on those in the earlier childbearing ages. No attempt is made to subdivide the population further into color-nativity or other component groups, a decision partly justified by increasing homogeneity of the population [124], but chiefly by expediency. The more limited time span under study makes it possible to base the present analysis largely on the invaluable population and labor force surveys of the past two decades, which provide fairly continuous data heretofore unavailable on the economic experience and demographic behavior of component groups in the population. In keeping with our interest in the longer-term movement rather than year-to-year fluctuations, these data have been smoothed, where possible, by a three-year moving average. For the most part, attention will center on comparisons between the period of the baby boom and that of the current fertility decline. Since it is only after World War II that most of the series become available annually, I have linked them with a prewar observation, usually for 1940, to fill out the picture for the earlier period.

In one respect, this analysis develops further the framework of Chapter 4. The analytical focus there was on the rate of change in fertility, thus making it possible to largely set aside considerations regarding the secular trend. This chapter, however, deals directly with the level of fertility; and, while not attempting a study of the long-term primary trend itself, does introduce one factor believed relevant to it, namely, the desired consumption level of those in early childbearing ages.

FERTILITY AND YOUNG ADULTS' CIRCUMSTANCES SINCE 1940

Fertility

The fertility pattern since 1940 will be lightly touched on only, since it is more than adequately treated elsewhere [201]. Figure 30 presents three-year moving averages of the total fertility rate and age-specific birth rates for females over the period 1940–63. Only a few observations require mention.

1. The increase from 1940–42 to the peak in the late 1950's is much greater for the age groups 15–19 through 25–29 than for the older ones. Indeed, together the three youngest age groups account for most of the rise in the total. If the rates for no other groups had changed, the rise to the 1957–59 peak in the total fertility rate would have been 44 per cent. This compares with an actual increase of 53 per cent.

2. Although there is no systematic difference between the younger and older age groups in the decline since 1957–59, the younger groups again account for most of the movement in the total (−4.3 versus −5.7 per cent, actual).

3. Within the younger age groups, there is a systematic difference by age in the recent decline. It occurs first and is greatest for those aged 15–19, followed by the 20–24, and finally, the 25–29. The peak for the 15–19 group occurs in 1956–58, ahead of that in the total, and the decline to 1961–63 is 12 per cent; for those aged 25–29, the peak is stretched out over 1957–61, and the decline to 1961–63 totals 3 per cent.

FIGURE 30

TOTAL FERTILITY RATE AND BIRTH RATE, BY AGE OF MOTHER, 1940–63 [a]
(INDEX: 1949–51 = 100)

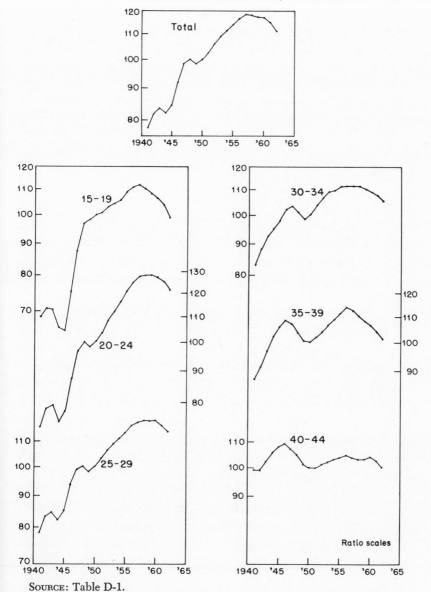

SOURCE: Table D-1.
[a] Three-year moving average.

FIGURE 31

PER CAPITA DISPOSABLE IN-
COME IN 1964 DOLLARS: TO-
TAL POPULATION, 1940 AND
1947–64 ᵃ
(INDEX: 1949–51 = 100)

FIGURE 32

MEDIAN TOTAL MONEY INCOME IN
1959 DOLLARS: MALE INCOME RE-
CIPIENTS, BY AGE, 1941 AND
1947–63 ᵃ
(INDEX: 1949–51 = 100)

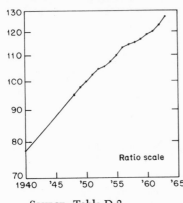

SOURCE: Table D-2.
ᵃ Three-year moving average.

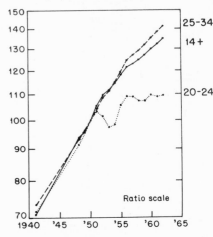

SOURCE: Table D-3.
ᵃ Three-year moving average.

Economic Condition

The income data assembled here are chiefly from the Current
Population Survey and accordingly follow the concepts used therein.[1]
Since nonmonetary income is omitted from the Survey, the position of
farmers is somewhat understated. Use is made here of the figures both
for income of persons, i.e., income recipients alone, and for families,
including individuals both with and without income. The figures have
been adjusted to a constant price level by the consumer price index.

These are the principal impressions which emerge from inspection
of the charts:

1. As previously noted, per capita disposable income, a commonly
used index of economic conditions in correlations with fertility, continues to grow throughout the last decade or so, though at a somewhat
lower rate than in the 1940's (Figure 31). If one considers all age

[1] Dorothy S. Brady and F. Gerard Adams have recently prepared comparable
estimates by age for 1941 [22], thus providing an invaluable prewar bench mark.
I am grateful for the opportunity to use a prepublication version of these estimates.

FIGURE 33

TOTAL MONEY INCOME IN 1959 DOLLARS: FAMILIES, BY AGE OF HEAD AND
RANK WITHIN AGE GROUP, 1947–63 [a]
(INDEX: 1949–51 = 100)

A. By Age of Head

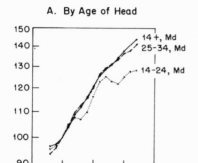

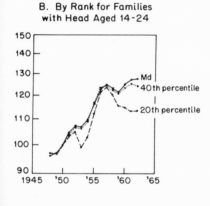

B. By Rank for Families
with Head Aged 14-24

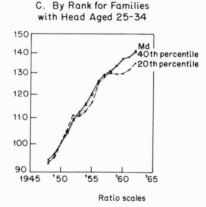

C. By Rank for Families
with Head Aged 25-34

Ratio scales

SOURCE: Table D-4.
[a] Three-year moving average.

groups 14 and over combined, the same is true of the median income
of male income recipients (Figure 32) and, for the somewhat shorter
span for which data are available, the median income of all families
(Figure 33, Part A).

2. Investigation of income experience by age makes clear that the
aggregative movement in recent years is not representative of the
experience of the younger age groups. This has typically been less
favorable. Moreover, the differences between the younger age groups

FIGURE 34

UNEMPLOYMENT RATE, BY SEX AND
AGE, 1940 AND 1947–63 [a]

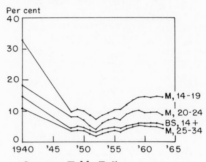

SOURCE: Table D-5.
[a] Three-year moving average.

in the timing and extent of departure from the general movement are
reminiscent of the pattern for fertility—the adverse departure is earlier
and greater for the younger group. Thus Part A of Figure 33 (the
figure presenting income information most immediately relevant to
fertility behavior) shows that the median income of families with head
aged 14–24 declined for several years after 1956–58, and by 1961–63
had recovered only to a slightly higher level than the 1956–58 peak.
For those with head aged 25–34, median family income in this period
continued to grow, but a gradual divergence from the aggregate movement becomes apparent after 1958–60.

3. As shown in Figure 34, the movement in unemployment rates
by age supports the impression that in recent years the experience of
younger groups has increasingly diverged in an unfavorable direction
from the average.

4. *Within* the younger age groups, disparate movements are
apparent in recent years between the lower and higher income segments. The poorest fifth of each younger age group has had less favorable income experience than the group average (Figure 33, Parts B
and C). Indeed, for the lowest fifth of the households with head aged
14–24, income has actually declined noticeably since 1956–58.

5. In the 1940's, in contrast, the age pattern of income and unemployment changes was the opposite of that which has recently developed. Income of younger age groups grew substantially more
rapidly than for others. This was because, relative to the average, the

proportion receiving income in these groups rose sharply, while relative income per recipient remained virtually constant (Figures 32 and 35).

Similarly unemployment rates of younger persons converged sharply toward the average (Figure 34). Finally, within the younger groups the lowest income segments experienced more rapid growth [22].

6. Since the economic situation of a family depends on more than its current income, other pertinent measures may be noted, though the information is more fragmentary and (for the measures noted in the second and third paragraphs below) of lower reliability.

Veteran status entails access to certain benefits and credit resources. For males aged 20–24, the proportion of veterans in civilian life rose to almost two-fifths in 1950; by the mid-1950's it had dropped to somewhat over one-fifth; and, by 1961–63, to almost zero (Figure 36). Roughly similar movements are apparent for those aged 25–29 and 30–34, but at a higher level and with a lag.

Housing conditions are sometimes considered relevant to fertility behavior. For nonfarm families in which the head was aged 18–24 or

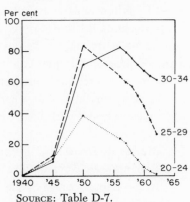

FIGURE 35

MALE MONEY INCOME RECIPIENTS AS A PERCENTAGE OF MALE POPULATION, BY AGE, 1941 AND 1947–63 [a]

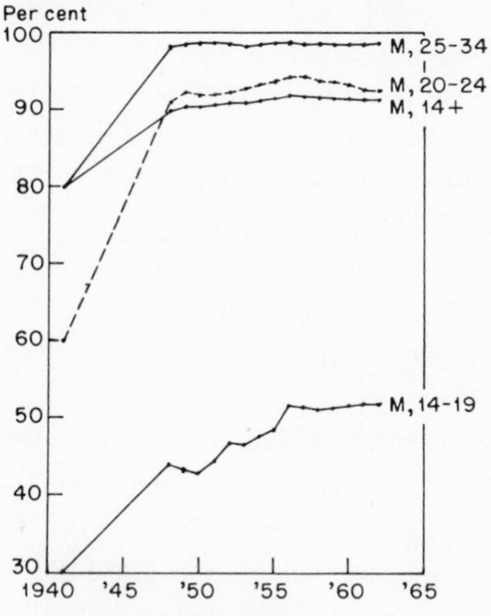

SOURCE: Table D-6.
[a] Three-year moving average.

FIGURE 36

VETERANS AS A PERCENTAGE OF MALE POPULATION, BY AGE, 1940, 1945, 1950, AND 1955–63 [a]

SOURCE: Table D-7.
[a] Three-year moving average.

TABLE 3. PERCENTAGE OF NONFARM FAMILIES OWNING HOMES, BY AGE, 1930–63

Age	1930	1940	1949	1954	1959	1960	1962 Jan–Feb	Dec [a]	1963
18 and over	46	41	51	56	58	58	56	59	61
18–24	11	12	21	17	16	14	7	12	15
25–34	26	22	35	42	42	44	44	42	47
35–44	44	37	53	57	63	64	66	60	71
45–54	55	48	59	63	64	69	67	71	72
55–64	64	56	62	66	69	62	67	69	63
65 and over	73	65	59	63	66	65	58	64	72

SOURCE: Through 1940, from census reports; 1949–59, from *Federal Reserve Bulletin*, September 1959, p. 1107, Supplementary Table 1; December 1962, from *Ibid.*, March 1964, p. 292; 1960, January–February 1962, and 1963, from George Katona et al, *Survey of Consumer Finances*, 1960, pp. 60–61, 1962, p. 89, 1963, p. 90.
[a] Includes farm families.

25–34, the percentage owning their own homes rose markedly between 1940 and 1949 (Table 3). Since that date, for those with head aged 18–24 the proportion has tended to drop off;[2] for those with head aged 25–34, it continued to rise noticeably through 1954, but thereafter edged up only slightly.

Between 1953 and 1962, the median net worth (in current dollars) of all spending units rose, but for those with head aged 18–24 or 25–34, it declined (Table 4). As a percentage of income, the adverse movement in the net worth position of younger persons is even more marked. Among all spending units, the proportion with net worth equal to or greater than one-half annual income decreases from 63 to 59 per cent; for those with head aged 18–24, the decrease is from 21 to 15 per cent, and with head aged 25–34, from 52 to 37 per cent.

Marriage, Household Formation, and Wives' Labor Force Participation

In the interpretation of the baby boom in Chapter 4, fertility was but one of several demographic variables markedly affected by the

[2] The low value for January–February 1962 is not supported by two subsequent surveys taken within twelve months of that date, and is most likely due to sampling variability.

exceptional economic situation. It is pertinent, therefore, to see whether these other variables have changed recently in a direction consistent with the earlier interpretation.

To turn, first, to marriage behavior, for the age groups under 25, the proportion ever-married rose sharply in the 1940's, leveled off in the 1950's, and, in recent years, shows evidence of a decline (Figure 37). As would be expected, for females this pattern is more pronounced at somewhat lower ages than for males. For the age groups over 25, following an initial rise, a leveling off is apparent but as yet there is no indication of a decline.

TABLE 4. PERCENTAGE DISTRIBUTION OF SPENDING UNITS BY AGE, BY NET WORTH, 1953 AND 1962

Net Worth (current dollars)	Age of Head					
	14 and Over		18–24		25–34	
	1953	1962	1953	1962	1953	1962
Negative	} 31	11	20	22	15	20
0–999		19	53	50	20	20
1,000–4,999	23	21	22	23	33	34
5,000–9,999	17	15	3	3	16	11
10,000–24,999	18	20	1	1	12	10
25,000 and over	11	14	1	1	4	5
Total	100	100	100	100	100	100
Median (dollars)	4,100	4,700	300	250	2,110	1,800
Net worth as percentage of pre-tax money income in previous year						
Zero or negative	16	17	25	33	19	25
1–49	21	24	54	52	29	38
50–99	11	13	13	9	16	16
100–199	15	15	6	3	17	12
200–499	20	17	1	1	15	6
500 and over	17	14	1	2	4	3
Total	100	100	100	100	100	100

SOURCE: George Katona et al, 1962, *Survey of Consumer Finances*, 1963, pp. 128–29, 133.

FIGURE 37

EVER-MARRIED PERSONS AS PERCENTAGE OF POPULATION, BY SEX AND AGE,
1940, 1947, and 1949–63 [a]

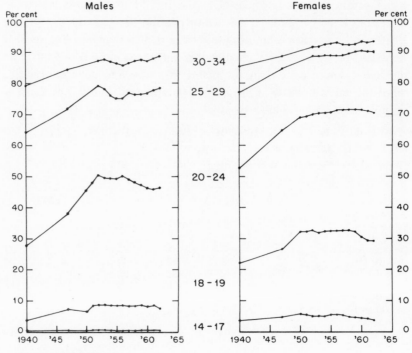

SOURCE: Table D-8.
[a] Three-year moving average.

The movement in household formation, shown in Figure 38, tends to lag behind that in marital status. For males aged 14–24 and 25–29, while there is no indication in recent years of a continuation of the earlier upsurge in the proportion heading husband-wife households, neither is there evidence as yet of a marked decline, although a slight downturn is perhaps indicated.

After increasing in the 1940's, the labor force participation rates of young wives tended to level off in the first half of the 1950's (Figure 39, Part B). More recently, however, they have started to climb again, so noticeably that the latest labor force projections embody a significant revision for this group. Two considerations suggest that the circumstances responsible for the recent rise differ from those underlying the earlier. In the 1940's unemployment rates for young females were declining; in the recent period, the increase in labor force participation has occurred in the face of rising unemployment rates (Part A). Second, in the earlier period the rates for wives with young children grew somewhat less than those for married women as a whole; in the recent period the rates for wives with young children are chiefly responsible for the upward movement for the group as a whole (Parts C and D). These observations suggest that, while the rise in labor force participation of young wives in the 1940's was induced by the increasing tightness of the labor market as a whole—both for younger men and women—in the 1950's it arose from a deterioration in the labor market for young men relative to that of young women,

FIGURE 38

PERCENTAGE OF MALE POPULATION
IN HUSBAND-WIFE HOUSEHOLDS, BY
AGE, 1940, 1947, AND 1950–63 [a]

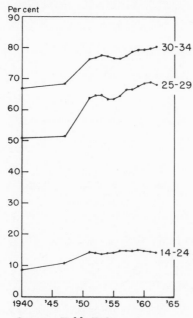

SOURCE: Table D-9.
[a] Three-year moving average.

FIGURE 39

UNEMPLOYMENT AND LABOR FORCE PARTICIPATION RATES OF FEMALES, BY
MARITAL, CHILD DEPENDENCY, AND AGE CLASSES

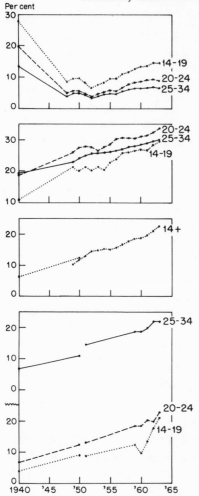

A. Unemployment Rate of Females, by Age, 1940, 1947–64 [a]

B. Labor Force Participation Rate, Married Females with Husband Present, by Age, 1940, 1948–64 [a]

C. Labor Force Participation Rate, Married Females with Husband Present, with Children under 6 and No Child 6–17, 1940, 1950, and 1948–64 [a]

D. Labor Force Participation Rate, Married Females with Husband Present, with Child under 6, by Age, Selected Years, 1940–63

SOURCE: Tables D-10 through D-13.
[a] Three-year moving average.

FIGURE 40

NEW HIGH SCHOOL GRADUATES NOT ENROLLED IN COLLEGE,[a] BY
SEX, MARITAL STATUS, AND EMPLOYMENT STATUS IN OCTOBER OF
YEAR OF HIGH SCHOOL GRADUATION: ANNUALLY, 1959–63
(thousands)

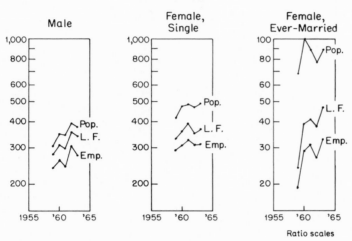

SOURCE: Table D-14.
[a] Civilian noninstitutional population.

which made it increasingly difficult for husbands to support a family
and correspondingly created pressures for increasing participation by
their wives.

For the last few years, insight into the experience of a somewhat
more homogeneous segment of the younger population—new high
school graduates who did not go on to college—is provided by recent
surveys of their employment status four months after graduation
(Figure 40). Although the size of the group is small and sampling
variability consequently greater, there is a striking rise in the employment and labor force figures for married females in this group; a finding at a more microscopic level consistent with the view just expressed.

Desired Consumption Level

In the discussion of income above, the concern was with the
absolute level, and the implied hypothesis was that fertility varies
directly with the absolute income level, other things being equal. One

of the considerations included in the *ceteris paribus* assumption is the consumption level *desired* by the husband and wife. It is generally recognized that in considering the potential uses of additional income, a rise in the per capita stock of consumer goods available to husband and wife is an alternative to expanding the size of the family [14, 45]. Holding income constant, one would expect that fertility would vary inversely with the desired consumption level.

But do desired consumption levels change, and if so, why? This question involves us in complex conceptual issues in the economics of consumer preferences. There is an understandable reluctance among economists to explain changes in behavior in terms of changes in "tastes," which are typically taken as given. There is, however, one generally accepted proposition of immediate relevance: If one of two families with equal current income previously received higher income than at present, that family would be expected to spend more on consumption [51, 130].[3] In other words, experience with previous higher income levels alters "tastes" and thereby consumption behavior.

This line of reasoning may be transferred with some modification to the present problem. Young persons currently in the childbearing ages a few years before were dependent members of their parents' households, and it seems plausible that the consumption levels experienced in the parents' households among other things served to shape their current preferences in much the same way a previous higher income level would affect those of a given household. Moreover, the situation in the parents' household when the children were in their teens would seem more relevant than when the children were quite young.

If this is so, an interesting implication follows. In a developing economy the second generation's income at age 20–24 is typically greater than the first generation's was at that age. The second generation could thus achieve the consumption level the first generation had at age 20–24 and have something left over for other purposes, such as saving or increased family size. But if the *desired* consumption level inherited by children from their parents relates to the parents' situation

---

[3] The pioneering contribution on the "relative income" hypothesis is Dorothy S. Brady and Rose D. Friedman [22a].

not at age 20–24 but at, say, 35–44, then it is less certain that the second generation's income at 20–24 will suffice to achieve the desired consumption level. In other words, there is an intergenerational effect tending to increase consumption at a given income level. Clearly by varying the parameters involved one could develop alternative models in which secular growth in absolute income was accompanied by increasing, decreasing, or constant fertility.

Given the purpose and scope of the present report, it is scarcely appropriate to pursue this suggestion regarding the secular trend at this point.[4] Two brief points may, however, be added. First, while the above clearly does not imply that such a model would suffice to explain the secular trend, it obviously bears on the oft-raised question of how to reconcile the apparent contradiction between the secular inverse (gross) association between income and fertility, on the one hand, and the shorter-term positive association, on the other. Second, it suggests that in an analysis of the secular trend the actual income of those in childbearing ages should be sharply distinguished from the factors behind the formation of their preference patterns. Under the latter heading would be included not only parents' income, but variables such as religion, nativity, and one currently the subject of increasing attention, farm-nonfarm origin.[5]

If sufficient historical data were available on income, tangible assets, and consumption expenditure by age, it would be possible to investigate various relations between parents' and children's incomes, and consider their bearing on fertility behavior. Unfortunately, the necessary information is scarce, and an attempt is made here only to present two largely illustrative analyses.

1. Column 2 of Table 5 shows the median income of families with head aged 14–24, the series plotted in index form in Figure 33. Column 4 gives the income five years earlier of families with head aged 35–44, presumably, the households in which most of those in column 2 were

----

[4] Note should be made, however, of recent major contributions on secular fertility trends by Kingsley Davis [46] and Ronald Freedman [67].

[5] See Otis Dudley Duncan [51a], and citations of earlier work by Goldberg and Freedman given therein. I have explored more fully these and other conceptual issues raised in this Part in a recent paper "Towards a Socio-Economic Theory of Fertility," which appeared in *Fertility and Family Planning: A World View*, a collection of papers prepared for the University of Michigan sesquicentennial celebration, November 15–17, 1967.

TABLE 5. TOTAL MONEY INCOME OF FAMILIES
WITH HEAD AGED 14–24 COMPARED WITH
THAT RECEIVED BY FAMILIES WITH HEAD
AGED 35–44 FIVE YEARS EARLIER, 1953–62
(Income figures are in 1959 dollars and are
three-year averages centered at indicated date.)

| Head Aged 14–24 | | Head Aged 35–44 | | Col. 2 ÷ Col. 4 |
Year (1)	Income (2)	Year (3)	Income (4)	Per Cent (5)
1953	3,405	1948	4,199	81.1
1954	3,496	1949	4,221	82.8
1955	3,701	1950	4,343	85.2
1956	3,912	1951	4,570	85.6
1957	3,981	1952	4,787	83.2
1958	3,916	1953	4,950	79.1
1959	3,887	1954	5,152	75.4
1960	3,984	1955	5,389	73.9
1961	4,068	1956	5,627	72.3
1962	4,077	1957	5,762	70.8

SOURCE: Same as for Table D-4.

living at that time.[6] Thus, column 2 is the actual income of young
families; column 4, an indicator of the desired consumption level
inherited by them from their parents' households. (Clearly some adjustment in the level of column 4 would improve it as a consumption
indicator, but our present interest is ultimately in the change rather
than level of the series.) Column 5 of Table 5 presents the ratio of
the two. In terms of the present framework this shows, e.g., that in
1953, on the average, young households were receiving incomes equal
to about four-fifths of what their parents received five years ago. As
was previously observed, and is shown here in column 2, absolute
income leveled off for this age group around 1956–58. What is suggested by column 5, however, is that relative to desired consumption,
income has been *falling* since about 1955–57 for this age group, a
development which would clearly serve to create greater downward
pressure on fertility.

[6] It would be desirable to experiment with lags of varying length as well as to
identify more precisely the relevant parent cohort, but longer time series and
greater age detail are needed for a thorough investigation.

TABLE 6. NET STOCK OF TANGIBLE ASSETS PER NONFARM
HOUSEHOLD, 1929–58
(1947–49 dollars)

Year	Assets Per Household	Year	Assets Per Household	Year	Assets Per Household
1929	12,210	1947	8,650	1953	9,210
1933	11,060	1948	8,690	1954	9,400
1939	9,580	1949	8,660	1955	9,780
1945	8,240	1950	8,840	1956	10,020
....					
1945	8,410	1951	8,920	1957	10,110
1946	8,470	1952	9,040	1958	10,200

SOURCE: For net tangible assets of nonfarm households, Raymond W. Goldsmith, *The National Wealth of the United States in the Postwar Period*, Princeton, 1962, p. 203. For number of nonfarm households, Bureau of the Census, *Current Population Reports: Population Characteristics*, Series P-20, No. 92. The two entries for 1945 arise from differing estimates of net assets, the first comparable to the pre-1945 values; the second, to the post-1945 values.

2. Table 6 is an attempt to develop a rough impression of the longer-term movement in desired consumption levels since 1929. The table shows the value in constant dollars of tangible assets per nonfarm household after allowance for depreciation.[7] Ideally, it would be desirable to have such information by age of household head. If, failing this, one takes the movement in the average as likely to be broadly indicative of the changing situation of the age group 35–44, then the series can be used to infer differences among successive younger cohorts in inherited consumption desires. Thus from 1929 through the late 1940's assets per household for all age groups, and presumably for those with head aged 35–44, declined and then leveled off. This suggests that the cohorts reaching childbearing age and establishing separate households toward the end of this period had been raised in less materially prosperous home environments than those reaching childbearing age earlier in the period and consequently had lower desired consumption levels. Indeed, the cohorts reaching childbearing age, say 15–19, when asset levels were lowest, roughly

[7] The figures comprise largely homes and consumer durables, whether owned or rented. Particularly prior to the postwar period the former dominates the total, so that the series might be viewed as a crude index of housing conditions, with the depreciation adjustment providing an allowance for age of housing.

in the decade 1940–50, include those that figured most prominently in the baby boom. Since the late 1940's average assets per household have moved up noticeably, which would imply that the most recent cohorts are reaching childbearing age with desired consumption levels significantly above those of their predecessors.[8]

Summary and Qualifications

Let us summarize the general impression emerging from this survey of the evidence, keeping in mind its preliminary nature. In recent years young persons' income has grown only hesitantly and their unemployment rates have risen. The situation has been most severe among the lowest-income segments of these groups. Home ownership has become less prevalent among households with head aged 18–24, although it has continued to edge up slightly for those 25–34. In both groups, however, net worth position has declined, suggesting heavier pressure of liabilities. Moreover, most of the special benefits associated with war veteran status are no longer available. The labor force participation of young wives with dependent children has risen noticeably, suggesting increasing economic stress on the family. Finally, the young cohorts of recent years have come from wealthier backgrounds than their predecessors in the 1940's, and in all likelihood are entering the childbearing ages with the more expensive tastes for consumer goods thereby acquired.

These developments contrast strikingly with the unusually favorable economic circumstances of young adults in the decade or so prior to the mid-1950's. They are consistent with the hypothesis that economic factors have been, at least in part, responsible, first, in the early postwar period for the abrupt declines in age at marriage and house-

---

[8] While the U-shaped movement in assets per household seems plausible (and it is this which provides the basis in the text for inferences about the movement in desired consumption levels), the noticeably lower level of the series in 1958 than in 1929 is puzzling. Differences between the two dates in the age distribution of households might account for a part of this. Also the fact that the present figures are mean rather than median values may be relevant. There is a great difference between the two (e.g., with regard to net worth, the mean value in 1962 was $14,600 compared to a median of $4,700). Since inequality declined between 1929 and the more recent period, the median figure for net assets would presumably show a smaller decline. Nevertheless, one has the impression that the present series is biased downward at later relative to earlier dates.

Subsequent to the preparation of this analysis, I discovered that in 1956 Victor R. Fuchs [72] predicted a decline in the U.S. birth rate, partly on the basis of reasoning similar to that advanced here.

hold formation and the associated rise in fertility, and second, for the more recent slowdown and gradual reversal of these demographic movements.

This conclusion, however, must be tempered by explicit recognition of the various shortcomings of the present analysis. While I have been able in this study—thanks to the new and growing fund of survey data since World War II—to probe perhaps more deeply into relevant economic circumstances than has typically been done in the past, no attempt has been made to assess the extent to which the quantitative magnitude of the fertility decline might be explained by economic factors. Further, separate examination would be desirable of various component groups in the population, for example, farm, nonwhite, and, as data become available, different socioeconomic classes. Study is needed also of the older groups in childbearing ages, even though their quantitative importance in the over-all period rates has not been great. Finally, an effort should be made at a cohort approach, though this is currently handicapped by the varying ways in which age detail is presented in the source materials.

IMPLICATIONS FOR FERTILITY PROJECTIONS

Period Rates

In view of the limited scope of the present analysis and manifest needs for further research, one may doubt the advisability of raising the question of prospective fertility changes. The justification for doing so arises from recognition that the use of economic factors in fertility projections is itself a pressing research problem. The current consensus is aptly stated by two of the authors of the recent census projections: "It is sometimes suggested that a considerable improvement in our projections of births could be achieved if account were taken of the relation between changes in fertility and economic changes. Our tentative view is that this approach is hardly feasible and that it may not achieve the end desired" [143].

Chapter 4 indicated that the postwar baby boom could be reconciled with longer-term historical experience; this chapter suggests that the recent shift from baby boom to fertility decline is consistent with the earlier interpretation. In both papers, economic factors were considered fundamental to fertility changes. Clearly, the implications of this viewpoint for the use of studies of economic factors in projections would be of interest, even though the discussion must necessarily be exploratory. Moreover, such a discussion might serve further to illustrate the framework and highlight research needs. What follows therefore is frankly speculative and is offered not as a prediction but for whatever value it may have in furthering research in this area.

The admirably detailed population projections recently released by the Bureau of the Census provide the point of departure [144]. These present not forecasts but the implications of alternative assumptions regarding the future course of the components of population change, particularly fertility. The framework thus provided for reflection about prospective developments is extremely valuable. For the foreseeable future, the potential contribution of the present approach would seem to lie not in supplanting such a framework, but in appraising the relative plausibility of the various assumptions and perhaps suggesting new possibilities. Thus, with reference to Figure 41, which shows the four series of projected fertility rates through 1975,[9] the pertinent question would be: Which, if any, of the projected paths is more consistent with the present analysis?

At the heart of the present explanation of postwar fertility movements are differences in income growth by age. Ideally, in looking to the future one would want projections of income by age based on a tested theory of the determinants of this distribution. Although there is no such theory available, the framework of Chapter 4 embodies a view, speculative though it may be, regarding these determinants; and we may perhaps utilize this to form some crude notion of prospective income trends for young adults compared to others. In this conception, the swing in the relative income position of young adults since 1940 has been chiefly due to corresponding swings from relatively favorable to unfavorable positions in three factors—aggregate demand, and the relative quantity and quality of younger persons. The first part of the period was characterized by high growth of aggregate demand associated with the war and early postwar boom, a relative shortage of young workers, and an unusual educational advantage of young over old; the second part, by slackened growth in aggregate demand, sub-

---

[9] For each date from 1965 on the points plotted refer, from top to bottom, to projections A, B, C, and D, respectively.

FIGURE 41

BIRTH RATE, BY AGE OF MOTHER AGED 15–19 THROUGH 25–29, AND SUMMARY
FERTILITY MEASURES: ANNUALLY, 1940–63, AND PROJECTED, QUINQUEN-
NIALLY, 1965–75

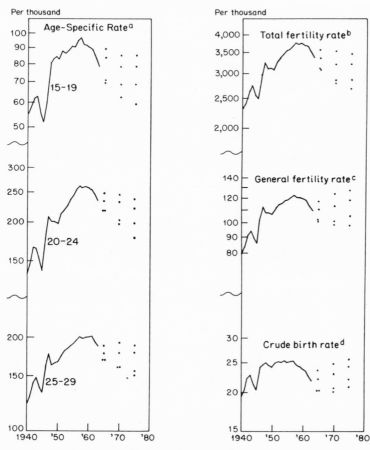

SOURCE: Table D-15.
ᵃ Per 1,000 female population in specified age group.
ᵇ Computed by summing age-specific rates for each five-year age group through
40–44 and multiplying the result by 5. The result is the completed fertility rate that
would arise if a hypothetical cohort experienced the age-specific rates of the given
date in the course of its reproductive history.
ᶜ Total live births divided by female population aged 15 to 44.
ᵈ Total live births divided by total population of all ages.

stantial growth in the relative number of younger persons, and deterioration in their educational advantage. Regarding the outlook over the next decade, the projections of educational attainment imply some additional decline in the relative advantage of younger persons in high school, though not college education (Figure 42). As for relative

FIGURE 42

PERCENTAGE OF THOSE AGED 25–29 AND
30–64 WITH SPECIFIED YEARS OF SCHOOL
COMPLETED: ACTUAL, DECENNIALLY, 1920–
60; PROJECTED, QUINQUENNIALLY, 1965–85

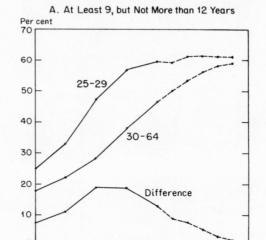

A. At Least 9, but Not More than 12 Years

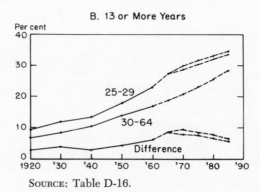

B. 13 or More Years

SOURCE: Table D-16.

FIGURE 43

ANNUAL RATE OF CHANGE OF MALE POPULA-
TION AGED 14–19,[a] 20–24, AND 25–29 COM-
PARED WITH THAT AGED 30–64: ACTUAL,
1940–64; PROJECTED, 1964–75 [b]

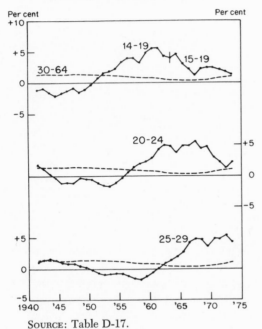

SOURCE: Table D-17.
[a] After 1964, aged 15–19.
[b] Three-year moving average.

quantity, the growth rate of those aged 15–19, which has been rising
for over a decade, will start to taper off in the next ten-year period,
but that for the two succeeding age groups will be cresting (Figure
43). These considerations tend, if anything, to suggest some possible
further deterioration in the relative income position of younger persons. On the other hand, it is possible (though by no means certain)
that aggregate demand growth will be higher than in the recent past
and the relative income position of younger persons will be consequently helped through an improvement in their relative employment situation. As shown in Table 7, however, the decline in relative
income position of young adults in the recent past has noticeably ex-

TABLE 7. INCOME AND EMPLOYMENT OF THOSE AGED 14–24 RELATIVE TO THOSE 35–44: AVERAGE FOR PEAK TO PEAK CYCLES, 1948–63 (per cent)

Cycle	Total Money Income (Ratio of Median for Families with Head 14–24 to That for Head 35–44) (1)	Civilian Employment as Percentage of Labor Force (Ratio of Rate for Males 14–24 Not Enrolled in School to That for Males 35–44) (2)
1948–53	72.4	96.5
1953–57	68.8	96.0
1957–60	65.2	93.3
1960–63 [a]	62.3	93.9

SOURCE: Col. 1, same as for Table D-4; col. 2, [202, March 1965, p. 205, Table A-12, and p. 222, Table B-8].

[a] Incomplete cycle.

ceeded what might have been expected as a result of the greater growth in unemployment among this group. Hence, under prospective supply conditions, even restoration of the earlier more favorable employment situation would probably only moderate the adverse relative income condition that has developed for young adults.

Altogether, the outlook for the next decade suggested by these considerations is that the relative income position of younger persons may show some further decline and then a leveling off, perhaps followed by a slight rise. As among the several age groups, those aged 15–19, which are furthest along with regard to the adverse impact of numbers on the labor market, might be expected to lead in this movement, with those aged 25–29 lagging behind. With regard to fertility rates for these age groups, one might correspondingly infer some further decline followed by a leveling off. Of the projections shown in Figure 41, this would suggest that series C and D are more consistent with the present analysis. As between the two, there is little to choose through 1975, but the tendency of series C to level off seems somewhat more in line with the suggested income movements. Since, as we have indicated, the movements in the age-specific rates for those under 30 typically dominate the movement in the summary measures for all ages, one might further infer that the total fertility rate would continue to decline between 1965 and 1970 and then level off (Figure 41). The substantial positive effect on fertility of prospective age composition shifts over this period is shown by the movements in the general fertility rate and crude birth rate. The latter would actually "bottom out" in 1965–70 and show a noticeable rise in 1970–75.

Completed Fertility

To this point the discussion has been concerned entirely with "period rates" of fertility, that is, measures of reproductive performance during a given chronological period. Important research by P. K. Whelpton and his colleagues in the postwar period has brought to the forefront a new set of fertility measures, namely, "cohort rates," in which the basic unit of study is not a chronological period but a population cohort, typically a group of women born in a given year(s). Thus a cohort fertility measure describes the reproductive history of the group up to a specified age. The "completed fertility rate" is a cohort measure showing the total number of live births per woman (or per thousand women), on the average, over the entire reproductive period of the cohort. For cohorts currently completing childbearing this is in the neighborhood of 3.0 births per woman.

It has been stressed that variations in period rates do not necessarily imply variations in completed fertility rates, since the former are also influenced by changes in the spacing of childbearing. For example, during much of the period of the baby boom (a period rate phenomenon at the time) it was often pointed out that the boom did not necessarily imply a rise in completed fertility (though this has in fact subsequently proved to be the case). Correspondingly, it might be asked whether the recent and prospective decline in period rates portends a decline in completed size of family?

A satisfactory answer to this calls for explaining the age-specific rates for the groups aged 30 and over, which is not attempted here.[10] However, just as the rates for ages under 30 dominate the summary period rates, so cumulative births for a cohort through age 29 com-

[10] A recent paper by Arthur A. Campbell provides a concise review of the postwar fertility experience from the cohort viewpoint [28]. Campbell suggests that the recent fertility decline at older ages is due to a change in spacing.

prise a large share of the cohort's completed fertility. For example, if the cohort of 1945–50, which will be aged 15–19 in 1965, were to show the relevant age-specific rates of the Census C projections as it aged to 25–29 in 1975, it would have had an average of 2.1 live births per woman by that age. Clearly, the present speculation regarding the outlook through 1975 for age-specific rates up to ages 25–29 carries this cohort through the main part of its reproductive period. If this cohort were to maintain the spacing pattern used in all the Census projections (which is to say if it were to continue on the C track through the remainder of its reproductive career), its completed fertility would be 2.8 births, well below the roughly 3.3 peak now anticipated for the cohort of 1930–35 (Table 8, column 4).

Is a movement like this toward lower completed fertility likely to occur, or is a major change in child-spacing toward later age in prospect? While significant shifts in child-spacing have occurred in past experience, most notably toward earlier childbearing in the past two decades, there is nevertheless a high positive correlation between cumulative fertility through age 29 and completed fertility. Presumably this is but one indication that by age 30 the life cycle pattern of most individuals has been well established. While some shift toward later childbearing seems possible, one may speculate that with the continued growth in the educational level of females and in opportunities for them in productive employment a major reversal toward later childbearing is unlikely to occur. On these (admittedly tenuous) grounds, I venture the guess that the current movements in period fertility do imply a reduction in completed fertility.

Recent surveys show that expectations regarding completed family size for cohorts currently entering the childbearing period do not differ significantly from those of cohorts further along [68]. These results appear to contradict the suggestion made here of an incipient decline in completed fertility, and to imply that the recent decline in fertility among younger persons involves merely postponement of births which will be made up at later ages. However, a suggestion is put forward by the authors of the survey report, and some supporting evidence noted, that postponement of births may be a first step toward revising expectations downward. If correct, this would reconcile the expectations results with my speculation.

However, it is not entirely clear that the survey results are in

TABLE 8. PROJECTED AND EXPECTED NUMBER OF BIRTHS PER
WOMAN FOR FIVE-YEAR BIRTH COHORTS OF WOMEN, BIRTH YEARS,
1920–25 TO 1955–60

Birth Cohort	Age in 1965 (1)	Projected A (2)	Projected B (3)	Projected C (4)	Projected D (5)	Birth Cohort (6)	Expected Survey Year '60 (7)	Expected Survey Year '62 (8)	Expected Survey Year '63 (9)	Expected Survey Year '64 (10)
1920–25	40–44	2.9			2.9	1921–25	3.0	n.a.	n.a.	n.a.
1925–30	35–39	3.2	3.1		3.1	1926–30	3.3	3.1	3.2	3.2
1930–35	30–34	3.5	3.4		3.3	1931–35	3.4	3.3	3.3	3.5
1935–40	25–29	3.5	3.4		3.2	1936–42	3.1	3.2	3.2	3.2
1940–45	20–24	3.5	3.3		3.0	1939–45	n.a.	n.a.	3,1	3.0 [a]
1945–50	15–19	3.4	3.2	2.8	2.7					
1950–55	10–14	3.4	3.1	2.8	2.5					
1955–60	5–9	3.4	3.1	2.8	2.4					

NOTE: (1) Cohorts below dotted line are those affected by projections for 1965 through 1975 of age specific rates for 15–19, 20–24, and 25–29. (2) Except for the youngest cohort, the expectation data refer only to those members of each cohort who would have been eligible for the 1960 GAF study. There is, therefore, an upward selection with respect to duration of marriage as these cohorts age.
SOURCE: Cols. 1–5, [144, Table A-1]; cols. 7–10, [68, Tables 3 and 7]. Unpublished 1964 survey data were provided by Ronald Freedman.
[a] Birth cohort of 1940–46.
n.a. = not available.

conflict with my view. In Table 8 the expectations of various cohorts reported in the survey have been matched with the census projections. If one reads columns 7 through 10 vertically, one finds a consistent picture of a rise in completed family size through the cohort of 1931–35, followed by a gradual decline for the two subsequent cohorts.[11] The close correspondence of the Census C and D projections with this pattern, not only in movement but in magnitude as well, is not exactly surprising since the projections utilized the surveys through 1962. The point is, however, that my analysis based on economic considerations, which relates to the cohorts below the break in the series, independently suggested the Census C series as the most plausible, and this is the one consistent with the expectations results.

[11] The original draft of the chapter was based on the 1960, 1962, and 1963 surveys. Subsequently, Ronald Freedman kindly supplied comparable 1964 data, which proved to show the same pattern of intercohort differences as the three previous surveys.

The apparent contradiction between the survey results and my suggestion of a prospective decline in completed fertility thus stems from the fact that the size of the sample does not permit attributing *statistical* significance to the decline indicated by the survey results, rather than the absence of such a decline. Some reassurance about the reliability of the differences in expectations for adjacent cohorts might perhaps be drawn from the fact that all four surveys indicate a larger completed rate for the 1931–35 cohort than for the 1926–30 cohort, and a smaller rate for the 1936–42 cohort than for the 1931–35 cohort, though the magnitude of the differences vary. Clearly what is needed, however, is an increase in sample size to permit finer judgments about statistically significant differences. In this connection, it would seem desirable to strive in addition for separate observations for the 15–19 group. The cohort of 1945–50 will reach this age in 1965 and the Census C series implies a further noticeable decline in the completed rate for this group. The current survey procedures, however, would not provide a reading on this group until it is 20–24.

Conclusions on Projections

The application of the cohort approach has resulted in significantly improved population projections in recent years. Surveys of fertility expectations are of value both in the development of new projections and in appraising existing ones, as well as in analyzing ongoing fertility changes. The present discussion of economic factors suggests that such an analysis may play a role in projections work similar to that performed by the expectations surveys. If my analysis is correct, each projection series implies a pattern of income change by age. To the extent this pattern can be made more explicit (perhaps tying in, for example, with recent work on income by age at HEW [22]) the more feasible it becomes to appraise the "realism" of individual projections, in much the same way as knowledge of the completed fertility rate implied by different projections helps in evaluating them. It hardly needs to be stressed that this is a goal, and that much more basic research is needed, including of course attention to differences among population components. The complementary use of expectations surveys and studies of economic factors, illustrated in this discussion, is an attractive possibility for the longer run.

PART III / LABOR FORCE ANALYSES

CHAPTER 6 / RECENT AND PROJECTED LABOR FORCE GROWTH IN THE LIGHT OF LONGER-TERM EXPERIENCE

It was shown in Chapter 3 that recent experience, like that in the past, has been marked by a long swing in the growth of population, labor force, and households. It was noted there, however, that the components of change principally responsible were different in the recent period, and reasons were suggested for this. Part II pursued the problem of reconciling recent and past experience with regard to population growth. The present part similarly follows up the swings in labor force growth. Here, as has been noted, the most recent swing is marked by the exceptional behavior of participation rates. The recent disproportionate contribution of participation-rate change to the swing in total labor force growth is the subject of the present chapter; the unusual rise in the rates of older women, the principal topic of the following chapter.

As the Gordon Committee Report [136] pointed out several years ago, research on the dynamics of labor force change has been lacking. Since that time, and partly in response to the Report, some important new work has appeared.[1] However, this research, like the current projections of future labor force, rests almost entirely on data for the period since 1947,[2] reflecting the initiation at that time of regular sample surveys. These surveys have provided a major new source of data, whose potential even now is only beginning to be exploited. But the census data, whose value has been amply demonstrated in several

[1] For example, see the papers and references in [80, 138]. The recently initiated *Manpower Report of the President* provides an annual review of the field and valuable current insights [202].

[2] A notable exception is Stanley Lebergott's work [110].

earlier monographs [12, 52, 106, 116, 126, 173] have not been brought to bear on the current discussion either. The present and following chapters may perhaps indicate the potential relevance of these historical materials to some of the current issues.

This chapter first reviews pertinent aspects of the record of swings in labor force growth. This can be done briefly, since many of these points have been covered before. Then an attempt is made to develop an explanation for recent experience consistent with earlier. Finally, as in the case of fertility, the discussion touches on the implications of the analysis for projections, one of the principal subjects of current controversy.

THE RECORD

The absolute magnitudes of total labor force at decennial or quinquennial intervals since 1870 are plotted in Figure 44. The outstanding feature is the continuous upward trend. Each successive interval in the ninety-five year period registered an increase, and by 1965 the labor force total was over six times the 1870 figure of 12.9 million.

However, while the trend in total labor force was continuously upward, the rate of growth was not constant. This is apparent from the changing slope and mild undulatory movement of the curve in Figure 44. This unevenness can be made more explicit if the successive decade percentage increases themselves are plotted, as in Figure 45. For a number of analytical problems, it is these *changes* in total labor force rather than the stock, that are directly relevant. Hence one should be careful not to infer that the seemingly mild variation in the total stock curve of Figure 44 is of little economic significance.

For most of the period, the general sweep of the curve in Figure 45 is downward, signifying a trend toward a declining rate of growth in labor force. But the movement occurs in a stepwise fashion, rather than smoothly. And—what is of particular significance—these fluctuations are of sizable magnitude. Thus, from its high of 29.3 per cent in 1870–80 to its low of 8.3 in 1930–40, the growth rate of the labor force declined from one decade to the next at a rate averaging around 3.5 percentage points. Of the six actual interdecade changes, however,

FIGURE 44

TOTAL LABOR FORCE, 1870–1965

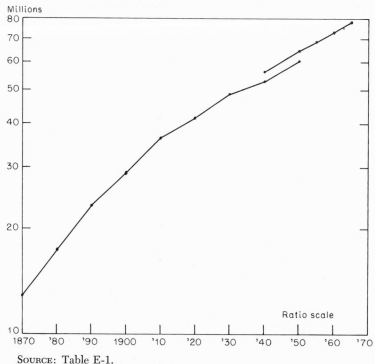

SOURCE: Table E-1.

three showed much higher declines, in the neighborhood of 7 to 9 percentage points, and three showed virtually no decline or even a slight rise. As a result, the mean deviation from the 3.5 average was 4.3 percentage points, higher than the average itself. Moreover, this fluctuation in the decade-to-decade growth rate has continued into the recent period. From 1930–40 to 1940–50, the growth rate per decade rose by 5 percentage points. From 1940–50 to 1950–60, it declined by 3.1 percentage points, and in the most recent quinquennium (1960–65) it has risen again by 2.8 points.

That these swings are not a statistical artifact has already been suggested by several considerations touched on in Part I. First, the swings in labor force growth exhibit a pattern broadly consistent with those in series relating to output, construction, population change,

FIGURE 45

AVERAGE GROWTH RATE OF TOTAL LABOR FORCE: DECENNIALLY, 1870–1950;
QUINQUENNIALLY, 1950–65

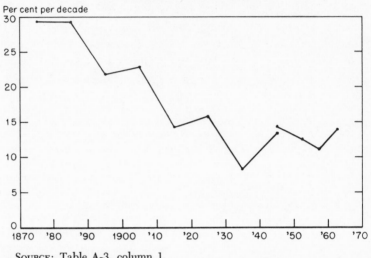

SOURCE: Table A-3, column 1.

and the labor market, most of which are estimated from data entirely independent of those on labor force. Second, if observations corresponding to decennial census intervals are selected from the entirely independent annual series on immigration, one obtains a sawtooth pattern similar to that shown by the labor force data for the period in which immigration was a significant factor in labor force change (Figure 1). Third, if instead of the aggregate, one studies the major industrial components of labor force, the sectors in which the swings appear are largely the same over time (Figure 8).

Nevertheless, because the historical census data relating to the labor force or the gainfully occupied are known to contain deficiencies which affect comparability over time, the specific bearing of these on the present analysis is considered in Appendix F. The conclusion reached there is that the defects do not invalidate the inference that longer-term fluctuations in labor force growth actually did occur.

Labor force growth may be subdivided into several underlying components, along the lines described in Part I, with a view to identifying the role of each component in the swing in total growth. When this is done, the following findings emerge (Figure 46). First, prior to the decade of World War I, the swings in total labor force growth were predominantly due to corresponding fluctuations in net immigration. Second, the upsurge in the 1920's was largely produced by the demographic component of aging and mortality, with the other two components contributing relatively little. This movement is of interest because experience since the late 1950's shows some similarity. (This is suggested by the terminal values plotted in Figure 46 and will be

FIGURE 46

AVERAGE GROWTH RATE OF LABOR FORCE BY COMPONENT OF CHANGE:
DECENNIALLY, 1870–1950; QUINQUENNIALLY, 1950–65

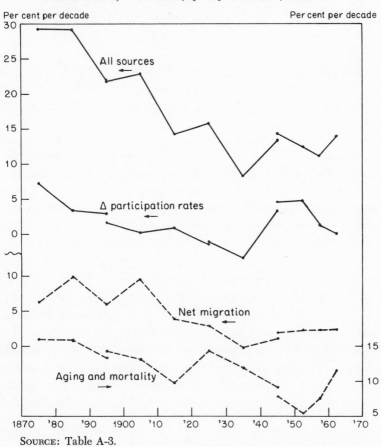

SOURCE: Table A-3.

developed somewhat more fully in the later section on projections.) By far the most striking movement among the components, however, and the one of primary interest, is the marked swing in the contribution of participation-rate change to labor force growth since the 1930's. It is this movement which is chiefly responsible for the upturn in labor force growth in the 1940's and its subsequent decline to a trough in 1955–60. Prior to the 1930's participation-rate change appears to have played an insignificant role in the swings. (There is even a suggestion of an inverse movement prior to World War I, but since the estimates for this period are rather crude, not much confidence can be placed in this observation.) The startling change in this component's role clearly raises the question whether the recent swing in labor force growth forms a logically consistent part of prior experience. It is to the analysis of this question that the subsequent section is principally devoted.

Before turning to this, however, one may ask how the emphasis here on variability of labor force growth can be reconciled with Clarence Long's widely known finding on the stability of the age-standardized labor force participation rate [116, especially Chapter 12]. One point highlighted by the present analytical scheme is that since participation-rate change is but one component of labor force growth fluctuations may occur because of movements in other components. As Figure 46 shows clearly, before World War I labor force projections based on such stability would have been wide of the mark unless they anticipated the varying role played by net immigration in labor force growth [71]. A second point relates to the criterion of stability.[3] A one-point increase over a decade in an over-all labor force participation rate of around 50 per cent has a different meaning depending on whether one's interest is in the labor force stock or the change therein. With regard to the stock, a one-point change alters the total by only one-fiftieth. But with regard to the labor force change, which in this century has averaged about 14 per cent per decade, a one-point change alters growth by around one-seventh. To illustrate, if between 1930 and 1940 the age-sex standardized rate had really been constant at 53.9 instead of declining "only" 1.7

[3] Lowell Gallaway has conducted a searching examination of this question with regard to the various component classifications of labor force [74, Appendix A].

points to 52.2, the labor force increase would have been almost 12 per cent, nearly one-half greater than the actual change of slightly over 8 per cent.[4]

EXPLANATION

The Model

The basic elements of the present model are quite simple:

Labor force growth is divided into two components: the first, that arising from the natural increase of the working-age population, is autonomous as regards current swings; the second, that due to the combined contribution of net migration and participation-rate change, is viewed as induced.[5]

The autonomous component depends on demographic processes, age changes and mortality, which shape the natural growth of the working-age population in a given period.

The induced component varies inversely with the unemployment rate. It is seen as comprising adjustment mechanisms for correcting labor market imbalances, mechanisms which are set in motion by changes in unemployment conditions.

The contribution of the autonomous component to labor force growth in any given period is largely predetermined by prior demographic developments, principally natural increase some ten to twenty years earlier. (Unanticipated developments in mortality during a given period could alter the size of this component, but such occurrences tend to be rare in modern experience.) The problem of explaining swings in total labor force growth thus devolves into explanation of the fluctuations in the induced component. The subsequent empirical tests consequently focus on this component. Beyond this, there remains the question of the changing role within the induced component of

---

[4] Note that the contribution of participation-rate change to labor force growth is roughly the same as the relative, not absolute, change in the over-all participation rate. Thus, *ceteris paribus*, a decline in the rate from 53.9 to 52.2 reduces labor force growth, not by 1.7, but by 3.2 per cent (1.7 ÷ 53.9).

[5] The analogy with a similar classification of investment in many models of growth and fluctuation is readily apparent. If the present distinction is valid, it would imply need for reconsideration of the typical treatment in these models of population or labor force (the two are often not even differentiated) as an autonomous variable.

migration versus participation-rate change. The present chapter attempts to suggest some pertinent considerations, but no attempt is made to incorporate them formally into the model.

Tests

As simple as the model is, it is not easy to test it empirically.[6] Two tests of the unemployment-induced component relation can, however, be presented.

First, the analysis in Chapter 2 of the causes of pre-World War I swings in immigration may be drawn on since, as has been seen, the swings in labor force growth in this period appear to have been almost entirely produced by immigration movements (Figure 46). The earlier discussion embraced a substantial part of the nineteenth century, since the aim was to judge, if only roughly, whether movements in domestic or foreign conditions were principally responsible for initiating the immigration swings. As for identifying the actual market mechanism to which immigrants were responding, however, the analysis must be confined to the last full swing before World War I, since only for this period are unemployment estimates and other pertinent data available on an annual basis.

In Figure 47, reference cycle averages for the period 1889–1915 are plotted for the growth rate of aggregate production, for both the annual level of the unemployment rate and the change in it as well as for the level of the immigration rate and real wage rate. A close correspondence is apparent, first, between the movement in the output growth rate and the change in unemployment rate (inverted); second, lagging noticeably behind the former association, between

------

[6] The basic problem is lack of annual estimates—for unemployment before 1890 and for the components of labor force change throughout the entire period. Lebergott [110] has made annual estimates of the labor force for 1890–1940, but these are derived by interpolation between decade observations. Though his procedure is an ingenious one, the estimates do not provide an adequate basis for developing components of change estimates relevant to the present purpose. His unemployment estimates, which are obtained as the difference between labor force and employment estimates, are less open to objection because the employment estimates reflect at least in part actual experience in each year. Meaningful annual estimates of the components of labor change could be developed for the period from around 1947 onward, when CPS data become available regularly in sufficient detail, but in the present study no attempt has been made to derive such estimates for periods shorter than a quinquennium (the three following 1950).

FIGURE 47

AVERAGE ANNUAL RATE OF CHANGE IN AGGREGATE PRODUCTION (ΔP) AND
UNEMPLOYMENT RATE (ΔU); AND AVERAGE LEVEL OF REAL WAGE RATE (W),
UNEMPLOYMENT RATE (U), AND IMMIGRATION RATE (I): NBER REFERENCE
CYCLES, 1890–1915

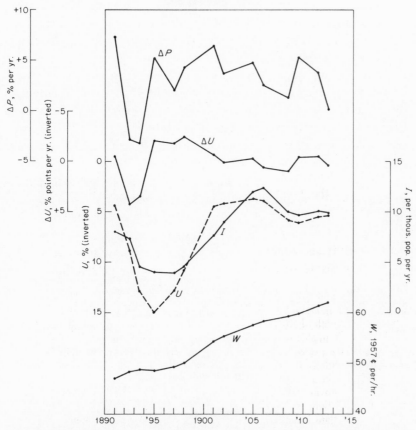

SOURCE: Table E-2 and, for aggregate production (nonperishable commodity
output), Table B-2, series 1 and 3.

the level of the unemployment rate (inverted) and that of the immigration rate. In the latter association, the unemployment rate leads
the immigration rate, a finding consistent with the view suggested by
the model that the induced component of labor force growth is a
function of unemployment conditions.

An alternative possibility, that the immigration rate was responding to changes in the U.S.-European wage differential, seems less likely. To derive an estimate of the differential would require wage estimates for a number of European countries, a task beyond the scope of this study. But one can see from Figure 47 that the U.S. side of this differential, the wage rate in this country, shows not a swing in absolute level but only retardation and acceleration in the upward trend. (The swing in wages becomes most apparent only when one uses the rate of change in the real-wage rate as in Figure 9.) Unless wage movements in Europe were large and synchronous among the various countries, it seems doubtful that the variations in the wage differential in the course of a long swing could have been large in relation to the average size of the differential. Rather, it seems more plausible, as Lebergott also argues, that while real-wage differentials contributed to establishing the direction and secular level of the flow, the fluctuations in the flow were chiefly governed by variations in the availability of jobs, as reflected in the unemployment rate.[7]

A second and more comprehensive test of the model is possible if the analysis is structured by the periods for which the present

[7] ". . . We find only a limited relationship between changes in [U.S.] nonfarm earnings and migration. The difference between wage levels in the two worlds was always substantial; short-term changes in wages (particularly small ones) made little difference in this ratio of advantage" [110, p. 40].

Harry Jerome's study in the 1920's showed the close association between unemployment conditions and immigration during the regular business cycle [96]. The conclusions of the Immigration Commission, created by Congress in 1907 to study immigration, provide additional support as to the immediate relevance of unemployment conditions to the flow of migrants [211, p. 25]:

"The immediate incentive of the great bulk of present day immigration is the letters of persons in this country to relatives or friends at home. Comparatively few immigrants come without some reasonably definite assurance that employment awaits them, and it is probably that as a rule they know the nature of that employment and the rate of wages."

Another alternative proposed by Kuznets, that the level of the immigration rate was a function of the rate of change in the flow of goods to consumers, is dubious on both conceptual and empirical grounds [103, pp. 32–33]. Kuznets himself recognizes the theoretical difficulty of assuming, in effect, that immigrant decisions were influenced not by the level of U.S. per capita consumption but by additions to the level, though he attempts to escape this problem by arguing that the additions were particularly relevant to lower-income groups [Ibid., pp. 32–33]. In any event, as Hickman points out [90, p. 496, n. 7] the scheme implies an extraordinarily long lag. This is shown in Figure VI-4 where the immigration rate lags behind the rate of change in aggregate production (a close approximation in timing to Kuznets' flow of goods to consumers) by a substantial period.

study has estimated the components of change in labor force growth, *viz.*, decennial intervals 1870 through 1950, and quinquennial thereafter. Lebergott's valuable attempt to rough out the unemployment magnitudes for the part of this period not covered by official estimates makes possible a direct comparison of the unemployment rate and induced component of labor force growth for eleven intervals (eight decennial and three quinquennial) since 1870.

Two series are plotted in the upper panel of Figure 48, the average unemployment rate (inverted) and the contribution of the induced component, net migration plus participation-rate change, to labor force growth in the corresponding interval. While there is some

FIGURE 48

LEVEL AND RATE OF CHANGE OF INDUCED COMPONENT OF LABOR FORCE GROWTH (L_n) AND UNEMPLOYMENT RATE (u): ACTUAL, 1870–1965; AND PROJECTED VALUES OF RATES OF CHANGE, 1965–70

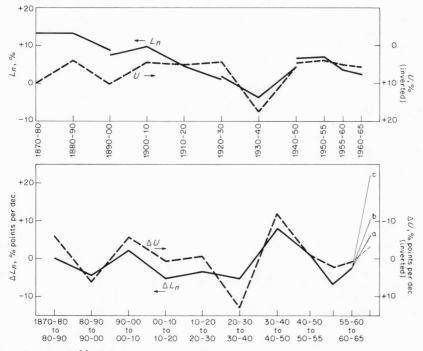

SOURCE: Table E-3.
ᵃ BLS.   ᵇ Tella.   ᶜ Strand-Dernburg.

semblance of similarity in movement, it is obscured by the downward trend in the induced component of labor force growth throughout much of the period. If one follows the procedure adopted in Chapter 4, where a similar problem occurred in the analysis of the birth rate, and plots the first differences in the two series, a striking correspondence emerges (lower panel). Fluctuations in the first differences of the induced component match those in the first differences of the unemployment rate on a one-to-one basis from the beginning of the period down to the present. The amplitudes of the movements in the two series conform less closely. Nevertheless, the extent of agreement is surprising when one considers the crudeness of the unemployment estimates for much of the period, and the uncertainty on the labor force side as to the degree of comparability of the census figures and the shift to the CPS concept after 1940, with its greater sensitivity to marginal groups. Indeed, there are some noteworthy similarities. The expansion phases (designated here according to the beginning date of the phase) fall in the following descending order when ranked according to the rise in the rate of change in the unemployment rate (inverted):

1. 1920–30 to 1930–40
2. 1880–90 to 1890–1900
3. 1900–10 to 1910–20

This is precisely the same order as that obtained when the phases are ranked according to the change in the induced component of labor force growth. Thus, in the upper panel of Figure 48, the mildness in the upswing of the induced component in 1920–30 compared with 1940–50 appears to trace back to differential movements in unemployment conditions. This is in turn perhaps partly attributable to the contrasting behavior of the autonomous component in the two periods—the rise in its contribution to labor force growth in the 1920's and the decline in the 1940's (see Figure 46)—which would have contributed to more rapid tightening of the labor market in the later period.

It is striking too how well recent experience falls in line with the historical pattern. The change in the induced component of labor force growth in the recent period is seen to trace a path much like the change in the unemployment rate (inverted), with both showing a common upturn in the expansion phase beginning 1950–55 to 1955–60.

On the whole, then, the findings seem consistent with the view that variations during this period in the induced component of labor force growth, which reflects the contributions of net migration and participation-rate change to the labor force, arose in substantial measure from variations in unemployment conditions. The similarity between this model and that developed for explanation of swings in the birth rate will be readily apparent (cf. especially Figure 29 and accompanying text). In the case of the birth rate, however, where a part rather than the total of the working-age population was the subject of analysis (those in family-building ages), it was necessary to introduce an additional explanatory variable indicative of the differential experience of that segment.[8]

Changes Within the Induced Component

There remains the question of the changing importance within the induced component of participation-rate change versus net migration, specifically, the rise in the relative importance of the former in recent decades. It is clear in general where the explanation is to be sought—in the occurrence of secular developments which on balance have operated to raise the relative responsiveness of participation-rate change as an adjustment mechanism. The most obvious, and perhaps sufficient, explanation is restrictive immigration legislation, which has tended to set a ceiling on immigration and also altered its composition. World Wars I and II would of course also be major exogenous events reducing the migration flow in their respective decades.

While these are plausible and probably important factors operating to reduce the importance of immigration, there are nevertheless

---

[8] This statement implies adoption of the analytical view of swings in the unemployment rate suggested in Chapter 4, footnote 21, as an alternative to that in the text on that page, namely, that the swings be viewed as reflecting the consensus of both aggregate demand and supply forces (though, for the most part, movements in aggregate demand have probably dominated the observed swings in the rate). An analysis of the unemployment rate itself calls for a fully articulated model of swings, a task beyond the scope of this study.

some puzzling aspects which must be recognized. The phrase "tended to set a ceiling" is used advisedly, since the quota laws did not apply to residents of the Western Hemisphere until the Act of October 3, 1965. Why did not immigration from this area, particularly Latin America, rise more noticeably? Some response is evident, notably from Puerto Rico, but also to some extent from Mexico and a few other areas not enjoying the favored political status of Puerto Rico. Possible explanations for the limited response come readily to mind— differences in language and culture, lack of education, financing and transportation difficulties, and so on. The trouble is that such explanations would seem equally if not more applicable to southern and eastern Europe before World War I. Yet means were devised to overcome such obstacles and an immense inflow to the United States from these areas resulted. Why not the same in the case of Latin America?

Another puzzling aspect arises from the fact that while the legislation has a dampening effect on an upswing in immigration, it clearly does not prevent immigration from declining or even becoming negative if conditions warrant. The virtual cessation of net immigration in the 1930's and an actual net outflow in a few years of that decade is illustrative of this. But the net migration component in the last two decades has been remarkably stable and has not shown the responsiveness to weakened employment conditions in the late 1950's evidenced by the participation-rate component (see Figure 46). It might be argued that this shows that the immigration level is substantially below its equilibrium value and that the weakening in the growth of aggregate demand has not been great enough to alter this situation. But the net movement from Puerto Rico, one of the flows included here in the migration component, did in fact drop off sharply. Yet the migration total did not. Why?

There is perhaps a tendency to assume that the study of United States immigration is of little current interest. Yet in the decade 1950–60, net immigration accounted for about one person in five added to the labor force. Clearly there are some important questions in this area that merit fuller study.

To turn to participation-rate change, have there been secular changes operating to increase the responsiveness of various population groups to market pressures? [9] A number of factors have been suggested as increasing the sensitivity of the female segment of the working age population—the secular decline in fertility and associated reduction in family responsibilities; a shortening of the work week making it easier for married women to accept outside employment; increased education; redistribution of the female population toward urban areas and thus closer proximity to markets for their services. There has also been a secular trend toward more white-collar jobs relative to blue-collar ones, a development which would probably favor domestic females as against immigrants (though the composition of immigration too shows adaptation in this direction [208]). On the other hand, the secular rise in husband's income has presumably worked in the opposite direction. And for the other groups in the population whose labor force attachment is similarly marginal, youths and the elderly population, secular changes have probably worked to reduce their responsiveness. For youths, the principal factor would be the rise in compulsory education. For the elderly, there would be, first, the shift from self-employed status in farming toward employee status in the nonfarm sector, a development that would increase dependence on others for employment, and, secondly, a secular rise in income level which would encourage earlier labor force withdrawal and the formalization of retirement plans.[10]

In the present state of knowledge, the question of whether the forces operating on the domestic population tended on balance to increase or decrease responsiveness to labor market pressures cannot be answered with assurance. Taken in conjunction with legislative and other impediments to foreign supply, however, it seems safe to say that the *relative* responsiveness of the domestic supply was increased. This is sufficient to account for the observed *direction* of shift in recent decades within the induced component of labor force

[9] Long [116] provides an extensive survey and analysis. More recently, Mincer [127, pp. 73–112; 128] has made important contributions relevant to secular trends.

[10] This discussion implies a trend toward an altered sex-age composition of those responding through participation-rate changes, a point which is developed in the following chapter.

growth in the roles of immigration and participation-rate change. Clearly, however, a fuller and quantitative analysis of this problem would be desirable.

PROJECTIONS

In recent discussions of both economic growth and stabilization, the prospective size and composition of the labor force has received increasing attention. Labor force projections are a fundamental point of departure in estimates of future economic growth [11]. A basic problem in public policy efforts to reduce recent unemployment has been the prospective need to create jobs, not only for those currently reported as unemployed but also for those who might enter the labor force as job opportunities expanded [35, pp. 138–140]. The bearing on future labor force growth of the interpretation of past experience offered here is therefore of substantial interest. This section first outlines the method currently used in official labor force projections, and then considers the bearing on these projections of two aspects of the analytical framework used here—the components-of-change technique and long swings.

The most recent projection (1964) indicates that labor force may grow to a total in 1970 of around 86 million; in 1975, almost 94 million; and in 1980, over 101 million [35]. The implied growth rate in each of the three quinquennia from 1965 to 1980 is around 16 per cent or more per decade. In contrast, the rates in each of the three quinquennia prior to 1965 were all less than this figure (Table 9, column 1). Indeed, comparison with the decade changes in this century (Table A-3) shows that the growth projected for 1965–75 is higher than in any corresponding period except 1900–10, the last decade of unobstructed immigration.

Present Method

The procedure underlying the official labor force projections is summarized as follows:

The projections described above represent the authors' best judgment as to the most reasonable pattern of labor force growth to 1980. It must

TABLE 9. LABOR FORCE GROWTH BY COMPONENT OF CHANGE, ACTUAL, 1940–50, AND QUINQUENNIALLY, 1950–65; PROJECTED, QUINQUENNIALLY, 1965–80
(per cent per decade)

| | | | Contribution of | | |
| | | | Population Growth Due to | | |
	Total Labor Force Growth (1)	All Sources (col. 3 + col. 4) (2)	Aging and Mortality (3)	Net Migration (4)	Participation Rate Change (5)
1940–50	14.2	9.7	7.8	1.9	4.5
1950–55	12.4	7.7	5.5	2.2	4.8
1955–60	11.1	9.8	7.5	2.3	1.3
1960–65	13.9	13.9	11.5	2.4	0
1965–70	18.6	14.9	13.1	1.8	3.7
1970–75	17.0	15.7	14.0	1.7	1.4
1975–80	15.9	14.5	12.9	1.6	1.5

SOURCE: Appendix Tables A-3, E-3 (1965–70), and B-7 (1970–80).

be stressed that these are long-term projections, reflecting anticipated changes in demographic composition and changes which might occur in the labor force activity of the several age-sex groups in the population.

The general approach was to project labor force participation rates for each age-sex group, to apply these rates to the future population, and thereby to derive total labor force by age and sex. The projections are greatly dependent upon the future size and age structure of the population.

Labor force participation rates for men age 25 to 59 have shown little variation in the postwar period. These were held constant at the average level of 1955–57, when over-all unemployment was about 4 per cent [35, pp. 134–135].

For other age groups where some consistent change in participation rates is apparent, selected social and demographic factors which limit or encourage labor force activities were taken into account. After specifying some of the changes which were assumed in demographic composition of the population and participation rates specific to certain groups, the bearing of unemployment conditions on the projection is explained:

Although there is some interest in a projection of the labor force at very low levels of unemployment—such as 3 per cent—the post-World War II experience from which data for these projections are drawn imposes some constraints.

Therefore, the projections made in this article more nearly represent a 4 per cent unemployment situation. . . . For age groups whose labor-force participation rates have been rising or falling consistently throughout the postwar period, it was assumed that past trends will continue but at a slower rate. These trends, however, were adjusted where it appeared that they might have been dampened in recent years by reduced job opportunities [ibid., pp. 137–138].

An important contrast between the labor force and population projections is apparent. In the latter case, a set of four alternative projections is presented, with a specific disclaimer to the effect that no single set is considered superior. On the other hand, in the case of the labor force projection, only one projection is presented and it is specifically identified as representing the authors' "best judgment." [11] The difference in approach perhaps reflects in part the greater number of specific assumptions that enter into a single labor force projection, and thus the problems of manageability and exposition that variant projections would raise. However, while the development of alternative projections of households poses similar difficulties, an attempt is nevertheless made to present several variants [182, No. 123]. In part, the differing approach in the labor force projection may simply reflect a smaller amount of resources available for such work. In any event, it is clear that while users of the projections may be pleased to have a single "best judgment" projection, there is a real disadvantage in relieving these users of the obligation of weighing basic assumptions so as to choose among alternatives, as is necessary in the case of the population and household projections.

Uses of a Components-of-Change Analysis

It may be suggested that formally incorporating in the labor force projection a components-of-change analysis such as that em-

---

[11] A footnote in the report indicates that an alternate projection was prepared; but it is not published, though mention is made of a few of its features.

ployed here would go some way toward meeting this objection.[12] Such a scheme helps both in appraising the projection and in considering alternative possibilities. For example, as has been noted, the current projection for the 1965–80 period seems to imply an unusually high growth rate. However, if a partition analysis by component of change were presented, as in columns 2 through 5 of Table 9, one would see immediately that the unusually high projected rate stems largely from the unusually high growth of the working-age population. Indeed, it is this component which is responsible for the upturn in labor force growth which occurred between 1955–60 and 1960–65. This lends more credence to the projection than if the rise in labor force growth to such a high level were found to be chiefly owing to an upsurge in the contribution of participation-rate change to labor force growth. Viewed against the longer perspective provided by Figure 46, experience in 1960–70 is seen as resembling that in 1920–30, though the size of the current movement is much greater.

The partition analysis further shows, however, that in the 1965–70 quinquennium the projection does imply a substantial rise in the contribution of participation-rate change along with a continued increase in the demographic component. It thus directs attention to the question of whether such a development seems plausible, a question accentuated by reference to the experience of the 1920's, when the rise in the demographic component was accompanied by declines in the others (Figure 46). The partition analysis makes clear too the part which current immigration is playing in labor force growth and thus points to the need for assessment of this factor's likely role. Thus, the components-of-change analysis helps alert users to elements in the projection which are critical to proper evaluation of it.

In addition to defining more sharply such basic issues, the components-of-change analysis readily lends itself to formulation of alternative estimates. The amount of labor force growth due explicitly to population change is identified, and this can in itself be viewed as

[12] Actually, reference is made, in describing the projections, to the contribution of population change to labor force growth among men, women, and youths [35, p. 129]. The proposal here is for a more formal and detailed presentation, and one that provides historical perspective as well. For an earlier discussion along these lines, see [53].

an alternative projection. Indeed, for the most recent quinquennium, 1960–65, a user who adopted this alternative would have been better off than with the official projection. As is shown in Table 9, column 5, in this period participation-rate change actually made, on balance, a zero contribution to labor force growth, whereas the official projection (made in 1962) implied a contribution from this source at a rate equivalent to 1.5 points per decade, and a total growth rate correspondingly higher [193]. This disparity, it may be noted, should not be viewed as implying that the official projection was incorrect, for the projection was explicitly based on the assumption of a lower unemployment rate than actually occurred. An analyst who favored a different projected contribution from participation-rate change might do so on either of two grounds—that the actual unemployment rate might differ from that assumed, or that the sensitivity of participation rates to unemployment changes might be different.

The assumption that the contribution of participation-rate change to labor force growth might be zero, and, hence, that labor force growth would depend on population change alone, is one alternative projection that comes directly out of the components-of-change analysis. But other assumptions could readily be made of the prospective value of the participation-rate change contribution, including the possibility of negative magnitudes.[13] Variant assumptions might be introduced too with regard to the potential contribution of net immigration. In principal, the same is true with regard to the demographic component, the contribution arising from natural increase of the working age population. But the likelihood of a poor projection for this component is small because the principal source of error

---

[13] An assumption that participation-rate change, on balance, would contribute zero to labor force growth (or some value other than that projected) does not necessarily imply that no change will occur in participation rates for individual age-sex groups. Actually, in 1960–65 the direction of participation-rate change for almost every age-sex group was correctly anticipated in the official projection. As it turned out, however, the magnitudes involved differed enough so that they summed to a zero rather than net positive addition to labor force growth, as had been anticipated. The judgment about a different aggregate contribution may thus be viewed as merely implying somewhat modified magnitudes of the changes projected for individual age-sex groups. (If a more precise judgment is desired with regard to individual groups, a possible procedure is suggested in the next chapter.)

(aside from data considerations) is unexpected developments in mortality. Indeed, an advantage of the present partition scheme is that, by breaking down the aggregate growth into its underlying components, it displays side-by-side the elements in the projection which are both strongest and weakest.

Recently, the official projections have come under fire for being too low. On the basis of a model estimated for quarterly data for 1947 to 1964, Alfred Tella projects a "full" employment (4 per cent unemployment rate) labor force in 1970 around one million higher than the BLS figure [154, 155]. Strand and Dernburg using a different model and monthly observations from July 1947 to December 1962 (tested through 1963) project a "full employment" 1970 labor force exceeding the BLS level by 3.6 million [49, 150]. The components-of-change analysis proposed here can be used to identify more specifically the differences among several such projections and thus make it easier to appraise their relative merits. Both of the private projections accept the population estimates (including the net migration component) used in the official labor force projection. Thus, assuming a 4 per cent unemployment rate were to materialize, the issue of whether total labor force growth in 1965–70 is likely to be at a rate of 18.6 per cent per decade (BLS), 20.7 per cent (Tella), or 26.6 per cent (Strand-Dernburg), becomes one of whether the net contribution from participation-rate change will be, respectively, 3.7, 5.8, or 11.7 points per decade. When it is realized that according to the estimates made in this study, the highest contribution observed in any preceding period was 4.8 points per decade in 1950–55, some serious doubts are immediately suggested about the realism of the Strand-Dernburg estimate, and even the Tella projection seems rather outsize.[14] The official projection, on the other hand, appears more plausible.

[14] The 1940–45 period witnessed a contribution at a rate higher than 4.8 points, but none of the projections under discussion here assumes wartime conditions, even to the extent of the Vietnamese situation, let alone World War II. In keeping with the reasoning given in Chapter 3, the period selected here for the components-of-change analysis, 1940–50, counterbalances intervals marked by the sharp rise in government expenditure and the subsequent decline to a more nearly postwar "normal."

Relevance of Long-Swings Analysis

To this point, I have tried in this discussion to suggest some of the advantages of explicitly including in the official projections a components-of-change analysis along the lines of that presented here. This proposal is independent of the question of the possible relevance of the long-swings conception to projections, and it is appropriate to turn now to this issue.

Skepticism on this score has been voiced by Edward Denison, who says: "Long-wave analysis tells little about future labor force behavior not shown directly by projections based on the age distribution of the population, school attendance, the retirement age, and so on" [47, p. 532], in other words, by projections developed along the lines of the official one. It is undoubtedly true that mechanical extrapolation of long swings is unwarranted. However, as was observed with regard to similar strictures by Denison relating to the household projections (cf. Chapter 3, footnote 22), if relevant aspects of the swings mechanism are at least partly known, then this approach may contribute useful insights, pertinent at least to appraising a projection, if not to developing an alternative one. The model developed in the preceding section suggests just such a mechanism and may easily be applied to evaluating the alternative projections, official and private.

The model indicates that first differences in the induced component of labor force growth (the sum of the contributions of migration and participation-rate change) are a function of first differences in the average unemployment rate. Appraising the projections to 1970 requires merely: (1) an assumption concerning the average unemployment rate that will prevail in 1965–70, and (2) calculation of the growth in labor force due to the induced component implied by each of the projections. Since all of the projections are tied to an assumed 4 per cent unemployment rate in 1970, it is assumed here that this rate would prevail, on the average, throughout the full quinquennium. The value of the induced component in each projection is obtained simply by adding to the implied contribution of participation-rate change the contribution due to net migration as indicated in the official projection, since as noted, all three projections accept the Census population projections. Thus, one obtains:

Implied Contribution to Labor Force Growth, 1965–70
(percentage per decade), due to

	Participation-Rate Change	Net Migration	Total (Induced Component)
BLS	3.7	1.8	5.5
Tella	5.8	1.8	7.6
Strand-Dernburg	11.7	1.8	13.5

The values in the third column above have been added to Appendix Table E-3 and the first differences, 1960–65 to 1965–70, derived. These are plotted along with the first difference in the unemployment rate, assuming 1965–70 = 4 per cent, in the lower panel of Figure 48 to facilitate comparison with past experience. Reference to this shows that both the Tella and Strand-Dernburg implied projections of the induced component appear exceptionally high if a relationship between the two series of an order of magnitude like that observed historically is assumed likely to persist in the 1965–70 quinquennium. The official projection seems more within the range of plausibility though even it might be viewed as tending toward the high side.

A corollary of the Tella and Strand-Dernburg analyses of recent and prospective labor force growth has been the view that public policy attempts to reach and maintain "full employment" would be seriously handicapped by the need to create jobs both for those now reported as unemployed and for members of a "disguised unemployment group" who were left out or kept out of the labor force by weakened employment conditions, but who would enter the labor force as job opportunities expanded. While my analysis agrees with these studies in its conclusion as to the *direction* in which unemployment variations affect labor force growth, the above finding implies that the *magnitude* of effect suggested by these studies is seriously exaggerated. Thus it adds historical support to a similar conclusion reached by Jacob Mincer in his appraisal of this work [127, pp. 73–112].

SUMMARY

Labor force growth may be divided into several components, that due to: (1) natural growth of the working-age population, (2) net immigration, and (3) participation-rate change. For the analysis of swings in labor force growth, it is useful to view the first component as autonomous, determined by natural increase some ten to twenty years earlier. The second and third may be grouped together as an induced component, first differences in which are a function of those in the unemployment rate, with the latter viewed as reflecting the net balance of aggregate demand and supply forces.

The marked swing in the contribution to labor force growth of participation-rate change since 1940 appears explicable in terms of two circumstances: (a) variations in labor market tightness operating via the unemployment rate to generate a corresponding movement in the induced component; and (b) a reduction in the responsiveness of foreign relative to domestic labor supply sources, probably due chiefly to legislative and other impediments to immigration. In attempting to appraise labor force projections, both the components-of-change technique and long-swings frameworks seem of value. The current official projection for 1970 has been criticized as being from 1 to 3.6 million too low. My evaluation, however, suggests that the official projection seems more plausible than those put forward by its critics, and that, if anything, it may be on the high rather than low side. Correspondingly, estimates of "disguised unemployment" offered by these critics seem excessive.

CHAPTER 7 / DIFFERENTIAL CHANGES IN SEX-AGE SPECIFIC PARTICIPATION RATES

Participation-rate changes in any given period differ both in sign and magnitude among the various sex-age groups of the working age population, and, over time, for any given sex-age group. The change in total labor force attributed to participation-rate movements is, therefore, an aggregate in which the shares of the various sex-age groups are unequal and changing over time. In the preceding chapter, the object of study was the magnitude of the aggregate itself. The problem of this chapter is the following: Assuming one knew the total contribution which participation-rate changes would make to labor force growth, could the sex-age structure of these changes be correctly predicted? (It will be noted that the sequence in which the issues of aggregate vs. sex-age specific changes are taken up in this Part is the opposite of that employed in the official projection technique, where estimates for individual sex-age groups are first made and then summed to obtain the estimate for the total labor force.) The most challenging recent observation calling for explanation is the remarkable rise in the rates of older women. As elsewhere in this study, an attempt is made to develop a model which can consistently explain both past and recent experience, and then to use this model to appraise current projections.

An important research tradition bearing on this question has grown up in demography, one which emphasizes the influence of changing population *composition* on participation rates, changes such as those in color-nativity, marital status, and rural-urban distribution [cf. 12, 52, 95, 218]. This work has contributed important insights into relevant secular factors, though it has generally led to the conclusion that "compositional" factors, as they are often termed, have not played a predominant role in the observed changes [12, p. 43; 52, Chapter 3;

FIGURE 49

LABOR FORCE PARTICIPATION RATE, BY SEX-AGE GROUP, DECENNIALLY,
1900–60

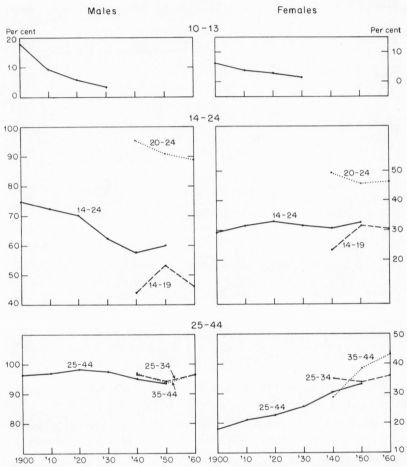

95, p. 295]. More recently, in several of the studies on the relation of
employment conditions to participation rates cited in the previous
chapter [35, 48, 150, 154, 155], the effect of market pressures on labor
force participation of individual sex-age groups has been explored,
but no attempt has been made to take systematic account of secular

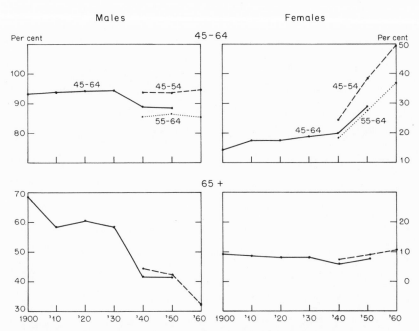

NOTE: Values for 1900–50, from Census; overlap values, 1940 on, from CPS.
SOURCE: Table G-1.

factors.[1] In the explanatory model developed in this chapter I attempt
to incorporate both sets of influences.

The record of participation-rate changes by sex and age since
1900 is first summarized. Then, the analytical model is presented, and
applied, first, to interpretation of past experience, and then to appraisal
of the official projection to 1970.

[1] Mincer's review of these studies and the relevant evidence concludes:
"To sum up: positive cycle sensitivity . . . is readily discernible in the annual
behavior of the secondary labor force. . . . But powerful trend factors and institutional changes continue to dominate the behavior of labor force groups. Much
more attention should be paid to these factors and changes" [127, p. 100].
Reference should also be made to the important contributions to this subject by
Lebergott and Long [110, 116].

THE RECORD

Figure 49 presents at decennial intervals from 1900 to 1960 the participation rates for the individual sex-age groups covered by this analysis. The variety of experience is readily apparent. Since our interest is in the rate *changes* in each decade, these are themselves plotted in Figure 50 in the form of age profiles. To facilitate summarization the four decade changes 1900–40 have been averaged, as have the two decade changes, 1940–60. Important deviations from the average within these two broad periods will be noted in the course of the discussion.

The principal features of the rate changes suggested by Figure 50 are as follows:

1. There is an important difference by sex in the direction of the rate changes. Both in the pre-1940 and post-1940 periods, the rate

FIGURE 50

AGE PROFILE OF CHANGE IN LABOR FORCE PARTICIPATION RATES, BY SEX: AVER-
AGE OF DECADES 1900–40 COMPARED WITH THAT OF DECADES 1940–60

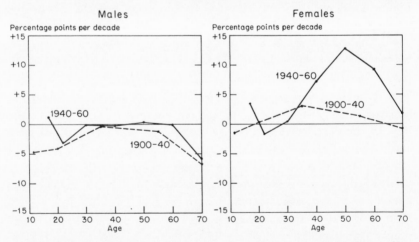

NOTE: Values are plotted at center of each age group, except for 65+, where they are plotted at age 70. For 1900–40, age groups are: 10–13 (1900–30 only), 14–24, 25–44, 45–64, and 65+. For 1940–60, age groups are: 14–19, 20–24, 25–34, 35–44, 45–54, 55–64, and 65+. Values for 1900–40, from Census; 1940–60, from CPS.

SOURCE: Table G-2.

changes for males are almost always around zero or below; for females, around zero or above. This means, of course, that where the over-all contribution to labor force growth of participation-rate change has been positive, this has been largely accomplished through higher female participation which has more than offset reduced male participation.

2. Both pre-1940 and post-1940 age profiles for males show relatively small rate changes from ages in the mid-twenties through mid-fifties, a feature reflecting the hard-core nature of this group in the labor force. In these age periods almost all males are in the labor force all of the time. A mild dip in the rates for those between 25 and 45 did occur between 1940–50 but was recouped in 1950–60 (Figure 49).

It is at the extreme ages, both lower and upper, that the negative rate changes of males have occurred. Thus, to the extent that increased female labor force participation has offset reduced male participation, it has done so primarily for the youngest and oldest males, as Long has particularly emphasized [116]. Post-1940 experience displays one exception, a positive change for males aged 14–19. Actually, as Figure 49 shows, this was confined to the 1940–50 decade, and was virtually eliminated by a return to the historical downtrend in 1950–60.

3. It is for females that the most striking difference occurs between the age profiles for the two periods. Before 1940, the female profile, like that for males, shows negative rate changes at the extreme ages, though of smaller magnitude. For the intervening age groups, however, and particularly for younger women, rate changes are positive. In the decades since 1940, rate changes for females between 20 and 34 have dropped to zero or negative levels, while those for older females have risen to unprecedentedly high positive levels. For females aged 14–19, the rate change has shifted from negative to positive, though, as in the case of males, the positive change was in fact confined to the 1940–50 decade (Figure 49). In general, these patterns signify that it is older females who have been largely responsible for the large rise in the contribution of participation-rate change to labor force growth in the last two decades, though youths aged 14–19 made some contribution in 1940–50.

The principal observations calling for explanation may now be summarized. First, there is the generally higher level of the rate changes for females than for males. Second, there is the tendency toward negative changes at both ends of the age profiles. Third, and most striking with regard to recent experience is the shift in the roles of younger and older women, and the amazingly high rate increases shown by the latter.

ANALYTICAL MODEL

The growth in total labor force attributable to participation-rate changes may be viewed as representing a "net requirement" for workers arising from the balance of aggregate demand and supply forces through a mechanism of the type described in Chapter 6. Given this net requirement, the question is, how would one predict the participation-rate changes for individual sex-age groups?

The model developed here rests on two basic ideas. First, the net requirement is transformed into a "gross requirement" through the addition of an estimate of the net withdrawal of workers due to compositional factors. Second, the share of any given sex-age group in supplying the gross requirement is taken as proportionate to its share in the domestic working-age population outside the labor force, after the latter is adjusted by eliminating several groups assumed to be unresponsive to pressures for labor market entry. These groups are persons aged 10–24 (14–24 from 1940 on) enrolled in school, persons aged 65 and over, and females aged 14–44 with dependent children under 6 years old. For any given sex-age group, the observed change in its participation rate reflects the net balance between the relevant compositional factors making for withdrawal, on the one hand, and market pressures making for entry (the group's share in supplying the gross requirement), on the other.

The key assumption, that the domestic working-age population outside the labor force may be divided into two groups, one wholly unresponsive to market pressures and the other uniformly positive in its response, is an extreme one. As shall be seen, such a simple assumption does not do badly in providing a basis for explaining actual experience—indeed, it serves surprisingly well—but the model could be improved by introducing more realistic variants.

Table 10 illustrates the technique in fuller detail for the 1940–50 decade:

The observed increase in total labor force due to participation-rate change, 2,731 thousand persons, is entered in the "both sexes" row of column 3. This is the "net requirement," the sex-age distribution of which is to be estimated by the model.

Next, the effect of each compositional factor on relevant individual sex-age groups is estimated. Three compositional factors are considered: (1) for youths aged 14–24, changes in school enrollment status, (2) for females aged 14–44, changes in marital and child dependency status, and (3) for males aged 55 and over, changes in OASDI status. For the first factor, the population in a given sex-age group was broken down into those enrolled in school and those not enrolled for each date, and the proportionate distribution calculated. The implications for participation-rate change of the changing proportions were then obtained by weighting them by participation rates specific to each enrollment class, usually fixed at the period average. Similar techniques were used for the second and third factors. No estimate was developed for the second factor before 1940–50 because of scarcity of data, but it is likely that the magnitude involved would have been small.

Columns 5 through 7 give the estimated magnitudes, in thousands of persons, of the effect of these compositional factors on each sex-age group. In every case, the direction of effect is toward withdrawal from labor force activity.

The combined effect of the three compositional factors on each sex-age group is then found by summing horizontally columns 5 through 7. The results (column 4) are totaled to obtain, for the working-age population as a whole, the net labor force withdrawal attributable to compositional factors. This is estimated at 2,079 thousand persons (cf. "both sexes" row of column 4).

The estimated net withdrawal due to compositional factors, 2,079 thousand persons, is added to the "net requirement" of 2,731 thousand persons, to obtain the "gross requirement" to be supplied via market pressures, 4,809 thousand persons (cf. "both sexes" row of column 8).

The next step is to estimate the sex-age distribution of this gross

TABLE 10. ILLUSTRATION OF PROCEDURE FOR PREDICTING PARTICIPATION RATE CHANGE BY SEX AND AGE, 1940–50

(all columns in thousands, except column 1, percentage points)

Sex-Age Class	Predicted Change in Participation Rate (col. 3 ÷ col. 2) (1)	Domestic Working Age Population 1950 [a] (2)	All Factors ("Net Requirement") (3)	Labor Force Growth Due to Participation Rate Change Arising from				Market Pressures ("Gross Requirement") (8)
				All (4)	Compositional Factors			
					School Enrollment (5)	Marital and Child Dependency Status (6)	OASDI (7)	
Both sexes, 14 and over	n.a.	n.a.	2,731	-2,079	-429	-1,465	-185	4,809
Males, 14 and over	n.a.	n.a.	-167	-601	-416	n.a.	-185	434
14–19	-2.9	6,439	-188	-212	-212	n.a.	n.a.	24
20–24	-3.6	5,666	-204	-204	-204	n.a.	n.a.	0
25–34	0.3	11,386	31	0	n.a.	n.a.	n.a.	31
35–44	0.7	10,414	70	0	n.a.	n.a.	n.a.	70
45–54	1.3	8,569	109	0	n.a.	n.a.	n.a.	109
55–64	3.0	6,677	201	0	n.a.	n.a.	n.a.	201
65 and over	-3.2	5,792	-185	-185	n.a.	n.a.	-185	0
Females, 14 and over	n.a.	n.a.	2,897	-1,478	-13	-1,465	n.a.	4,375
14–19	2.1	6,300	132	-26	-13	-13	n.a.	158
20–24	-6.6	5,714	-377	-474	0	-474	n.a.	97
25–34	-2.5	11,892	-299	-785	n.a.	-785	n.a.	486
35–44	9.1	10,738	973	-193	n.a.	-193	n.a.	1,166
45–54	15.7	8,607	1,348	0	n.a.	n.a.	n.a.	1,348
55–64	16.9	6,640	1,119	0	n.a.	n.a.	n.a.	1,119
65 and over	0	6,429	0	0	n.a.	n.a.	n.a.	0

NOTE: n.a. = not applicable.
SOURCE: See text and Appendix G.
[a] Actual population in 1950 less survivors of net immigration, 1940–50.

TABLE 11. PERCENTAGE DISTRIBUTION BY SEX AND AGE OF 1950
DOMESTIC WORKING-AGE POPULATION NOT IN LABOR FORCE [a]

| | Males | | Females | |
	Total (1)	Total Excluding Specified Groups [b] (2)	Total (3)	Total Excluding Specified Groups [b] (4)
14 and over	18.5	9.0	81.5	91.0
14–19	7.2	0.5	9.6	3.3
20–24	0.5	0	5.8	2.0
25–34	0.8	0.6	15.3	10.1
35–44	0.7	1.4	15.2	24.2
45–54	1.0	2.3	13.0	28.0
55–64	1.9	4.2	10.8	23.3
65 and over	6.4	–	11.8	–

SOURCE: See text and Appendix G.
[a] Assumes no participation-rate changes, 1940–50, except those due to compositional factors.
[b] Excluding persons 65 and over, youths 14–29 in school, and females 14–44 with dependent children under 6.

requirement. Columns 1 and 3 of Table 11 shows for 1950 the sex-age composition of the domestic working-age population [2] outside the labor force that would have prevailed in the absence of participation-rate changes other than those due to compositional factors. This is the "pool" from which the gross requirement must be supplied. From this are eliminated persons over 65, persons 29 or under enrolled in school, and females aged 14–44 with dependent children under 6 years old, on the grounds that such persons are less likely than others to enter the labor force, because of poorer job qualifications as viewed by employers or higher opportunity costs in the sense of child-care responsibilities or educational opportunities foregone. The resulting distribution of this reduced pool (Table 11, columns 2 and 4) is used to distribute the gross requirement total for both sexes (Table 10, column 8, top line) among the individual sex-age groups. Since older women make up such a large share of this pool, a correspondingly large share of the gross requirement is assigned to them.

[2] The population of 1950 less survivors of net immigration, 1940–50.

The sex-age distribution of the net requirement total in column 3 is then obtained by horizontal summation of the corresponding distributions in columns 4 and 8, since the net change for any given group reflects the balance between the effect of compositional factors on the group and its share in supplying the gross requirement.

For each sex-age group the net requirement in thousands of persons is converted to the implied change in participation rate by dividing by the population total for that group (Table 10, columns 1 and 2).

Table 12 brings together the totals of columns 3 through 7 obtained by this procedure for the various decades. Column 1 is the observed change in labor force in each decade attributed to participation-rate change. As can be seen, this "net requirement" was positive in all decades but two, 1920–30 and 1930–40. Columns 2 through 5 show the individual and combined effect of the compositional factors. In the periods studied, each operated to produce labor force withdrawal. As a result, the algebraic value of the "gross requirement" in column 6 exceeds that of the net requirement in column 1 and is posi-

TABLE 12. LABOR FORCE GROWTH DUE TO PARTICIPATION-RATE CHANGE, BY SOURCE, 1900–10 TO 1960–70 (thousands)

| | All Factors ("Net Requirement") (1) | Compositional Factors | | | | Market Pressures ("Gross Requirement") (col. 1 − col. 2) (6) |
		All (cols. 3 + 4 + 5) (2)	School Enrollment (3)	Marital-Child Dependency Status (4)	OASDI (5)	
			Census			
1900–10	104	−372	−372			476
1910–20	254	−442	−442			696
1920–30	−684	−1,411	−1,411			727
1930–40	−1,736	−539	−539			−1,197
			CPS			
1940–50	2,731	−2,079	−429	−1,465	−185	4,809
1950–60	2,048	−2,222	−814	−874	−534	4,270
1960–70	843	−2,145	−898	−266	−981	2,988

SOURCE: See text and Appendix G.

tive in all decades except 1930–40. Thus, after allowance for compositional influences, market forces were exerting pressures for entry on those outside the labor force in all decades but one. Before 1930 the magnitude involved was fairly small, but since 1940 it has been quite large.

The negative figure for 1930–40 in column 6 raises a special problem since it implies that in this decade market forces were operating not to pull new workers into the labor force but to push out some of those already in. Since the question thus becomes one of the sex-age incidence of the market pressures for *withdrawal*, a question to which the present model is not applicable, 1930–40 has been excluded from the subsequent analysis.

RESULTS

Past Experience

For each decade except 1930–40, a comparison of the actual age profile of rate changes with that predicted by the present analysis is given in Figure 51. How well does the model anticipate the actual changes?

1. The tendency for the average level of rate changes for females to lie above zero and that of males below is correctly anticipated. According to the model, this difference arises primarily from the overwhelming share of females in the "pool" from which added labor requirements must be supplied. This may be seen for the 1940–50 decade by reference to Table 10. For both sexes the effect of compositional factors is to depress the rates for certain age groups and consequently in the aggregate (column 4). However, the offsetting positive change induced by market pressures redounds very largely to the benefit of females because of their disproportionate share in the number available to satisfy these requirements (Table 10, column 8, and Table 11, column 4). As a result, the negative influence of compositional factors predominates in the male rates, and the positive influence of market pressures in the female rates (Table 10, column 3).[3]

[3] As shown in Table 12, the 1940–50 decade is exceptional in that the negative effect of the change in marital and child-dependency status of females was unusually high. Before 1940 the compositional factors considered here tended to depress the rates for males more than those for females.

FIGURE 51

PREDICTED AND ACTUAL AGE PROFILE OF CHANGE IN LABOR FORCE
PARTICIPATION RATES, BY SEX, DECENNIALLY, 1900–60 [a]

——— Actual
------ Predicted

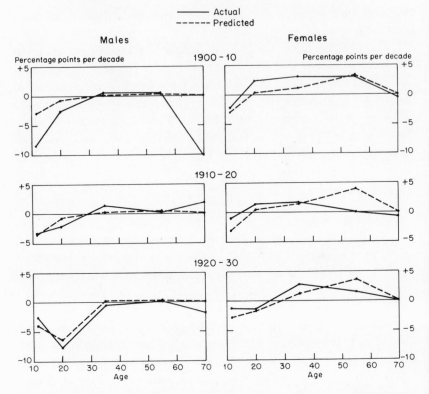

2. For males the shape of the predicted curve in each decade reproduces fairly well that of the actual curve, showing negative changes at the younger and (after 1940) older extremes and little change for the intervening age groups. This reflects basically the impact on these extremes of the compositional factors, respectively, of school enrollment and OASDI (cf. Table 10, columns 4, 5, and 7).[4]

Aside from those aged 65 and over in 1900, there are two noticeable differences between the actual and predicted values. First for the 14–19 group in 1940–50, the shift of the rate change from negative to positive is not anticipated by the model. This reflects chiefly the

[4] Valuable analyses of the impact of OASDI appear in [74, 135].

Males   Females

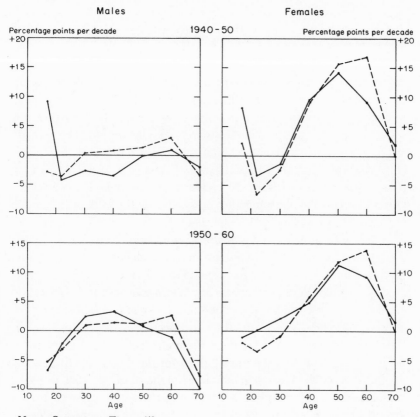

NOTE: See note to Figure 50.
SOURCE: Table G-3.
a Except 1930–40.

assumption underlying the model that those in school do not share in the opportunities for higher labor force participation induced by market pressures. The other discrepancy is the failure of the model to predict the 1950 dip in the rates of those between 25 and 44. As Gertrude Bancroft points out, this was due largely to the temporary impact of unusual educational opportunities for this group in the early post-World War II period created by the G.I. Bill; this influence is excluded from the model since the compositional effect of school enrollment is confined to those under 25 [12, p. 29].

3. For females, the predicted curve also provides a fairly good

approximation to the actual one. Particularly noteworthy is the fact that the model correctly anticipates the change in the shape of the profile between the pre-1940 and post-1940 periods. Further, it predicts the persistence into 1950–60 of the high increases for older females and the disappearance of such increase for the 14–19 group.

According to the model, the change after 1940 in the shape of the age profile is due to the influence of exceptionally high market pressures making for positive participation-rate change, coupled with the removal of younger females to an unusual extent through a rise in child dependency (cf. Table 10, columns 6 and 8, and Table 12, columns 4 and 6). As a result, the incidence of the market pressures falls very largely on the older females who comprise the bulk of the remaining labor reserve (Table 11, column 4).

The most noticeable departure of predicted from actual values is a tendency for the model to overestimate the change at older ages and underestimate it for younger ages. Possible reasons for this come readily to mind. Younger females are better educated than older. Also, employers may consider the oldest group among females over 35 a poorer investment as regards their prospective period of service than those that are younger. Neither of these circumstances is provided for in the model. Nor does the model allow for the possibility that females in school or with dependent children might share at least in part in the opportunities for higher labor force participation induced by market pressures, as has in fact been the case in the two recent decades.

All in all, the model does provide a picture of the structure of rate changes roughly consonant with the actual course of experience, including some of the startling departures in recent decades. Further experimentation—particularly with regard to the assumptions governing the shares of various groups in the opportunities for higher labor force participation induced by market pressures—would probably eliminate some of the remaining discrepancies.

In general, what interpretation does this analysis suggest regarding the principal factors which have governed differential participation-rate changes? On the one hand the spread of education has operated persistently to reduce labor force participation at younger ages. More recently, the growth of OASDI has tended to reduce that of older men. Offsetting, partly or wholly, the tendency of these factors to withdraw persons from the labor force, however, have been the labor requirements arising from market pressures. The principal beneficiaries of such requirements have been females, largely for the reason that they comprise by far the largest share of those not in the labor force. In recent decades, when the withdrawal of young females from the labor force occurred to an unusual extent because of the baby boom, the impact of these requirements fell largely on older females.

How does this compare with Clarence Long's interpretation [116]? First, it rejects the idea that females pushed youths and older men out of the labor force. According to the model the trends for youths and older males can be largely explained by school enrollment and OASDI without reference to females entry into the labor force. On the other hand, it does imply that the withdrawal of youths and older men accentuated the pressure for female entry, and to that extent the former contributed to "pulling" the latter in. But it further indicates that in most decades the general aggregate demand-supply situation exerted pressures for entry on both males and females. This is an influence largely disregarded by Long because of his preoccupation with the supposed stability in the over-all labor force participation rate. Moreover, in the last two decades, when the rise in female labor force participation has been greatest, it is this factor which has been the most important one.

In another study, Jacob Mincer has explained the trend toward rising labor force participation of married women in terms of the price alternatives with which they are confronted [128]. There is no contradiction between his results and the present model. Rather, his results may be viewed as illustrating the market mechanism by which the underlying demand and supply influences considered here induced the necessary changes.

Projected Rate Changes
The implications of the present model as to rate changes for 1960–70 can be compared with the changes projected by BLS [35]. For this purpose, the contribution to labor force growth implied by all participation-rate changes combined is taken at the level officially projected.

In general, the age profiles predicted by the model are fairly close to the projected ones (Figure 52). A continued growth in the rates for older females is predicted, though not as great as in the two preceding decades. Where the changes projected by BLS differ from those predicted by the model, they generally differ in the same direction as actual experience in the past deviated from the model's prediction, suggesting that any shortcomings are more likely to rest with the model. As in Chapter 6 therefore, the present analysis provides general support for the official projection.

The most noticeable discrepancy between projected and predicted changes is for females 20–24, where an upward kink appears in the BLS projections. This kink, which virtually reverses the 1940–50 situation for this group (cf. Figure 51), did not appear in the BLS projections published in 1959 and 1962 [192, 193]. It reflects the sudden rise since 1960 observed in the rate for this group [cf. 53, p. 388]. In Chapter 5, it was shown that within the 20–24 group, this rise has chiefly characterized married women with dependent children, a change excluded, of course, from the predictions of the present model by virtue of its underlying assumptions, and it was suggested that this phenomenon reflects the recent weakening of the labor market for young men. Since the latter situation would be moderated by a return

FIGURE 52

PROJECTED AND PREDICTED AGE PROFILE OF CHANGE IN LABOR FORCE
PARTICIPATION RATES, BY SEX, 1960–70

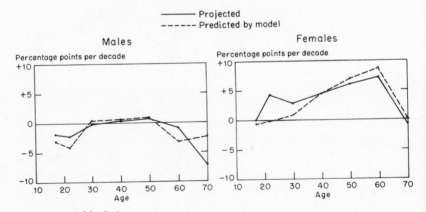

SOURCE: Table G-4.

to a 4 per cent general unemployment rate such as that assumed in the projections, one might consider this in part a transient phenomenon. There are, however, features pointing to the persistence of rate changes for younger women higher than in the 1940–60 period. Comparing the rate changes since 1940 for females aged 20–24, one observes a gradual disappearance of the negative effect caused by the shift to a high fertility pattern and associated rise in child dependency (Figures 51 and 52). Moreover, if the speculations advanced in Chapter 5 regarding prospective fertility are correct, the predictions of my model here do not provide sufficiently for a reversal of this fertility pattern, because they are based, as are the official projections, on the Census B series rather than the more probable (and lower fertility) C series. If the C series had been used, predicted participation rate changes for women aged 20–34 would be higher than those foreseen by my present model.

More generally, compared with the profiles for previous decades, the new BLS projection (though not the earlier ones) can be viewed as presenting a situation intermediate between the pre-1940 picture, when rate changes for younger females exceeded those for older, and the 1940–60 picture, when those for older females soared to levels much above those for younger. Thus, if one focuses not on the kink at age 20–24 itself but views it in terms of the profile as a whole, the new projection implies in some measure a shift back toward (though not a complete return to) the pre-1940 pattern. The likelihood that a shift of this type will occur is supported by the succession of age profiles predicted by my model.[5]

SUMMARY

The most tantalizing development in this century in sex-age specific participation rates has been the sharply accelerated increase in the rates for older women since 1940; the question of its prospective continuation is equally provocative. Also of interest is the generally higher level of rate changes for females than for males, and the tend-

---

[5] This holds true even more when one takes account of the model's persistent tendency to underestimate rate changes for younger women relative to those of older.

ency toward negative rate changes at both younger and older ends of the working-age span for each sex.

The model developed here takes as given (by considerations such as those discussed in Chapter 6) the aggregate growth in total labor force attributable to participation-rate changes. It seeks to predict the contribution to this of individual sex-age groups, first, by taking account of "compositional factors" of the type traditionally analyzed by demographers (specifically, school enrollment status, marital and child-dependency status, and OASDI status), and, second, by assuming that the domestic working-age population outside the labor force may be divided into two groups, one wholly unresponsive to market pressures (youths in school, females with small-child-care responsibilities, and persons aged 65 and over) and the other uniformly positive in its response.

Although this assumption is patently extreme, the model does not do badly in anticipating the striking recent developments involving rates for older females as well as the longer-run differentials by sex and age. Specifically, it implies that the rate declines for youths are due to changes in enrollment status, and those for older men to changes in OASDI status. Partially or entirely offsetting the tendency for these factors to withdraw persons from the labor force have been market pressures for labor force entry on the working-age population; the principal beneficiaries of this have been females, chiefly because they comprise the largest share of those not in the labor force. Since 1940 the impact of these market requirements, which were exceptionally high in this period, fell particularly on older women because of the unusual withdrawal of younger females associated with the decline in age at marriage and accompanying baby boom. As for prospective changes through 1970, the model tends to support the BLS projection, which suggests a shift back in the direction of the pre-1940 pattern, with rate changes for older women still above those of younger, but by a smaller amount.

PART IV / DATA, SOURCES, AND METHODS

A / APPENDIX FOR CHAPTER 2

TABLE A-1. TEN-YEAR MOVING AVERAGE OF NET IMMI-
GRATION AND OF ANNUAL CHANGE IN TOTAL POPULA-
TION AND GROSS CONSTRUCTION (KUZNETS), 1869–1950

	Net Immigration (thousands per year)		Annual Change in	
Midpoint of Period	Net Arrivals (1)	Net Migrants (2)	Total Population (thousands per year) (3)	Gross Construction (millions of 1929 dollars per year) (4)
1874	221.7		969.7	73.5
1875	227.5		999.0	79.4
1876	262.0		1,033.9	148.7
1877	299.3		1,071.3	84.3
1878	317.0		1,091.9	101.8
1879	339.9		1,114.5	146.9
1880	355.0		1,132.0	123.0
1881	370.0		1,162.5	181.6
1882	404.5		1,208.5	201.6
1883	439.4		1,255.0	182.7
1884	457.7		1,285.8	168.1
1885	448.1		1,292.1	335.8
1886	426.2		1,290.5	232.9
1887	399.0		1,285.5	390.3
1888	379.2		1,285.9	249.7
1889	345.5		1,276.6	209.1
1890	326.6		1,278.6	251.5
1891	322.1		1,284.2	109.4
1892	291.0		1,269.3	161.6
1893	259.3		1,253.0	138.1
1894	247.9		1,255.6	113.1
1895	253.6		1,271.6	11.1
1896	239.8		1,278.0	120.8
1897	230.4		1,286.1	39.4
1898	245.5		1,292.2	129.4
1899	284.8		1,324.4	132.5
1900	341.5		1,373.0	137.0
1901	390.7		1,419.7	287.1
1902	456.9		1,467.3	255.6
1903	465.8		1,527.2	237.8
1904	500.1		1,583.9	360.5
1905	543.4		1,637.0	267.2
1906	565.8		1,633.7	143.7
1907	567.4		1,622.3	131.6
1908	595.7		1.664.4	224.7

(continued)

TABLE A-1 (*concluded*)

	Net Immigration (thousands per year)		Annual Change in	
			Total Population (thousands per year)	Gross Construction (millions of 1929 dollars per year)
Midpoint of Period	Net Arrivals (1)	Net Migrants (2)	(3)	(4)
1909	619.6		1,699.9	7.6
1910	558.4		1,677.3	−60.5
1911	501.3		1,656.9	−83.2
1912	446.3	516.8	1,637.4	−195.9
1913		479.6	1,579.5	−182.0
1914		428.7	1,452.0	−217.1
1915		358.9	1,408.8	−282.0
1916		356.3	1,470.1	−133.7
1917		316.9	1,475.1	48.8
1918		272.1	1,474.9	77.4
1919		243.6	1,502.0	405.1
1920		251.4	1,530.7	570.3
1921		257.2	1,545.7	599.0
1922		260.5	1,572.4	660.9
1923		281.8	1,605.3	659.2
1924		301.2	1,681.1	489.3
1925		306.1	1,663.1	393.8
1926		253.9	1,552.3	111.6
1927		236.1	1,481.3	−392.3
1928		186.2	1,366.2	−598.0
1929		122.2	1,229.8	−653.8
1930		101.7	1,145.9	−704.0
1931		79.0	1,069.9	−547.8
1932		55.1	983.6	−515.9
1933		36.5	937.8	−488.3
1934		21.0	916.8	−251.0
1935		6.8	893.9	−28.7
1936		6.8	925.0	418.5
1937		15.7	990.2	727.0
1938		23.3	1,103.5	325.3
1939		26.6	1,189.2	43.9
1940		30.1	1,254.1	3.0
1941		39.2	1,319.3	208.6
1942		49.3	1,515.2	330.1
1943		60.0	1,665.0	522.3
1944		70.7	1,814.6	459.2
1945		87.9	1,956.1	670.6

TABLE A-2. AVERAGE GROWTH RATE OF POPULA-
TION BY COMPONENT OF CHANGE, QUINQUEN-
NIALLY, 1870–1964
(per thousand per year)

Period	Total Increase (1)	Net Migration (2)	Birth Rate (3)	Death Rate (4)
1870–75	25.5	6.7	40.8	21.8
1875–80	18.3	3.4	38.8	23.8
1880–85	25.4	10.1	36.9	21.0
1885–90	19.9	5.8	35.3	20.6
1890–95	20.1	4.5	34.3	19.5
1895–1900	16.3	2.8	31.6	18.8
1900–05	18.5	6.0	30.0	17.6
1905–10	19.8	6.9	29.6	16.6
1910–15	17.5	5.3	27.5	14.7
1915–20	10.5	1.1	26.1	16.2
1920–25	16.9	3.6	25.0	11.3
1925–30	12.5	2.0	21.5	10.6
1930–35	7.0	−0.4	18.3	11.0
1935–40	7.2	0.2	18.3	11.3
1940–45	10.6	0.5	21.2	10.9
1945–50	15.6	1.3	24.5	9.9
1950–55	16.9	1.2	25.2	9.6
....				
1950–55	17.2	1.8	24.8	9.5
1955–60	17.0	1.8	24.6	9.4
1960–64	15.3	2.0	22.7	9.4

TABLE A-3. AVERAGE GROWTH RATE OF LABOR FORCE BY COMPONENT OF CHANGE, 1870–1965
(per cent per decade)

	Labor Force Growth Due to			
Period	All Sources (1)	Net Migration (2)	Aging and Mortality (3)	Change in Participation Rates (4)
1870–80	29.3	6.2	16.0	7.1
1880–90	29.2	9.9	15.9	3.4
1890–1900	21.9/21.7	5.8/6.0	13.2/14.2	2.9/1.5
1900–10	22.8	9.5	13.1	0.2
1910–20	14.2	3.7	9.6	0.9
1920–30	15.5/15.9	2.8/2.8	14.2/14.2	−1.5/−1.1
1930–40	8.3	−0.2	11.9	−3.4
1940–50	13.3/14.2	1.0/1.9	9.0/7.8	3.3/4.5
....				
1950–55	12.4	2.2	5.5	4.8
1955–60	11.1	2.3	7.5	1.3
1960–65	13.9	2.4	11.5	0

TABLE A-4. AVERAGE GROWTH RATE OF POPULATION BY RESI-
DENCE, DECENNIALLY, 1870–1950
(per cent per decade, initial year as base)

Period	Total (1)	Non-farm (2)	Farm (3)	Urban (4)	Rural (5)	Standard Metropolitan Areas (6)	Nonstandard Metropolitan Areas (7)
1870–80	30.1	–	–	42.7	25.7	–	–
1880–90	25.5	35.5	12.7	56.5	13.4	–	–
1890–1900	20.7	20.8	20.6	36.4	12.2	–	–
1900–10	21.0	29.9	7.4	39.3	9.0	32.0	13.7
1910–20	14.9	23.7	−1.4	29.0	3.2	25.3	6.9
1920–30	16.1	24.6	−3.7	27.3	4.4	27.2	6.2
1930–40	7.2	9.5	0.3	7.9	6.4	8.5	5.9
1940–50	14.5	26.0	−23.6	19.5	7.9	21.8	6.3

TABLE A-5. AVERAGE GROWTH RATE OF LABOR FORCE BY AGRI-
CULTURAL–NONAGRICULTURAL SECTOR AND URBAN–RURAL RES-
IDENCE, DECENNIALLY, 1870–1950
(per cent per decade, initial year as base)

Period	Total (1)	Nonagriculture (2)	Agriculture (3)	Urban (4)	Rural (5)
1870–80	34.8	35.3	34.0	–	–
1880–90	36.3	56.4	16.0	–	–
1890–1900	22.7	33.6	7.1	37.6	15.1
1900–10	26.9	39.0	5.1	47.7	8.1
1910–20	12.3	19.4	−1.9	27.0	2.3
1920–30	17.1	25.7	−5.7	24.2	7.9
1930–40	9.5	15.3	−11.5	9.4	5.8
1940–50	12.7	19.7	−22.0	24.8	−4.0

TABLE A-6. AVERAGE GROWTH RATE OF URBAN POPULATION BY GEOGRAPHIC DIVISION, DECENNIALLY, 1870–1950

(per cent per decade, initial year as base)

Division	1870–80 (1)	1880–90 (2)	1890–1900 (3)	1900–10 (4)	1910–20 (5)	1920–30 (6)	1930–40 (7)	1940–50 (8)
United States	42.7	56.5	36.4	39.3	29.0	27.3	7.9	19.5
New England	35.7	37.6	32.5	25.3	17.0	12.3	1.7	7.8
Middle Atlantic	35.1	40.0	36.7	36.5	22.0	21.5	3.7	7.1
East North Central	56.2	66.0	41.2	33.2	35.7	28.7	3.9	14.6
West North Central	53.1	106.2	27.7	31.3	22.2	17.6	7.9	17.1
South Atlantic	34.3	53.0	29.2	38.5	40.2	31.4	21.5	30.0
East South Atlantic	21.5	74.3	38.4	39.2	26.7	39.3	13.9	28.9
West South Central	55.2	71.2	47.7	85.0	51.8	49.1	17.5	48.0
Mountain	262.0	152.6	52.2	74.5	28.9	19.7	21.5	39.8
Pacific	86.2	99.5	39.3	112.3	45.3	60.0	14.8	43.3

TABLE A-7. AVERAGE GROWTH RATE OF NONAGRICULTURAL LABOR FORCE BY GEOGRAPHIC DIVISION, DECENNIALLY, 1870–1950

(per cent per decade, initial year as base)

Division	1870–80 (1)	1880–90 (2)	1890–1900 (3)	1900–10 (4)	1910–20 (5)	1920–30 (6)	1930–40 (7)	1940–50 (8)
United States	45.0	53.4	31.7	44.9	20.1	23.9	12.6	23.2
New England	29.2	35.9	22.9	27.6	14.3	6.9	5.5	11.1
Middle Atlantic	43.0	42.4	30.6	39.2	16.1	20.6	6.6	10.7
East North Central	46.8	59.0	36.9	40.2	27.4	25.1	8.1	22.0
West North Central	74.8	86.5	27.9	42.1	11.0	14.9	8.7	15.9
South Atlantic	38.0	50.6	33.4	44.0	24.2	26.8	29.8	32.5
East South Atlantic	28.1	61.2	35.8	44.0	13.2	27.8	23.3	25.4
West South Central	55.0	70.9	52.5	94.6	35.2	39.0	22.0	34.0
Mountain	145.2	70.9	27.0	69.1	11.1	15.0	18.0	38.6
Pacific	64.0	78.4	26.8	105.2	27.7	54.9	18.2	53.6

TABLE A-8. AVERAGE GROWTH RATE OF LABOR FORCE BY INDUSTRY, DECENNIALLY, 1870–1950 (per cent per decade, initial year as base)

Sector	1870–80 (1)	1880–90 (2)	1890–1900 (3)	1900–10 (4)	1910–20 (5)	1920–30 (6)	1930–40 (7)	1940–50 (8)
Total	34.8	36.3	22.7	26.9	12.3	17.1	9.5	12.7
Agriculture	34.0	16.0	7.1	5.1	-1.9	-5.7	-11.5	-22.0
Forestry and fishing	59.3	88.2	18.0	17.0	16.0	-5.3	13.0	-7.3
Mining	58.5	51.0	60.0	39.0	16.8	-6.5	-4.6	-12.8
Manufacturing and independent hand trades	41.1	49.8	33.6	29.8	32.2	1.0	10.9	29.7
Construction	10.4	74.1	15.1	38.1	-5.7	39.8	2.9	20.1
Transportation and public utilities	32.1	80.9	37.9	49.0	32.0	14.9	-15.3	32.8
Trade	47.1	58.0	35.0	36.9	20.6	48.2	16.0	34.0
Finance, insurance, and real estate	46.2	158.0	85.5	71.0	53.9	78.5	5.5	26.0
Professional service and amusements	52.8	70.0	39.0	49.6	39.2	54.5	29.4	26.2
Domestic service	15.0	40.8	14.8	23.7	-21.0	37.1	2.2	-33.7
Personal service	44.0	78.0	51.7	56.9	7.1	52.7	24.0	20.2
Government service	58.0	50.6	34.1	62.1	43.9	29.5	22.4	73.0
Nonagriculture	35.3	56.4	33.6	39.0	19.4	25.7	15.3	19.7

TABLE A-9. AVERAGE LEVEL OF NET IMMIGRATION RATE AND UNEMPLOYMENT RATE, NBER REFERENCE CYCLES, 1890–1907 AND 1908–15

Reference Cycle (fiscal years)	Net Immigration Rate (per thousand total population per year)	Reference Cycle (calendar years)	Unemployment Rate, Manufacturing and Transportation, Douglas (per cent)
1908–11	6.72	1890–92	5.00
1910–13	6.87	1891–94	8.15
1911–15	6.84	1892–95	11.37
		1894–96	13.95
		1895–99	13.38
		1896–1900	11.72
		1899–1903	4.98
		1900–04	4.55
		1903–07	4.52

TABLE A-10. AVERAGE RATE OF CHANGE OF BURNS' CONSTANT-PRICE-BUILDING-PERMITS AND STANDARD-TREND CYCLE,[a] KUZNETS' GROSS CONSTRUCTION IN 1929 PRICES, AND MALE POPULATION OF WORKING AGE, DECADES ENDING IN 0 AND 5, 1870–1950 (per cent per year)

Decades Ending in 0 and 5	Gross Construction (1)	Building Permits (2)	Standard Trend Cycle (3)	Male Population of Working Age (4)
1870–80	4.7		−0.4	2.5
1875–85	5.0	5.9	1.4	2.6
1880–90	8.9	3.3	−0.6	2.7
1885–95	5.8	−2.3	−1.6	2.3
1890–1900	0.2	−5.5	−1.1	2.1
1895–1905	2.2	−1.1	2.4	2.1
1900–10	3.9	0.9	0.2	2.4
1905–15	−0.9	−5.2	−0.1	2.1
1910–20	−4.1	−10.3	0.6	1.3
1915–25	6.2	10.9	−1.6	1.3
1920–30	5.3	3.4	0.3	1.7
1925–35	−8.2			1.4
1930–40	−0.3			1.2
1935–45	0.1			1.2
1940–50	5.4			1.0
1945–55	11.9			0.9

[a] Both of Burns' series are trend adjusted.

TABLE A-11. AVERAGE TREND-ADJUSTED RATE OF CHANGE OF SELECTED BASIC COMMODITY SERIES, DECADES ENDING IN 0 AND 5, 1870–1930

(per cent per year)

Series [a]	1870–80 (1)	1875–85 (2)	1880–90 (3)	1885–95 (4)	1890–1900 (5)	1895–1905 (6)	1900–10 (7)	1905–15 (8)	1910–20 (9)	1915–25 (10)	1920–30 (11)
Standard-trend cycle	-0.4	1.4	-0.6	-1.6	-1.1	2.4	0.2	-0.1	0.6	-1.6	0.3
25 Bituminous coal	-4.2	3.8	-1.4	-1.2	-0.1	4.3	1.6	0.3	0.2	-1.9	-1.2
68 Tin-plate consumption	0.5	3.9	0.5	-4.7	-2.5	0.6	0.0	0.7	0.8	-0.4	0.7
71 Cottonseed oil	-0.1	2.0	0.5	-1.2	0.0	-0.1	-3.2	1.6	-1.5	-3.6	5.7
56 Pig iron	-3.2	1.5	1.6	-1.5	-0.9	4.1	0.8	0.2	0.5	-2.9	-0.1
72 Nails	-1.2	2.5	0.7	-2.0	-2.0	1.9	1.3	0.9	-0.5	-0.6	-1.1
36 Cement, total	—	—	0.6	-4.8	-2.5	7.2	5.6	-1.1	-6.5	0.3	1.2
83 Tobacco consumption	—	—	0.6	-0.5	-1.6	1.6	0.8	-0.6	-0.6	-0.7	0.7
92 Building permits	—	5.9	3.3	-2.3	-5.5	-1.1	0.9	-5.2	-10.3	10.9	3.4
38 Gypsum	—	—	-3.0	-2.0	-4.5	11.2	6.1	-2.8	-6.1	2.0	-0.9
93 Coastal trade	-1.7	-0.4	0.7	1.3	-0.2	2.0	1.7	-1.2	-3.7	1.2	0.5
21 Cod and mackerel	-0.2	1.7	0.3	-0.5	-1.1	0.2	1.1	-4.0	-1.6	2.4	1.9
50 Fermented liquors	-2.4	1.5	0.9	0.6	-1.8	0.8	1.9	-0.2	-1.2	—	—
69 Tobacco and snuff	-1.6	1.2	1.2	-0.3	-1.5	1.3	1.5	0.4	-0.2	-1.8	-0.4

[a] Numbers at left are those designating series in source.

TABLE A-12. AVERAGE RATE OF CHANGE OF TOTAL MANUFACTURING CAPITAL IN 1929 PRICES,[a] BY SELECTED MAJOR MANUFACTURING INDUSTRIES, 1880–1961
(per cent per year)

Period	All Manu-facturing (1)	Metal and Its Products (2)	Iron and Steel Products (3)	Machinery, Excluding Transportation (4)	Forest Products (5)	Stone, Clay, and Glass Products (6)	Printing and Publishing (7)
1880–90	8.8	10.4	9.2	10.9	8.7	10.1	12.5
1890–1900	5.3	5.1	3.3	5.2	3.9	6.1	5.6
1900–04	6.5	9.4	13.8	7.9	3.7	10.9	3.5
1904–09	6.3	7.6	8.3	6.2	6.2	9.1	6.2
1909–14	3.1	4.0	3.7	3.3	-0.6	2.0	2.7
1914–19	4.7	7.1	5.5	5.4	-1.9	-2.9	1.5
1919–29	3.2	1.2	-0.1	1.0	2.6	4.5	5.8
1929–37	-1.6	-0.4	0.1	-1.9	-5.7	-3.2	-1.1
1937–48	3.2	4.1	3.3	6.3	1.3	0.7	0.2
1948–53	4.9	n.a.	n.a.	5.8	2.0	4.2	0.3
·········							
1948–53	4.6	6.1	3.5	5.9	2.1	4.3	0.4
1953–57	3.1	2.4	2.2	1.1	2.8	6.4	1.9
·········							
1953–57	3.7	4.1	2.9	2.1	3.1	7.8	2.9
1957–61	0.6	-0.2	n.a.	-0.2	-1.6	4.6	4.2

[a] Except last two lines of table, which relate to *fixed* capital in *1954* prices.
n.a. = not available.

SOURCES AND METHODS

Table A-1

Net arrivals: [107, Table B-1, pp. 95–96] arrivals less departures. Net migrants: [ibid., p. 96, immigrants less emigrants]. Total population: unpublished annual estimates underlying [102, p. 624, Table R-37, col. 9]. Gross construction: [1, p. 142, series 2 (unpublished data for 1869–88 were used)].

Table A-2

The break in series in 1950–55 is due to the shift in sources described below.

1870–1955. Except as noted subsequently, the basic source was [103, p. 37, Table 1, col. 4; p. 39, Table 3, col. 5; p. 41, Table 5, col. 7; and p. 43, Table 6, col. 5 (underlying unrounded quinquennial estimates were used)]. However, for net migration, 1910–40 data were from [107, pp. 95–96, Table B-1]. For 1940–55, estimates for all series were revised somewhat, the chief differences from the original source being inclusion of armed forces deaths overseas and keeping the scope of the net migration estimate the same as for the pre-1940 period.

The sum of the components does not exactly equal total increase, because net migration refers to alien arrivals less departures and thus includes some nonmigratory movements. Pure migration estimates are not available prior to 1910.

1950–64. [183, No. 302, p. 8]. Estimates for fiscal year were divided by January 1 population to obtain annual rates, which were then averaged for periods shown.

Table A-3

Computations of the components of labor force change were done for the most detailed classifications available (identified below for each period) with higher levels of aggregation being obtained by summation. The break in series in 1890–1900 is chiefly due to the replacement of a regional by an age classification in the calculations; in 1940–50, by a shift from census to Current Population Survey data.

The derivation of component contributions to total change involves familiar issues, variously characterized as "index number" or "standardization" problems. The method adopted here is not claimed to be definitive, but alternative procedures would not significantly alter the results. The "aging and mortality" component was obtained by multiplying the numerical change of a population group due to sources other than current migration by its beginning-of-decade participation rate; the result is the change in labor force that would have occurred in the absence of migration or participation rate change. The contribution of participation-rate change for each age-sex group was obtained by multiplying the end-of-decade population attributable to sources other than current migration by the excess of the end-of-decade over beginning-of-decade participation rates. The migration contribution was obtained as the product of the end-of-decade participation rate and population change due to net immigration during the decade. Thus computed, the three components sum exactly to the actual labor force growth.

1870–1900. The series cover all population classes except nonwhites other than Negroes. For 1870–90, the calculations were done separately for native born and foreign born in each of the four census regions (no separation by sex was possible); for 1890–1900, for native white, Negroes, and foreign-born white, by sex, in each of the four regions. An overlap comparison for 1890–1900 of the pre-1890 and post-1890 methods yielded similar results with regard to total U.S. change and the two sets of calculations were therefore treated as continuous. The sources of the basic data necessary for the calculations were as follows.

Labor force: 1870, 1880, census reports; 1890, 1900, tabulations of census data prepared by Ann R. Miller, University of Pennsylvania Population Studies Center. For the present study, the 1870 data were adjusted for underenumeration in the South as estimated by Alba M. Edwards [173, p. 141]; the 1890 data, for underenumeration of children aged 10–15 as described in [172, pp. lxvi–lxxi, cviii, clv].

Population: All dates from census reports. Data for 1870 were adjusted for underenumeration in South as estimated by Edwards [173].

Migration: [111, Table P-1].

1890–1950. All classes of the population are covered. The calculations were done separately for each sex-age class of native whites, nonwhites, and foreign-born whites. Through 1930 the population aged 10 and over is included, thereafter, that 14 and over. An overlap for 1920–30 indicates the negligible effect of eliminating those aged 10–13. Other age classes used were 14–19, 20–24, 25–44, 45–64, 65 and over.

Labor force: 1890–1940, from unpublished unrounded data underlying [116, Appendix A]; 1950, the estimate was built up from the census reports, and the total differs slightly from that shown by both Long and the census because it was obtained by summing components which included estimates. The latter were necessitated by lack of complete count data or sufficient component detail in the census.

Population: 1890–1940, tabulations of census data by Everett S. Lee, University of Pennsylvania Population Studies Center. 1950, data taken directly or estimated from census report.

Migration: [111, Table P-1]. Migration for those aged 14–19 was assumed same as that for those aged 15–19. Age groups 15–19 and 20–24 were from unpublished underlying data.

1940–65. Covers total population including armed forces overseas. The calculations were done separately for each sex-age class, but no color-nativity or geographic components were distinguished. The age classes were 14–19, 20–24, ten-year groups through 55–64, and 65 and over, except that for the period after 1960, the 14–19 were subdivided into 14–15, 16–17, and 18–19.

Labor force: 1940, [181, No. 2 (no date), p. 11]. Unpublished age detail comparable to 1950 was kindly provided by Gertrude Bancroft, Bureau of Labor Statistics. To these figures were added 150,000 members of the armed forces who were outside the continental United States in 1940. See [ibid., p. 1] and [191, Vol. 6, No. 1 (July 1959), p. 1, n. 1]. The age-sex distribution for this group is from [183, No. 98 (August 13, 1954), pp. 7 and 15]. 1950, [181, No. 85 (June 1958), p. 5]. Published estimates were adjusted upward in same way as for 1940. For explanation, see references cited for 1940. 1955, [192, p. 53]. 1960 (excluding Alaska and Hawaii), [191, Vol. 7, No. 7 (January 1961), p. XII, Table 2]. 1960 (including Alaska and Hawaii), [143, p. 4]. 1965, [191, Vol. 12, No. 7, January 1966, p. 74, Table A-10, col. 1].

Population: 1940, [183, No. 98 (August 13, 1954), p. 15]; 1950, [ibid., No. 146 (November 12, 1956), p. 10]. 1955, [192, p. 52]; 1960 (excluding Alaska and Hawaii), unpublished estimates prepared with reference to 1950 census. These data, provided by Bureau of Labor Statistics, are consistent in latter regard with the 1960 labor force estimates excluding Alaska and Hawaii. Alaska and Hawaii were eliminated by deducting 1960 census data for these states. 1960 (including Alaska and Hawaii), [193, p. 4]; 1965, [183, No. 321, p. 11].

Migration: 1940–50, migration total from [183, No. 223 (January 26, 1961), p. 4]. Age-sex distribution was assumed to be in same proportions as in [*ibid.*, No. 98 (August 13, 1954), p. 18]. A small deduction was made to allow for mortality among migrants between year of immigation and end of decade, based on survival rates employed in [*ibid.*, No. 187 (November 10, 1958) p. 13]. 1950–60, total and age-sex distribution of migrants (excluding Alaska and Hawaii) surviving to end of decade from unpublished estimates made by Gladys Bowles, kindly provided by Bureau of Census. For all age groups, the decade total was distributed between quinquennia according to the proportions shown for total migration in [*ibid.*, No. 302 (March 11, 1965), p. 8]. 1960–65, migration total from *ibid.*, assuming the 1964–65 value was the same as that for 1963–64. Age-sex distribution was assumed same as that of migrants used in 1964 population projections [183, No. 286 (July 1964), p. 27].

Table A-4

Total population: [186, series A-20]. *Farm population:* [184, p. 31], except 1940, from [175, p. 45]. *Nonfarm population:* by subtraction. *Urban and rural population:* [176, p. 1–5, Table 4]. *SMA and non-SMA population:* [203, p. 13, Table 1, class VI (125 principal SMA's)].

Table A-5

Total, agricultural and nonagricultural labor force: see sources for Table A-8. *Urban and rural labor force:* [116, Appendix A, Table A-3].

Table A-6

[176, pp. 1–17 and 1–18, Table 15].

Table A-7

[111, pp. 609 ff., except 1940, p. 389].

Table A-8

[13, p. 5], except 1930, where [31, p. 47] was used, with data for those aged 10 and over taken as comparable with 1920 and for those aged 14 and over, comparable with 1940. For 1940 and earlier, forestry and fishing was separated from agriculture as in *ibid.*, and domestic service from personal service, following [*ibid.*, p. 42]. For 1950, similar subdivisions were provided by [176, Table 130]. Nonagriculture was obtained by subtracting agriculture from total labor force, and thus includes industry not specified. As explained in [1, pp. 232–235], the 1940 estimate for labor force in construction shown in [13] and [31], is greatly overstated. In the present table the 1930–40 and 1940–50 changes computed from the latter have been replaced by Abramovitz's estimate [1, p. 125].

Table A-9

Net immigration: [107, Table B-1, p. 96], immigrants less emigrants. *Unemployment:* [50, p. 445].

Table A-10

Gross construction: [1, pp. 142 ff., series 2], except 1870 and 1880, unpublished estimates. *Building permits:* [27, p. 316, series 92]. *Standard-trend cycle:* [*ibid.*, p. 324]. *Male population of working age (15–64):* census dates, from census reports; mid-census dates: for native white and nonwhite, from an unpublished memorandum prepared by Everett S. Lee of the University of Pennsylvania Study of Population Redistribution and Economic Growth providing age detail underlying the quinquennial series published by Kuznets [103, p. 37]; for foreign born white, estimated by applying to mid-decade total for all ages as estimated in [107, p. 102, Table B-6] the estimated share of those 15–64, obtained by averaging the shares at the preceding and subsequent census dates.

Table A-11

Standard-trend cycle: [27, p. 324, Table 52]. All other series: [*ibid.*, p. 313–316, Table 47].

Table A-12

Total capital in 1929 prices: 1880–1953, [38, p. 25], overlapped, 1948–57, by [36, pp. 79–83, Table G-1, G-2]. *Fixed capital in 1954 prices:* 1953–61, [37, pp. 44–47, Table A-2].

B / APPENDIX FOR CHAPTER 3

TABLE B-1. UNPROCESSED ANNUAL DATA ON OUTPUT, INCORPORATIONS, RESIDENTIAL CONSTRUCTION, IMMIGRATION, AND NET CAPITAL IMPORTS, 1820–1964

Year	Industrial and Commercial Production (1899 = 100) Series 1	Gross National Product (bill. 1954 $) Series 2	Incorporations		Nonfarm Residential Construction		Rate of Alien Immigration (per 1,000 total population)		Net Capital Imports (mill. current $) Series 9
			Evans (1925 = 100) Series 3	Dun and Bradstreet (units) Series 4	Production of Housekeeping Dwelling Units (thous.) Series 5	Number of Dwelling Units Started (thous.) Series 6	Gross Series 7	Net Series 8	
1820							0.87		−1
1821							0.92		−5
1822							0.67		8
1823							0.60		−2
1824							0.72		−1
1825							0.91		−7
1826							0.94		3
1827							1.58		−10
1828							2.24		11
1829							1.79		−2
1830							1.81		−8
1831							1.70		14
1832							3.52		7
1833							4.14		14
1834							4.48		19
1835							3.02		30
1836							4.94		59

APPENDIX B / 205

Year					
1837	22	5.01			
1838	3	2.39			
1839	49	4.08			
1840	−31	4.91			
1841	8	4.53			
1842	−6	5.70			
1843	−22	3.68			
1844	−4	4.02			
1845	−4	5.67			
1846	−1	7.43			
1847	−19	10.98			
1848	2	10.29			
1849	−3	13.12			
1850	29	12.72	138		
1851	6	15.75	135		
1852	16	14.92	142		
1853	56	14.32	−103		
1854	42	16.11	98		
1855	15	7.34			
1856	12	7.10			
1857	17	8.65			
1858	−23	4.12			
1859	26	3.95			
1860	−7	4.88	90	1.06	13
1861	103	2.84	72	0.67	13
1862	−1	2.77	70	0.88	13
1863	13	5.18	76	1.66	15
1864	111	5.55	57	4.15	17

(continued)

TABLE B-1 (continued)

| Year | Industrial and Commercial Production (1899=100) Series 1 | Gross National Product (bill. 1954 $) Series 2 | Incorporations | | Nonfarm Residential Construction | | Rate of Alien Immigration (per 1,000 total population) | | Net Capital Imports (mill. current $) Series 9 |
			Evans (1925=100) Series 3	Dun and Bradstreet (units) Series 4	Production of Housekeeping Dwelling Units (thous.) Series 5	Number of Dwelling Units Started (thous.) Series 6	Gross Series 7	Net Series 8	
1865	17		7.00		86		6.95		59
1866	19		0.26		131		8.72		95
1867	19		5.22		153		8.45		145
1868	20		5.52		171		7.27		73
1869	22		5.54		162		8.83		176
1870	23		5.30		148		9.48		100
1871	25		6.03		175		7.66		101
1872	28		6.37		158		9.39		242
1873	29		6.13		162		10.38		167
1874	28		5.75		140		6.90		82
1875	28		6.73		139		4.90		87
1876	28		5.31		109		3.60		2
1877	29		4.91		107		2.96		-57
1878	30		4.76		84		2.84		-162
1879	34		5.36		97		3.58		-160

Year								
1881	43		13.9	189		12.81		−41
1882	46		13.9	205		14.66		110
1883	48		14.4	244		10.92		51
1884	47		12.6	252		9.17		105
1885	46		12.5	273		6.85		34
1886	54		15.0	294		5.68		137
1887	60		19.4	335		8.16		231
1888	61		18.8	309		8.92		287
1889	65		22.9	354		7.11		202
1890	71		25.9	278		7.14		194
1891	74		27.1	252		8.60		136
1892	78		29.5	323		8.69		41
1893	74		24.9	226		6.46		146
1894	71		24.4	225		4.12		−66
1895	81		26.5	262		3.67		137
1896	77		23.8	218		4.79		40
1897	83		26.3	247		3.17		−23
1898	92		25.8	222		3.10		−279
1899	100		36.9	239		4.15		−229
1900	103		37.8	230	189	5.89		−296/−218
1901	114		50.2	330	275	6.29		−245
1902	126		53.1	320	240	8.19		−135
1903	131		56.0	347	253	10.63		−21
1904	129		55.5	403	315	9.89		−50
1905	148		63.6		507	12.24		−83
1906	162		70.6		487	12.88		68
1907	168	104.1	68.6		432	14.77		71
1908	144		57.9		416	8.82	4.37	−46
1909	177		71.5		492	8.31	5.81	59

(continued)

TABLE B-1 (concluded)

Year	Industrial and Commercial Production (1899 = 100) Series 1	Gross National Product (bill. 1954 $) Series 2	Incorporations Evans (1925 = 100) Series 3	Incorporations Dun and Bradstreet (units) Series 4	Nonfarm Residential Construction Production of Housekeeping Dwelling Units (thous.) Series 5	Nonfarm Residential Construction Number of Dwelling Units Started (thous.) Series 6	Rate of Alien Immigration (per 1,000 total population) Gross Series 7	Rate of Alien Immigration (per 1,000 total population) Net Series 8	Net Capital Imports (mill. current $) Series 9
1910	186	106.8	65.7			387	11.27	9.08	255
1911	180	109.5	67.2			395	9.36	6.21	48
1912	206	116.1	70.7			426	8.78	5.29	23
1913	215	117.0	70.9			421	12.31	9.15	87
1914	206	112.1	62.6			421		9.22	−72
1915		111.4	67.7			433		1.22	−1,129
1916		120.0	77.5			437		1.66	−2,355
1917		120.5	77.1			240		2.21	−3,886
1918		132.9	53.1			118		0.15	−4,002
1919		132.6	100.5			315		0.16	−2,712
1920		125.6	112.8			217		1.33	−1,007
1921		114.9	91.2			449		5.13	−562
1922		133.2	100.1			716		1.01	−784
1923		149.2	99.3			871		3.94	13
1924		149.0	89.9			893		5.52	−553
1925		161.8	100.0			937		1.73	−649
1926		170.8	100.3			849		1.93	−277
1927		170.5	102.8			810		2.20	−406

Year						
1932	130.1	95.1		134	−0.54	−195
1933	126.6	88.5		93	−0.45	−342
1934	138.5	73.7		126	−0.08	425
1935	152.9	74.5		216	−0.03	1,512
1936	173.3	75.4		304	0	1,208
1937	183.5	70.7		332	0.18	877
1938	175.1	62.6		394	0.33	441
1939	189.3	63.0		458	0.43	1,498
1940	205.8	61.8		530	0.37	1,457
1941	238.1	53.3		620	0.26	−1,031
1942	266.9	33.9		301	0.16	−92
1943	296.7	33.6		184	0.14	1,078
1944	317.9	40.8		139	0.17	377
1945	314.0	68.1	132,916	208	0.22	516
1946	282.5	138.6	112,638	662	0.64	−4,417
1947	282.3	101.1	96,101	846	0.86	−7,691
1948	293.1	86.5	85,491	914	1.02	−1,578
1949	292.7			989	1.09	−1,133
1950	318.1		92,925	1,352	1.46	491
1951	341.8		83,649	1,020	1.17	−646
1952	353.5		92,819	1,069	1.55	34
1953	369.0		102,545	1,068	0.92	560
1954	363.1		117,164	1,202	1.09	−64
1955	392.7		139,651	1,310	1.25	−67
1956	400.9		140,775	1,094	1.78	−1,815
1957	408.6		136,705	993	1.77	−3,442/−3,770
1958	401.3		150,781	1,142	1.45	−2,631
1959	428.6		193,067	1,343	1.47	1,147
1960	440.2		182,713	1,105	1.48	−2,429
1961	447.9		181,535	1,154	1.48	−2,528
1962	474.8		182,057	1,293	—	−1,926
1963	492.6		186,404	1,421		—
1964			166,167	1,363		

TABLE B-2. AVERAGE ANNUAL RATE OF CHANGE IN AGGREGATE PRODUCTION, AGGREGATE CONSTRUCTION, WAGE RATE, AND HOURS; AND AVERAGE LEVEL OF IMMIGRATION RATE, NONFARM HOUSEHOLD GROWTH RATE, AND UNEMPLOYMENT RATE, NBER REFERENCE CYCLES, 1830–1964 [a]

| Reference Cycle Dates (calendar year) | Rate of Change of Aggregate Production | | | | Rate of Change of Aggregate Construction | | |
| | Nonperishable Commodity Output (1860 $) Series 1 | Industrial and Commercial Production (1899 wts.) Series 2 | Gross National Product | | Gross New Construction (1860 $) Series 5 | Physical Volume of Construction Series 6 | Gross New Construction (1929 $) Series 7 |
			Kendrick (1929 $) Series 3	Commerce (1954 $) Series 4			
1829–34	—						
1832–36	8.83						
1834–38	4.17				14.17		
1836–39	–2.21				12.59		
1838–43					–5.45		
1839–45	7.69				3.62		
1843–46	16.53				19.26		
1845–47	15.74				10.02		
1846–48	10.06				1.00		
1847–53	10.16				10.72		
1848–55	8.92				10.15		
1853–56	2.14				4.75		
1855–58	–0.57				–2.83		
1856–60						0.86	
1858–61						–6.02	
1860–64		6.67				–3.35	
1861–67		6.25				15.45	
1864–69		5.13				17.55	
1867–70		6.35				9.07	
1869–73	5.29	6.86			2.79	–0.68	
1870–78	2.15	3.30			–1.76	–8.79	
1873–82	4.96	5.04			1.90	–3.87	
1878–85	6.30	—			6.41		

1888–91	6.24			9.32	
1890–92	7.24			10.76	
1891–94	−2.85			0.64	
1892–95	−3.23			−8.99	
1894–96	5.13			−8.82	
1895–99	2.06			−3.89	
1896–1900	4.28			3.70	
1899–1903	6.38			6.30	
1900–04	3.63	3.84		3.34	4.36
1903–07	4.76	4.60		4.62	4.83
1904–08	2.46	2.77			3.08
1907–10		1.34			0.76
1908–11		5.26			0.80
1910–13		3.88	3.04		2.51
1911–14		0.18	0.78		−4.53
1913–20			1.01		−6.93
1914–21			0.35		−0.79
1920–23			5.73		18.76
1921–24			8.61		17.20
1923–26			4.50		9.28
1924–27			4.48		5.54
1926–29			2.08		−4.40
1927–32			−5.38		−17.91
1929–37			0.12		−4.88
1932–38			4.92		6.92
1937–48			4.18		4.19
1938–49			4.57		4.85
1948–53			4.59		6.31
1949–54			4.29		6.54
1953–57			2.55		3.66
1954–58			2.50		2.17
1957–60			2.48		3.64
1958–61			3.66		4.67
1960–64			3.95		4.10

(continued)

TABLE B-2 *(continued)*

| Reference Cycle Dates (calendar year) | Rate of Change of Wage Rate | | Rate of Change of Average Hours of Work per Week in Manufacturing | | Rate of Change of Nonfarm Households (per 1.000 nonfarm households per year) Series 13 |
	Money Daily Wages, Erie Canal Series 8	Real Hourly Wages, Manufacturing (1957 cents) Series 9	Jones Series 10	Bureau of Labor Stat. Series 11	
1829–34	0				
1832–36	3.84				
1834–38	4.54				
1836–39	4.44				
1838–43	–3.64				
1839–45	–4.76				
1843–46	0				
1845–47	7.69				
1846–48	7.69				
1847–53	2.22				
1848–55	1.90				
1853–56	0				
1855–58	0				
1856–60	0				
1858–61	0				
1860–64		–7.90			
1861–67		–1.32			
1864–69		6.92			
1867–70		4.84			
1869–73		3.54			
1870–78		1.44			
1873–82		1.18			
1878–85		2.41			
1882–87		3.08			
1885–88		2.49			

Period	(1)	(2)	(3)	(4)
1890–92	0.32			
1891–94	0.92			
1892–95	0.90			
1894–96	0.83			
1895–99	1.35			
1896–1900	1.97			
1899–1903	2.45			
1900–04	1.20	−0.64		2.73
1903–07	1.20	0		2.83
1904–08	1.40	−1.59		2.16
1907–10	0.39	−1.31		2.21
1908–11	1.61	0.92		3.27
1910–13	1.73	−0.84		3.33
1911–14	0.59	−1.05		3.00
1913–20	3.57	−0.81		2.80
1914–21	4.01	−1.44		2.30
1920–23	1.79	0.55		1.40
1921–24	2.66	0.94		1.58
1923–26	0.39	−0.76		1.98
1924–27	−0.41	0.57		2.48
1926–29	2.15	0.14		2.68
1927–32	0.69	−4.40		3.42
1929–37	3.41	−2.94		2.96
1932–38	5.09	−1.37		2.25
1937–48	2.32	0.21		2.20
1938–49	2.54	0.75		2.13
1948–53	3.27	−0.10	0.25	2.15
1949–54	2.72	−0.11	0.25	2.04
1953–57	2.68	−0.52	−0.44	
1954–58	2.26		−0.26	
1957–60	1.53		−0.08	
1958–61	1.98		0.51	
1960–64	1.62		0.62	

(continued)

TABLE B-2 (concluded)

Reference Cycle Dates (calendar year)	Unemployment Rates		Reference Cycle Dates 1829–1869: Calendar Yr. 1867–1913: Fiscal Yr.	Rate of Gross Alien Immigration (per 1,000 total population per year) Series 12
	Lebergott (per cent of civilian labor force) Series 14	Bureau of Labor Stat. Series 15		
1829–34			1829–34	2.86
1832–36			1832–36	3.97
1834–38			1834–38	4.10
1836–39			1836–39	3.97
1838–43			1838–43	4.45
1839–45			1839–45	4.62
1843–46			1843–46	5.08
1845–47			1845–47	7.88
1846–48			1846–48	9.92
1847–53			1847–53	13.24
1848–55			1848–55	13.68
1853–56			1853–56	11.39
1855–58			1855–58	7.16
1856–60			1856–60	5.68
1858–61			1858–61	4.10
1860–64			1860–64	4.00
1861–67			1861–67	5.80
1864–69			1864–69	7.72
1867–70			1867–71	8.41
1869–73			1869–73	9.04
1870–78			1871–78	6.20
1873–82			1873–82	6.57
1878–85			1878–85	9.28
1882–87			1882–87	8.81
1885–88			1885–88	7.24
1887–90			1887–90	7.89

1891–94	8.87		1891–94	7.17
1892–95	12.80		1893–96	4.47
1894–96	15.05		1894–97	4.03
1895–99	12.85		1896–1900	3.94
1896–1900	10.78		1897–1901	4.47
1899–1903	3.68		1900–03	7.58
1900–04	3.15		1901–04	8.97
1903–07	2.73		1903–07	11.93
1904–08	3.09		1904–08	12.31
1907–10	5.85		1907–10	10.05
1908–11	6.15		1908–11	9.56
1910–13	5.52		1910–13	9.98
1911–14	5.57			
1913–20	5.03			
1914–21	5.28			
1920–23	7.70			
1921–24	6.50			
1923–26	4.02			
1924–27	3.57			
1926–29	3.68		1926–29	9.21
1927–32			1927–32	17.57
1929–37				
1932–38			1932–38	19.87
1937–48			1937–48	7.93
1938–49			1938–49	6.86
1948–53			1948–53	4.19
1949–54			1949–54	4.07
1953–57			1953–57	4.45
1954–58			1954–58	4.78
1957–60			1957–60	5.75
1958–61			1958–61	5.95
1960–64			1960–64	5.85

[a] Per cent per year, except as noted for series 12–15.

TABLE B-3. AVERAGE GROWTH RATE OF TOTAL AND NONFARM
HOUSEHOLDS AND OF TOTAL HOUSEHOLDS BY COMPONENT OF
CHANGE, 1880–1964
(per cent per decade)

	Growth of		Contribution to Total Household Growth of		
Period	Nonfarm Households (1)	Total Households (2)	Net Migration (3)	Aging and Mortality (4)	Change in Headship Rates (5)
1880–90	31.5	24.2	8.2	18.6	–
1890–1900	22.9	22.9	5.1	18.1	−2.1
1900–10	30.8	23.7	7.1	16.2	0.8
1910–20	25.6/23.2	18.4/19.2	3.3	14.5	1.5
1920–30	27.4	20.3	2.6	15.7	1.3
1930–40	18.5	15.8	−0.3	14.7	1.1
1940–50	28.4	21.7	1.8	13.1	6.8
1950–55	25.0	18.9	1.9	10.1	6.9
1955–60	22.4	18.4	2.0	8.0	8.4
1960–64	20.4	15.6	1.9	7.8	5.9

TABLE B-4. MALE POPULATION AGED 15–
29 AND 30–64, ACTUAL AND PROJECTED,
1920–85

Year	Males 15–29 (1)	Males 30–64 (2)	Col. 1 ÷ Col. 2 (3)
	Actual		
1920	13,739	20,607	.667
1930	15,955	24,550	.650
1940	17,442	27,664	.630
1950	17,216	31,671	.544
1955	16,772	33,781	.496
1960	17,794	35,478	.502
	Projected		
1965	21,074	36,339	.580
1970	25,114	37,008	.679
1975	28,657	38,645	.742
1980	30,393	41,687	.729
1985	30,851	45,505	.678

TABLE B-5. PERCENTAGE OF POPULATION AGED 25–29 AND 30–64 WITH 9–12 AND 13 OR MORE YEARS OF SCHOOL COMPLETED, ACTUAL AND PROJECTED, 1920–85

| | With 9–12 Years of School Completed | | | With 13 or More Years of School Completed | | |
| | Age | | Excess of 25–29 Over 30–64 | Age | | Excess of 25–29 Over 30–64 |
Year	25–29	30–64		25–29	30–64	
			Actual			
1920	24.9	17.6	7.3	9.2	6.7	2.5
1930	32.9	22.0	10.9	11.9	8.2	3.7
1940	47.3	28.3	19.0	13.2	10.3	2.9
1950	56.8	38.0	18.8	17.9	13.8	4.1
1960	59.4	46.5	12.9	23.0	17.0	6.0
			Projected			
1965	59.1	50.2	8.9	27.2	18.7	8.5
1970	61.1	53.3	7.8	29.8	20.7	9.1
1975	61.2	56.0	5.2	31.4	23.0	8.4
1980	61.0	58.0	3.0	32.9	25.6	7.3
1985	60.9	58.9	2.0	34.6	28.4	6.2

TABLE B-6. CONTRIBUTION OF POPULATION CHANGE TO LABOR FORCE AND HOUSEHOLD GROWTH, ACTUAL AND PROJECTED, 1930–80 (per cent per decade)

| | Contribution of Population Change to | |
Period	Labor Force Growth (1)	Household Growth (2)
	Actual	
1930–40	11.7	14.4
1940–50	9.7	14.9
....		
1950–55	7.7	12.0
1955–60	9.8	10.0
	Projected	
1960–65	13.9	10.2
1965–70	15.5	12.4
1970–75	16.0/15.7	15.2
1975–80	14.5	16.7

TABLE B-7. AVERAGE GROWTH RATE OF LABOR FORCE AND HOUSE-
HOLDS DUE TO ALL SOURCES AND THAT DUE TO POPULATION
GROWTH ALONE, ACTUAL AND PROJECTED, 1930–80
(per cent per decade)

	Labor Force Growth Due to		Household Growth Due to	
Period	All Sources (1)	Population Growth (2)	All Sources (3)	Population Growth (4)
Actual				
1930–40	8.3	11.7	15.8	14.4
1940–50	14.2	9.7	21.7	14.9
....				
1950–55	12.4	7.7	18.9	12.0
1955–60	11.1	9.8	18.4	10.0
1960–64	13.0	13.2	15.6	9.7
Projected				
1960–65	15.4	13.9	16.7	10.2
1965–70	16.4	15.5	16.2	12.4
1970–75	16.4/17.0	16.0/15.7	17.6	15.2
1975–80	15.9	14.5	16.6	16.7

SOURCES AND METHODS

Table B-1

Series 1: [70, p. 127].

Series 2: 1900–28, [207, pp. 138–139, Table 1–16, line 5]; 1929–62, [58 (January 1964), p. 210, col. 1]; 1963, [58 (January 1965), p. 192, col. 1].

Series 3: 1860–1941, [60, p. 34]; 1942–48, NBER files.

Series 4: NBER files.

Series 5: [1, pp. 151–152, series 21a].

Series 6: [1, pp. 151–153, series 21]. Extrapolated from 1959 to 1964 by annual per cent change in [58 (January 1965), p. 234, col. 4].

Series 7: *Immigration:* [186, series C-88]. *Population:* 1820–68. [186, series A-2]; 1869–99, [102, unpublished annual estimates underlying pp. 624–626, Table R-37, col. 9]; 1900–07, [183, No. 250, p. 6], adjusted to include armed forces overseas by unpublished annual estimates underlying [102, *ibid.*, col. 8].

Series 8: *Immigration:* 1908–45, [107, p. 96, immigrants minus emigrants], extended to 1961 via [186, 187, series C-140 and C-156]. *Population:* 1908–16, 1920–29, same as for series 7 for 1900–07; 1917–19, 1930–61, [183, No. 250, p. 6, Tables 2, 3].

Series 9: 1820–1957, [186, sum of series U-185–190]; 1957–62, [190, 1963, p. 854]. For 1900 and 1957, first entry is comparable to preceding years; second entry, to later years.

Table B-2

Series 1: Preliminary unpublished annual estimates (as of April 1964) in millions of 1860 dollars by Robert E. Gallman, underlying [34, pp. 27, 34]. Nonperishable commodity output is the sum of consumers' semidurables and durables, manufactured producers' durables, and gross new construction.

Series 2: [70, p. 127].

Series 3: [99, pp. 293–294, col. 11].

Series 4: Same as for Table B-1, series 2.

Series 5: Same source as for series 1.

Series 6: [1, pp. 141–142, series 5, segment I].

Series 7: 1900–58, [1, pp. 142–145, series 2]; extrapolated from 1954–58 to 1957–60 and 1958–61 assuming change in rates between successive periods was same as that shown by [58 (January 1964), p. 210, col. 7], and, for 1960–64, [58 (January 1965), p. 192, col. 7].

Series 8: [147, p. 303].

Series 9: 1900–58, [115, pp. 150–151, col. 5]; 1959–64, col. 1 of same source was extrapolated on basis of absolute annual change in [191 (March 1966), p. 59, col. 3], and col. 4 via [58 (January 1965), p. 244, col. 1].

Series 10: [97, p. 375].

Series 11: [191 (April 1965), p. 33, col. 2].

Series 12: Same as for Table B-1, series 7.

Series 13: [186, 187, series A-243]; 1964 value from [182, No. 130, p. 1].

Series 14: 1890–99, [110, p. 522]; 1900–32, [171, p. 215].

Series 15: [191 (March 1966), p. 23].

Table B-3

For 1940 on, the procedure used to disaggregate household growth was the same as that for labor force growth (Table A-3), except that headship rather than participation rates were used. Prior to 1940 it was necessary to follow a much more approximate procedure, described below.

1880–1940. *Nonfarm households:* 1880–1920, total households minus farm households [184, p. 6]; 1910–40, [186, series A-243]. The break in 1910–20 reflects a shift from census levels to estimates consistent with those of the Current Population Survey.

Total households: 1880–1920, [186, series A-255]; 1910–40, [*ibid.*, series A-242].

With regard to components of change, although estimates are available for the total number of households at each census date, lack of detail by sex and age for several of the censuses prevented use of the partition technique employed for Table A-3. After some experimentation, the following procedure for approximating the components was adopted:

(a) *Contribution of aging and mortality:* For each decade the absolute change due to aging and mortality in the population of both sexes aged 25 and over was weighted by .44, and in the population 20–24 by .10, with the weights representing the approximate headship rates for these population groups. Summation of the results gave an estimate of the absolute change in households due to this population component. This was then converted to a percentage change by dividing by the average of the initial and terminal number of households for the decade.

(b) *Contribution of net migration:* Assumed the same as the contribution of net migration to the percentage change in population aged 25 and over.

(c) *Contribution of headship rate change:* Assumed the same as the change in the age-standardized proportion of males aged 14 and over married. The absolute change over the decade was converted to a percentage basis by dividing by the average of the initial and terminal marriage proportions for the decade.

Estimates of the components of population change by sex and age (needed for the aging and mortality and net migration components), prepared for the University of Pennsylvania Study of Population Redistribution and Economic Growth, were kindly provided by Dr. Hope T. Eldridge. The headship rate weights of .10 and .44 are approximately those for the age groups 20–24 and 25 and over in the 1890 and 1930 censuses. The age-standardized percentage of males married was from [186, series A-216].

The rationale of the procedures is that the contribution to household growth of the two demographic components—aging and mortality and net migration—tends to conform closely to their contribution to growth of the population of household forming age. For the first component, an allowance is needed for differences among age groups in household headship. With regard to the rate component, marriage and household headship among males tend to be closely associated. Hence the movement in the former provides an approximation to the latter.

An indication of the validity of the approximation may be obtained by comparing the sum of the components estimated in this way with the actual change in households for each decade 1870–1940. The results correspond fairly closely for each period, and, of particular importance for the present purpose, the general pattern of change over time is quite similar. A second test is provided by applying the approximation technique to 1940–50 and comparing the results with those of the more refined procedure:

Household Growth (Per Cent) Due to

	All Sources	Sum of Components	Aging and Mortality	Net Migration	Headship Rate Change
Refined procedure (1940–50 data in Table B-3)	21.7	21.7	13.1	1.8	6.8
Approximation	—	23.1	14.4	0.7	8.0

Although there are small differences, the approximation procedure leads correctly to the inference that the source of the sharp rise in household growth from 1930–40 to 1940–50 (Table B-3) was the movement in the headship rate component, and that the demographic components played a negligible part.

1940–64. The method followed for estimating components of change was the same as that for labor force, described in the sources and methods for Table A-3. Household data refer to the civilian noninstitutional population plus members of the armed forces living off post or with their families on military reservations; population data, to the total population, including armed forces overseas. Calculations were done separately for each sex-age class of the total population. Age classes were 14–24, 25–29, 30–34, ten year groups through 55–64, and 65 and over. Alaska and Hawaii are omitted in calculations referring to periods through 1960, but are included in those for 1960 on.

Households: 1940, [179, p. 1–458]. 1950, [182, No. 33 (February 12, 1951), p. 15]. 1955, [ibid., No. 67 (May 2, 1956), p. 11]. 1960, [ibid., No. 106 (January 9, 1961), p. 13]. An estimate excluding Alaska and Hawaii was obtained by deducting 1960 census data for these states. 1964, [ibid., No. 139 (June 11, 1965), pp. 17–18].

Population and migration: Same as for Table A-3, 1940–65, except that the

1965 population data were replaced by those for 1964 from [194, p. 130], and the 1960–65 migration total was replaced by that for 1960–64 from [183, No. 302 (March 11, 1965), p. 8].

Table B-4

1920–30, [176, pp. 1–93]; 1940–50 [183, No. 98, p. 15]; 1955, [*ibid.*, No. 265, p. 25]; 1960–85, [*ibid.*, No. 286, p. 42, series C].

Table B-5

1920–40, [176, pp. 1–238]. The 1920 and 1930 values were inferred from those for the appropriate cohorts as reported in 1940, the first date at which data on educational attainment were collected. 1950, [*ibid.*, pp. 1–236]; 1960–85, [183, No. 305, pp. 7–10].

Tables B-6 and B-7

For periods through 1960–64, values are same as those in Tables A-3 and B-3, except for the 1960–64 labor force change by component, for which 1964 population and 1960–64 migration data were from sources shown for Table B-3, and 1964 labor force data from [194, p. 130]. The "population growth" component is the contribution due to net migration plus that due to aging and mortality.

The method by which the quinquennial projections from 1960–65 through 1975–80 were partitioned is that described above for Table A-3. Scope and classification detail for labor force were the same as those for the 1960–65 period described under the head of 1940–65 calculations of Table A-3; for households, same as those for the 1940–64 calculations of Table B-3. Sources of basic data were as follows.

Labor force: 1965–75 (based on 1962 population projection), [193, p. 4]. 1970–80 (based on 1964 population projection), [194, p. 130].

Households: 1965–80 (based on 1962 population projection), [182, No. 123 (April 11, 1963)]. Unpublished distributions by age and sex were provided by the Bureau of the Census.

Population: 1965–75 (1962 population projection), [193, p. 4]. 1980 (1962 population projection), [183, No. 251 (July 6, 1962), p. 4, Series II]. 1970–80 (1964 population projection), [194, p. 130].

Migration: 1960–75 (1962 population projection), quinquennial projection from [183, No. 187 (November 10, 1958), p. 13]. In accordance with assumption used in census projections, all migrants were assumed to survive to the end of the quinquennium in which they immigrated. 1960–80 (1964 population projection), annual projection in [183, No. 286 (July 1964), p. 27] was cumulated and aged to end of quinquennium, assuming no mortality among migrants.

C / APPENDIX FOR CHAPTER 4

TABLE C-1. AVERAGE GROWTH RATE OF TOTAL WHITE POPULATION, 1870–1959
(per cent per quinquennium)

Period	Rate of Change	Period	Rate of Change
1870–75	13.0	1915–20	5.6
1875–80	9.9	1920–25	8.6
1880–85	13.5	1925–30	6.3
1885–90	10.4	1930–35	3.5
1890–95	10.2	1935–40	3.6
1895–1900	8.2	1940–45	5.1
1900–05	9.7	1945–50	7.1
1905–10	10.6	1950–55	7.9
1910–15	9.2	1955–59 [a]	8.1

[a] Adjusted to rate of change per quinquennium.

TABLE C-2. LEVEL AND RATE OF CHANGE OF CRUDE BIRTH RATE OF TOTAL WHITE POPULATION, 1855–1959

| | Average Annual Crude Birth Rate (per thousand) | | Change in Crude Birth Rate Since Preceding Period (per cent per quinquennium on base of given and preceding period) | |
Period	Zelnik (1)	Official (2)	Zelnik (3)	Official (4)
1855–59	46.5	–	–	–
1860–64	41.5	–	–11.4	–
1865–69	39.7	–	–4.4	–
1870–74	39.7	–	0	–
1875–79	38.0	–	–4.4	–
1880–84	36.1	–	–5.1	–
1885–89	35.3	–	–2.2	–
1890–94	34.0	–	–3.8	–
1895–99	31.2	–	–8.6	–
1900–04	28.8	–	–8.0	–
1905–09	29.4	–	+2.1	–
1910–14	28.2	29.1	–4.2	–
1915–19	26.9	27.6	–4.7	–5.3
1920–24	25.2	26.0	–6.5	–6.0
1925–29	21.5	22.4	–15.8	–14.9
1930–34	18.3	18.9	–16.1	–16.9
1935–39	–	18.0	–	–4.9
1940–44	–	20.4	–	+12.5
1945–49	–	23.4	–	+13.7
1950–54	–	23.8	–	+1.7
1955–59	–	23.7	–	–0.04

TABLE C-3. LEVEL AND RATE OF CHANGE OF FERTILITY RATIO, 1865-1929, AND OF GENERAL FERTILITY RATE, 1920-58: TOTAL WHITE POPULATION, BY NATIVITY

Period	Fertility (per thousand)			Change in Fertility Since Preceding Period (per cent per quinquennium on base of given and preceding period)		
	Total White (1)	Native White (2)	Foreign-Born White (3)	Total White (4)	Native White (5)	Foreign-Born White (6)
	Fertility Ratio [a]					
1865–69	877	–	–	–	–	–
1870–74	855	–	–	−2.5	–	–
1875–79	812	771	971	−5.2	–	–
1880–84	783	743	938	−3.6	−3.7	−3.5
1885–89	744	706	889	−5.1	−5.1	−5.4
1890–94	723	672	927	−2.9	−4.9	+4.2
1895–99	665	628	819	−8.4	−6.8	−12.4
1900–04	636	606	768	−4.5	−3.6	−6.4
1905–09	632	601	754	−0.6	−0.8	−1.8
1910–14	610	566	793	−3.5	−6.0	+5.0
1915–19	614	575	792	+0.7	+1.6	−0.1
1920–24	586	574	648	−4.7	−0.2	−20.0
1925–29	505	508	486	−14.8	−12.2	−28.6
	General Fertility Rate [b]					
1920–24	111.4	106.4	–	–	–	–
1925–29	95.7	93.4	–	−15.2	−13.0	–
1930–34	79.6	79.4	–	−18.4	−16.2	–
1935–39	74.7	75.6	–	−6.4	−4.9	–
1940–44	85.2	87.4	–	+13.1	+14.5	–
1945–49	100.7	102.6	–	+16.7	+16.0	–
1950–54	108.6	109.2	–	+7.5	+6.2	–
1954–58	114.8	115.4	–	+6.9 [c]	+6.9 [c]	–

[a] Number of children under 5 years old per 1,000 women 20 to 44 years old.
[b] Annual average total live births per 1,000 women 15 to 44 years old.
[c] Adjusted to rate of change per quinquennium.

TABLE C-4. WHITE CHILDREN UNDER 5 YEARS OLD BY NATIVITY AND PARENTAGE, 1870–1930

Date	Total White (1)	Native White, Total (2)	Native White of Native Parentage (3)	Native White of Foreign or Mixed Parentage (4)	Native White of Foreign Parentage (5)	Native White of Mixed Parentage			Foreign-Born White (9)
						Total (6)	Mother Native (7)	Mother Foreign (8)	
1870	5,333	5,243	–	–	–	–	–	–	90
1875	5,872	5,774	–	–	–	–	–	–	98
1880	6,246	6,179	4,379	1,800	1,238	563	329	234	67
1885	6,809	6,669	4,748	1,921	1,279	642	375	267	140
1890	7,348	7,252	5,084	2,167	1,436	732	428	304	96
1895	7,995	7,922	5,471	2,450	1,611	839	490	349	73
1900	8,177	8,123	5,721	2,403	1,559	843	493	351	54
1905	8,606	8,546	6,125	2,420	1,561	859	518	341	60
1910	9,664	9,558	6,827	2,731	1,858	872	543	330	106
1915	10,332	10,231	7,198	3,033	2,174	858	534	324	101
1920	10,950	10,902	7,893	3,009	2,158	851	530	322	48
1925	11,306	11,236	8,622	2,614	1,681	933	604	329	70
1930	10,543	10,508	8,464	2,044	1,171	872	586	286	35

TABLE C-5. WHITE FEMALES 20–44 BY NATIVITY, 1870–1930

Date	Total White (1)	Native White (2)	Foreign-Born White (3)
1870	6,084	4,550	1,534
1875	6,869	5,276	1,593
1880	7,692	6,105	1,587
1885	8,692	6,894	1,798
1890	9,869	7,803	2,066
1895	11,062	8,870	2,192
1900	12,292	9,894	2,398
1905	13,523	10,967	2,556
1910	15,302	12,258	3,044
1915	16,946	13,668	3,278
1920	17,845	14,654	3,191
1925	19,281	16,070	3,211
1930	20,892	17,820	3,072

TABLE C-6. LEVEL AND RATE OF CHANGE OF FERTILITY RATIO BY RURAL-URBAN RESIDENCE: NATIVE WHITE POPULATION, 1885–1929; TOTAL WHITE POPULATION, 1925–58

Period	Fertility Ratio in Specified Quinquennium (per thousand)			Change in Fertility Ratio Since Preceding Period (per cent per decade, on base of given and preceding period)		
	Total (1)	Urban (2)	Rural (3)	Total (4)	Urban (5)	Rural (6)
Native White						
1885–89	671	434	818	–	–	–
1895–99	631	400	809	−6.1	−8.2	−1.1
1905–09	606	407	797	−4.0	+1.7	−1.5
1915–19	565	407	757	−7.0	0	−5.1
1925–29	503	384	686	−11.6	−5.8	−9.8
Total White						
1925–29	485	388	658	–	–	–
1935–39	400	311	551	−19.2	−22.1	−17.7
1945–49	551	479	673	+31.7	+42.5	+19.9
1954–58	651	566	n.a.	+18.5 [a]	+18.5 [a]	–

[a] Adjusted to rate of change per decade.

TABLE C-7. RATIO OF MALES AGED 25–34
TO FEMALES AGED 20–29, AND PERCENT-
AGE OF LATTER MARRIED: FOREIGN-BORN
WHITE POPULATION, 1890–1930

Date	Ratio of Males 25–34 to Females 20–29 at Specified Date (per cent)	Females 20–29, Per Cent Married at Specified Date
1890	126	60.4
1900	129	61.3
1910	147	67.0
1920	154	75.3
1930	137	66.1

TABLE C-8. LEVEL AND RATE OF CHANGE OF FERTILITY RATIO;
AND OF RATIO OF MALES AGED 25–34 TO FEMALES 20–29, AND OF
FEMALES AGED 20–34 TO FEMALES 20–44: FOREIGN-BORN WHITE
POPULATION, 1875–1930

	At Following Census or Mid-census Date (per cent)			Change Since Preceding Date (per cent per quinquennium, on base of given and preceding period)		
Period	Fertility Ratio (per thousand) (1)	Ratio of Males 25–34 to Females 20–29 (2)	Ratio of Females 20–34 to Females 20–44 (3)	Fertility Ratio (4)	Ratio of Males 25–34 to Females 20–29 (5)	Ratio of Females 20–34 to Females 20–44 (6)
1875–79	971	140.1	56.9	–	–	–
1880–84	938	126.7	59.1	−3.5	−10.0	+3.8
1885–89	889	126.4	63.1	−5.4	−0.2	+6.5
1890–94	927	138.0	64.0	+4.2	+8.8	+1.4
1895–99	819	128.8	61.9	−12.4	−6.9	−3.3
1900–04	768	135.9	59.9	−6.4	+5.4	−3.2
1905–09	754	147.0	62.3	−1.8	+7.9	+3.9
1910–14	793	152.2	62.3	+5.0	+3.5	0
1915–19	792	153.6	57.6	−0.1	+0.9	−7.8
1920–24	648	147.8	54.4	−20.0	−3.8	−5.7
1925–29	486	137.1	50.5	−28.6	−7.5	−7.4

TABLE C-9. LEVEL AND RATE OF CHANGE OF FERTILITY RATIO OF RURAL WHITE POPULATION AND REAL GROSS FARM INCOME PER ENGAGED, 1885–1929

| Period | Fertility Ratio (per thousand) (1) | Real Gross Farm Income per Engaged in Quinquennium Approximately 1.25 Years Earlier (1924–28 = 100) (2) | Change Since Preceding Period (per cent per quinquennium, on base of given and preceding period) | |
			Fertility Ratio (3)	Real Gross Farm Income per Engaged (4)
1885–89	845 [a]	55.4	–	–
1895–99	836	56.0	–0.6 [a]	+0.6
1905–09	821	81.9	–0.9	+18.8
1915–19	781	118.8	–2.5	+18.4
1925–29	686	100.0	–6.5	–8.6

[a] Adjustment of the figure in column 1 to reflect underenumeration of children under 5 in excess of the National Resources Committee allowance of 5 per cent yields a value of 887. The rate of change in column 3 based on this adjusted 1885–89 figure is –3.0 per cent.

TABLE C-10. LEVEL AND RATE OF CHANGE OF CRUDE BIRTH RATE OF TOTAL FARM POPULATION AND REAL NET FARM INCOME PER HEAD OF FARM POPULATION, 1920–58

| Period | Crude Birth Rate, Annual Average (per thousand) (1) | Real Net Farm Income per Head of Farm Population in Quinquennium 1.25 Years Earlier (1924–28 = 100) (2) | Change Since Preceding Period (per cent per quinquennium on base of given and preceding period) | |
			Crude Birth Rate (3)	Real Net Farm Income per Head (4)
1920–24	26.0	85.0	–	–
1925–29	25.1	100.0	–3.6	+16.2
1930–34	22.7	76.9	–9.7	–26.1
1935–39	22.6	96.3	–0.5	+22.4
1940–44	23.9	149.0	+5.4	+43.0
1945–49	25.5	217.6	+6.4	+37.4
1950–54	24.8	185.5	–2.6	–15.9
1954–58	25.1	167.3	+1.5 [a]	–12.9 [a]

[a] Adjusted to rate of change per quinquennium.

TABLE C-11. LEVEL AND RATE OF CHANGE OF URBAN NATIVE WHITE FERTILITY RATIO,[a] UNEMPLOYMENT RATE OF CIVILIAN LABOR FORCE, AND RATE OF CHANGE OF TOTAL WHITE MALE POPULATION AGED 20–29: 1885–1958

				Change Since Preceding Period		
Period	Fertility Ratio [a] (per thousand) (1)	Percentage of Civilian Labor Force Unemployed in Quinquennium Approximately 1.25 Years Earlier (2)	Change in Total White Male Population Aged 20–29 (per cent per quinquennium) (3)	Fertility Ratio (per cent per decade on base of given and preceding quinquennium) (4)	Percentage of Civilian Labor Force Unemployed (percentage points) (5)	Change in Total White Male Population Aged 20–29 (percentage points) (6)
1885–89	434	5.0	11.4	–	–	–
1895–99	400	11.7	7.4	−8.1	+6.7	−4.0
1905–09	407	3.8	15.8	+1.7	−7.9	+8.4
1915–19	407	5.7	−2.2	0	+1.9	−18.0
1925–29	384 [a]	4.0	7.7	−5.8	−1.7	+9.9
1935–39	311	18.4	3.3 [c]	−22.0	+14.4	−4.4
1945–49	479	2.8 [b]	−0.4	+42.5	−15.6	−4.0
1954–58	566	4.3	−2.6	+18.5 [d]	+1.7 [d]	−2.4 [d]

[a] For 1935–39 on figures are for urban total white. The overlap value for 1925–29 comparable to later dates is 388.

[b] Figures for 1954–58 are from a different source than those for earlier dates. The overlap value for 1945–49 comparable to 1954–58 is 2.9.

[c] Figures for 1945–49 on are from a different source than those for earlier dates. The overlap value for 1935–39 comparable to later dates is 3.6.

[d] Adjusted to rate of change per decade.

TABLE C-12. NATIVITY COMPONENTS OF CHANGE IN TOTAL WHITE
FERTILITY RATIO, 1875–1929

	Fertility Ratio (per thousand)			Change in Total White Fertility Ratio Since Preceding Period Attributable to Contribution of				
					Change in Fertility Ratio of		Change in Nativity Distribution of White Females Aged 20–44	Interaction Terms
Period	Total White (1)	Native White (2)	Foreign-Born White (3)	All Factors (4)	Native White (5)	Foreign-Born White (6)	(7)	(8)
1875–79	812	771	971	–	–	–	–	–
1880–84	783	743	938	−29	−22	−7	–	–
1885–89	744	706	889	−39	−29	−10	–	0
1890–94	723	672	927	−21	−27	+8	−2	0
1895–99	665	628	819	−58	−35	−21	−1	−1
1900–04	636	606	768	−29	−18	−10	−1	0
1905–09	632	601	754	−4	−4	−3	+2	+1
1910–14	610	566	793	−22	−28	+8	−1	−1
1915–19	614	575	792	+4	+7	–	−3	0
1920–24	586	574	648	−28	−1	−26	−3	+2
1925–29	505	508	486	−81	−55	−27	−1	+2

Columns 1, 2, and 3: Table C-3, columns 1 through 3.

Columns 5, 6, and 7: The values of all components were held constant at their beginning-of-period levels except for the component whose contribution was being assessed, and the change in the total that would have resulted from the change in this component alone was computed.

Column 8: Column 4 minus columns 5 through 7.

TABLE C-13. URBAN-RURAL COMPONENTS OF CHANGE IN NATIVE WHITE FERTILITY RATIO, 1885–1929

| | Fertility Ratio in (per thousand) | | | Change in Native White Fertility Ratio Since Preceding Period Attributable to Contribution of | | | | |
| | | | | | Change in Fertility Ratio of | | Change in Urban-Rural Distribution of Native White Females Aged 20–44 | Inter-action Terms |
Period	Total Native White (1)	Urban Native White (2)	Rural Native White (3)	All Factors (4)	Urban Native White (5)	Rural Native White (6)	(7)	(8)
1885–89	671	434	818	–	–	–	–	–
1895–99	631	400	809	−40	−13	−6	−20	−1
1905–09	606	407	797	−25	+3	−7	−24	+3
1915–19	565	407	757	−41	0	−20	−21	0
1925–29	503	384	686	−62	−13	−32	−20	+3

Columns 1 through 3: Table C-6, columns 1 through 3.
Columns 5 through 8: See explanation for Table C-12, columns 5 through 8.

SOURCES AND METHODS

Detailed notes explaining the underlying sources and methods and precise time reference of the observations are published in *The American Baby Boom in Historical Perspective*, New York, National Bureau of Economic Research, Occasional Paper 79, 1962, Appendix C.

D / APPENDIX FOR CHAPTER 5

TABLE D-1. TOTAL FERTILITY RATE AND BIRTH RATE BY AGE OF
MOTHER, 1940–63 [a]
(Index: 1949–51 = 100)

Year (mid-point of average)	Total Fertility Rate (1)	Birth Rate by Age of Mother					
		15–19 (2)	20–24 (3)	25–29 (4)	30–34 (5)	35–39 (6)	40–44 (7)
1941	77.4	68.3	73.2	77.9	82.9	87.5	99.3
1942	81.8	71.3	77.9	82.9	88.1	91.4	99.3
1943	83.6	70.2	78.9	84.4	92.2	96.8	102.0
1944	82.1	66.3	74.6	82.3	94.8	102.4	105.9
1945	84.5	65.3	77.5	85.0	97.8	106.0	107.9
1946	92.0	75.2	87.0	92.8	102.2	108.8	109.2
1947	98.5	87.5	97.1	99.0	103.3	107.3	107.2
1948	100.2	97.0	100.1	99.8	101.1	103.9	104.6
1949	98.3	97.9	98.0	97.9	98.6	100.2	101.3
1950	100.0	100.0	100.0	100.0	100.0	100.0	100.0
1951	102.6	100.7	103.1	103.0	103.4	101.7	100.0
1952	106.1	103.1	107.9	106.5	106.4	104.3	101.3
1953	109.0	104.1	112.0	109.3	108.9	107.1	102.0
1954	111.4	105.9	115.9	111.3	109.6	109.1	103.3
1955	114.1	108.5	120.5	113.6	110.7	111.0	103.9
1956	116.5	110.9	124.4	116.0	111.1	112.1	104.6
1957	117.9	111.7	127.1	117.6	111.2	111.4	103.9
1958	118.1	110.3	128.1	118.6	111.0	110.3	103.3
1959	117.3	108.2	128.0	118.3	109.8	108.2	103.3
1960	117.0	107.2	127.6	118.5	109.5	107.1	103.9
1961	114.9	104.0	125.3	117.0	107.7	104.3	102.6
1962	111.4	98.9	120.8	114.6	105.5	101.1	100.0

[a] Three-year moving average.

TABLE D-2. PER CAPITA DISPOSABLE INCOME IN 1964 DOLLARS: TOTAL POPULATION, 1940 AND 1947-64 [a]
(Index: 1949-51 = 100)

Year (mid-point of average)	Index	Year (mid-point of average)	Index	Year (mid-point of average)	Index
1940	77.4	1952	104.4	1958	115.4
		1953	105.4	1959	116.4
1948	95.2	1954	107.7	1960	118.4
1949	97.9	1955	110.1	1961	120.3
1950	100.0	1956	113.1	1962	122.9
1951	102.6	1957	114.2	1963	126.6

[a] Three-year moving average.

TABLE D-3. MEDIAN TOTAL MONEY INCOME IN 1959 DOLLARS: MALE INCOME RECIPIENTS, BY AGE, 1941 AND 1947-63 [a]
(Index: 1949-51 = 100)

Year (midpoint of average)	Age of Male Income Recipients		
	14 and over (1)	20-24 (2)	25-34 (3)
1941	70.7	71.6	73.3
1948	93.6	91.5	93.0
1949	95.9	95.7	96.4
1950	100.0	100.0	100.0
1951	105.5	103.5	104.5
1952	109.6	101.8	108.8
1953	111.5	97.5	111.4
1954	114.3	98.5	114.9
1955	118.1	105.8	119.3
1956	121.8	109.2	124.6
1957	123.2	109.1	127.2
1958	124.7	107.5	129.4
1959	126.8	107.6	132.0
1960	130.0	109.8	135.8
1961	132.3	109.1	138.3
1962	135.1	109.4	141.9

[a] Three-year moving average.

TABLE D-4. TOTAL MONEY INCOME IN 1959 DOLLARS: FAMILIES, BY AGE OF HEAD AND RANK WITHIN AGE GROUP, 1947–63 [a] (Index: 1949–51 = 100)

Year (mid-point of average)	14 and Over Median (1)	Age of Head and Rank Within Age Group					
		14–24			25–34		
		Median (2)	20th Per-centile (3)	40th Per-centile (4)	Median (5)	20th Per-centile (6)	40th Per-centile (7)
1948	96.9	95.9	97.0	97.0	94.0	93.3	92.8
1949	97.5	97.0	96.9	96.8	96.2	95.2	95.7
1950	100.0	100.0	100.0	100.0	100.0	100.0	100.0
1951	103.9	104.6	103.3	104.2	104.2	104.7	104.1
1952	108.8	107.4	104.6	107.1	109.6	111.3	109.2
1953	111.9	106.9	98.9	106.2	112.3	110.6	111.5
1954	116.4	109.8	102.7	109.2	116.0	112.5	115.4
1955	120.6	116.2	112.2	116.6	120.2	116.5	119.5
1956	125.7	122.8	121.9	123.5	126.1	125.4	125.4
1957	128.4	125.0	123.7	124.7	129.1	129.2	128.2
1958	130.8	123.0	120.2	122.2	131.0	129.8	130.8
1959	134.1	122.0	115.8	121.1	133.2	129.5	133.4
1960	137.8	125.1	115.0	123.9	136.5	129.7	136.6
1961	140.5	127.7	113.6	125.6	137.8	131.5	137.8
1962	143.8	128.0	113.7	124.5	141.0	134.4	140.3

[a] Three-year moving average.

TABLE D-5. UNEMPLOYMENT RATE, BY SEX AND
AGE, 1940 AND 1947–64 [a]
(per cent)

Year (mid-point of average)	Both Sexes 14 and Over (1)	Males 14–19 (2)	Males 20–24 (3)	Males 25–34 (4)
1940	14.6	32.8	18.1	10.9
1948	4.5	9.8	8.0	3.5
1949	5.0	10.4	8.0	3.8
1950	4.6	10.0	7.0	3.6
1951	3.9	8.5	5.1	2.7
1952	3.1	7.1	3.9	1.9
1953	3.9	8.5	6.0	2.7
1954	4.3	9.3	7.0	3.1
1955	4.7	10.2	7.7	3.4
1956	4.3	10.3	7.0	3.1
1957	5.1	12.0	8.9	4.2
1958	5.5	13.4	9.7	4.8
1959	6.0	14.3	10.1	5.3
1960	5.9	14.4	9.4	5.1
1961	6.0	14.2	9.5	5.0
1962	6.0	14.7	9.5	4.9
1963	5.5	14.4	8.6	4.2

[a] Three-year moving average.

TABLE D-6. MALE MONEY INCOME RECIPIENTS AS A PERCENTAGE OF MALE POPULATION, BY AGE, 1941 AND 1947–63 [a]

Year (mid-point of average)	Age of Males			
	14 and Over (1)	14–19 (2)	20–24 (3)	25–34 (4)
1941	78.0	30.0	60.0	80.0
1948	89.8	44.1	91.0	98.0
1949	90.2	43.6	92.1	98.3
1950	90.3	43.0	91.9	98.7
1951	90.6	44.3	91.9	98.7
1952	90.9	46.7	92.2	98.5
1953	90.9	46.4	92.8	98.2
1954	91.2	47.5	93.3	98.4
1955	91.4	48.3	93.6	98.5
1956	91.9	51.6	94.1	98.6
1957	91.8	51.4	94.1	98.4
1958	91.6	51.0	93.7	98.4
1959	91.5	51.3	93.5	98.3
1960	91.4	51.6	93.1	98.4
1961	91.3	51.8	92.6	98.4
1962	91.3	51.8	92.4	98.6

[a] Three-year moving average.

TABLE D-7. VETERANS AS A PERCENTAGE OF MALE POPULATION, BY AGE, 1940, 1945, 1950, AND 1955–63 [a]

Year (mid-point of average)	Age of Males		
	20–24 (1)	25–29 (2)	30–34 (3)
1940	0	0	0
1945	10.54	12.63	9.21
1950	38.04	83.11	71.29
1956	23.79	63.21	82.38
1957	20.41	60.00	79.34
1958	14.43	57.15	75.74
1959	10.00	51.43	71.47
1960	5.35	44.65	67.56
1961	2.37	35.93	64.04
1962	0.76	26.57	61.31

[a] Three-year moving average.

TABLE D-8. EVER-MARRIED PERSONS AS PERCENTAGE OF POPULATION, BY SEX AND AGE, 1940, 1947, AND 1949-63 [a]

Year (mid-point of average)	Males by Age					Females by Age				
	14-17 (1)	18-19 (2)	20-24 (3)	25-29 (4)	30-34 (5)	14-17 (6)	18-19 (7)	20-24 (8)	25-29 (9)	30-34 (10)
1940	0.3	3.7	27.8	64.0	79.3	3.6	22.2	52.8	77.2	85.3
1947	0.4	7.2	38.0	72.0	84.2	4.7	26.7	64.8	84.6	88.5
1950	0.4	6.6	45.5			5.6	32.1	68.8		
1951	0.5	8.3	48.0			5.5	32.1	69.2		
1952	0.6	8.6	50.4	79.1	87.2	4.9	32.7	69.9	88.6	91.5
1953	0.6	8.7	49.6	78.2	87.6	5.0	31.9	70.1	88.6	91.7
1954	0.4	8.5	49.4	76.2	86.9	4.9	32.2	70.2	88.8	92.3
1955	0.3	8.4	49.3	75.1	86.4	5.5	32.3	70.5	88.8	92.5
1956	0.3	8.5	50.1	75.1	85.8	5.5	32.4	71.1	88.8	92.9
1957	0.4	8.2	49.0	76.9	86.4	5.3	32.6	71.1	88.9	92.3
1958	0.3	8.2	48.2	76.4	87.1	4.7	32.7	71.2	89.4	92.2
1959	0.4	8.6	47.3	76.5	87.3	4.5	32.3	71.2	90.0	92.3
1960	0.4	8.2	46.3	76.7	87.1	4.3	30.5	71.2	90.2	93.1
1961	0.5	8.5	45.9	77.8	87.9	4.1	29.3	70.9	90.0	92.9
1962	0.4	7.6	46.3	78.3	88.6	3.7	29.2	70.2	90.0	93.2

[a] Three-year moving average.

TABLE D-9. PERCENTAGE OF MALE POPULATION
IN HUSBAND-WIFE HOUSEHOLDS, BY AGE, 1940,
1947, AND 1950–63 [a]

Year (mid-point of average)	Age of Males		
	14–24 (1)	25–29 (2)	30–34 (3)
1940	8.6	50.8	66.8
1947	10.7	51.3	68.3
1951	14.1	63.8	76.3
1952	14.0	64.6	76.8
1953	13.7	64.7	77.5
1954	14.0	63.3	77.2
1955	14.1	63.4	76.5
1956	14.8	64.4	76.4
1957	14.8	66.3	77.3
1958	14.8	66.5	78.7
1959	15.0	67.5	79.3
1960	14.8	68.4	79.4
1961	14.6	68.7	79.7
1962	14.3	68.0	80.3

[a] Three-year moving average.

TABLE D-10. UNEMPLOYMENT RATE, FEMALES, BY AGE, 1940 AND 1947–64 [a]

(per cent)

Year (mid-point of average)	Age of Females		
	14–19 (1)	20–24 (2)	25–34 (3)
1940	27.8	19.9	13.3
1948	8.5	5.0	4.0
1949	9.6	5.7	4.8
1950	9.7	5.6	4.9
1951	8.3	4.7	4.2
1952	6.8	3.8	3.4
1953	7.7	4.7	3.9
1954	8.3	5.2	4.5
1955	9.6	5.9	4.9
1956	9.7	5.7	4.8
1957	11.0	6.8	5.6
1958	11.8	7.7	6.2
1959	12.8	8.4	6.5
1960	13.3	8.7	6.5
1961	13.6	9.1	6.7
1962	14.6	9.3	6.9
1963	14.6	8.9	·6.6

[a] Three-year moving average.

TABLE D-11. LABOR FORCE PARTICIPATION
RATE: MARRIED FEMALES WITH HUSBAND PRES-
SENT, BY AGE, 1940 AND 1948–64 [a]
(per cent)

Year (mid-point of average)	Age of Females		
	14–19 (1)	20–24 (2)	25–34 (3)
1940	10.7	18.6	19.0
1949	21.3	26.0	22.9
1950	20.1	27.4	24.0
1951	21.2	27.8	24.9
1952	20.1	27.7	25.4
1953	21.2	26.5	25.6
1954	20.5	27.7	25.8
1955	22.8	28.6	26.2
1956	23.8	30.2	26.5
1957	25.8	30.6	26.9
1958	26.0	30.5	27.7
1959	26.4	30.4	27.9
1960	27.1	31.0	28.5
1961	26.9	31.3	28.8
1962	28.4	32.4	29.5
1963	29.5	33.8	30.0

[a] Three-year moving average.

TABLE D-12. LABOR FORCE PARTICIPATION RATE: MARRIED FE-
MALES WITH HUSBAND PRESENT, WITH CHILDREN UNDER 6 AND
NO CHILD 6–17, 1940, 1950, AND 1948–64 [a]
(per cent)

Year (mid-point of average)	Females Aged 14 and Over	Year (mid-point of average)	Females Aged 14 and Over	Year (mid-point of average)	Females Aged 14 and Over
1940	6.5	1952	14.4	1958	17.5
1950	11.1	1953	14.6	1959	18.3
		1954	15.1	1960	18.7
1949	10.1	1955	15.0	1961	19.6
1950	11.6	1956	15.5	1962	21.0
1951	12.8	1957	16.6	1963	22.4

[a] Three-year moving average.

TABLE D-13. LABOR FORCE PARTICIPATION RATE:
MARRIED FEMALES WITH HUSBAND PRESENT, WITH
CHILD UNDER 5 OR 6, BY AGE, SELECTED YEARS,
1940–63
(per cent)

| Year | Color-Nativity Group | Age of Females | | |
		14–19 (1)	20–24 (2)	25–34 (3)
		With Child Under 5		
1940	Native White	3.9	6.8	6.8
1950	Total White	9.0	12.4	10.8
		With Child Under 6		
1951	All	8.7	13.0	14.5
1959	All	12.3	18.3	18.6
1960	All	9.7	18.3	18.6
1961	All	13.5	20.1	19.9
1962	All	17.7	19.8	21.9
1963	All	21.0	22.7	21.9

TABLE D-14. NEW HIGH SCHOOL GRADUATES NOT
ENROLLED IN COLLEGE [a]: BY SEX, MARITAL STATUS,
AND EMPLOYMENT STATUS IN OCTOBER OF YEAR OF
HIGH SCHOOL GRADUATION; ANNUALLY, 1959–63
(thousands)

Employment Status	1959 (1)	1960 (2)	1961 (3)	1962 (4)	1963 (5)
	Male				
Population	304	348	345	392	379
Labor Force	279	308	297	356	340
Employed	239	262	242	305	275
	Female, Single				
Population	418	473	482	469	489
Labor Force	331	359	392	352	368
Employed	291	308	326	309	311
	Female, Ever-Married				
Population	68	100	89	77	89
Labor Force	24	39	41	38	47
Employed	19	29	31	27	33

[a] Civilian noninstitutional population.

TABLE D-15. BIRTH RATE BY AGE OF MOTHER, AGED 15–19 THROUGH 25–29, AND SUMMARY FERTILITY MEASURES: ANNUALLY, 1940–63, AND PROJECTED QUINQUENNIALLY, 1965–75 (per thousand)

	Age of Mother			Completed (total) Fertility Rate (4)	General Fertility Rate (5)	Crude Birth Rate (6)
Year	15–19 (1)	20–24 (2)	25–29 (3)			
1940	54.8	135.6	122.8	2,301.3	79.9	19.4
1941	57.6	145.4	128.7	2,399.1	83.4	20.3
1942	61.8	165.1	142.7	2,628.2	91.5	22.2
1943	62.5	164.0	147.8	2,718.3	94.3	22.7
1944	55.1	151.8	136.5	2,567.6	88.8	21.2
1945	51.9	138.9	132.2	2,491.2	85.9	20.4
1946	60.0	181.8	161.2	2,942.7	101.9	24.1
1947	80.2	209.7	176.0	3,273.5	113.3	24.6
1948	82.8	200.3	163.4	3,108.6	107.3	24.9
1949	84.4	200.1	165.4	3,110.1	107.1	24.5
1950	82.6	196.6	166.1	3,090.5	106.2	24.1
1951	87.9	212.6	174.3	3,268.0	111.3	24.9
1952	86.3	219.1	180.5	3,357.4	113.6	25.1
1953	88.4	225.9	183.9	3,424.5	114.8	25.0
1954	90.8	237.4	188.5	3,541.5	117.6	25.3
1955	90.6	242.8	190.8	3,578.6	118.0	25.0
1956	95.1	254.3	195.4	3,688.5	120.8	25.2
1957	97.0	261.0	200.4	3,767.4	122.7	25.3
1958	92.4	258.9	198.8	3,703.3	120.1	24.5
1959	91.6	260.4	200.4	3,712.9	120.1	24.3
1960	90.3	259.9	200.7	3,694	119.2	23.8
1961	89.3	255.4	201.1	3,668	118.4	23.4
1962	83.1	246.3	193.3	3,509	113.3	22.6
1963	78.4	233.8	187.4	3,369	109.6	21.8
			Projected			
Series A						
1965	89.8	248.5	189.1	3,587	117.9	23.5
1970	85.5	245.1	192.8	3,528	124.2	24.8
1975	85.5	238.5	189.3	3,473	127.4	25.7
Series B						
1965	83.9	232.8	178.2	3,350	110.3	22.1
1970	78.2	231.8	178.7	3,209	113.7	23.0
1975	78.2	221.1	179.0	3,209	117.9	24.3
Series C						
1965	70.7	217.5	170.0	3,100	101.5	20.3
1970	68.7	201.8	160.3	2,847	100.6	20.6
1975	68.7	198.5	156.1	2,852	104.7	22.1
Series D						
1965	69.6	217.5	170.0	3,095	101.2	20.3
1970	62.4	196.5	160.3	2,789	98.0	20.1
1975	59.5	178.1	151.5	2,681	97.7	20.8

TABLE D-16. PERCENTAGE OF THOSE AGED 25–29 AND 30–64 WITH
SPECIFIED YEARS OF SCHOOL COMPLETED: ACTUAL, DECENNIALLY,
1920–60; PROJECTED, QUINQUENNIALLY, 1965–85

	At Least Nine, but Not More Than Twelve Years			Thirteen or More Years		
	Both Sexes		Excess of 25–29 Over 30–64	Both Sexes		Excess of 25–29 Over 30–64
Year	25–29 (1)	30–64 (2)	(2)–(3) (3)	25–29 (4)	30–64 (5)	(5)–(6) (6)
1920	24.9	17.6	7.3	9.2	6.7	2.5
1930	32.9	22.0	10.9	11.9	8.2	3.7
1940	47.3	28.3	19.0	13.2	10.3	2.9
1950	56.8	38.0	18.8	17.9	13.8	4.1
1960	59.4	46.5	12.9	23.0	17.0	6.0
			Projected			
1965	59.1	50.2	8.9	27.2	18.7	8.5
1970A	61.1	53.3	7.8	29.8	20.7	9.1
1970B	60.5	53.3	7.2	28.5	20.7	7.8
1975A	61.2	56.0	5.2	31.4	23.0	8.4
1975B	60.8	55.9	4.9	30.3	22.8	7.5
1980A	61.0	58.0	3.0	32.9	25.6	7.3
1980B	60.5	57.8	2.7	32.0	25.3	6.7
1985A	60.9	58.9	2.0	34.6	28.4	6.2
1985B	60.5	58.7	1.8	33.4	27.8	5.6

TABLE D-17. ANNUAL RATE OF CHANGE OF MALE
POPULATION AGED 14–19,[a] 20–24, AND 25–29 COM-
PARED WITH THAT OF AGED 30–64: ACTUAL, 1940–
64; PROJECTED, 1964–75 [b]
(per cent, initial year as base)

Year (mid-point of average)	Males by Age			
	14–19 [a] (1)	20–24 (2)	25–29 (3)	30–64 (4)
Jan. 1942	−1.10	1.64	1.08	1.33
1943	−0.98	1.12	1.43	1.39
1944	−1.53	0.32	1.61	1.38
1945	−2.05	−0.37	1.27	1.31
1946	−1.72	−1.29	0.98	1.28
1947	−1.36	−1.13	0.78	1.33
1948	−0.84	−1.25	0.77	1.42
1949	−1.52	−0.36	0.48	1.42
1950	−1.01	−0.55	0.21	1.41
1951	−0.22	−0.59	−0.22	1.32
1952	0.83	−1.12	−0.73	1.25
1953	1.57	−1.64	−1.01	1.18
1954	1.84	−1.66	−0.98	1.13
1955	2.22	−1.16	−0.80	1.08
1956	3.43	−0.40	−0.84	1.01
1957	3.91	0.55	−1.17	0.92
1958	3.93	1.47	−1.61	0.84
1959	3.15	1.96	−1.81	0.82
1960	4.81	2.24	−1.40	0.77
1961	5.56	2.86	−0.76	0.71
1962	5.56	4.36	0.17	0.56
1963	4.25	4.92	0.94	0.47
	Projected			
1964	3.97	4.83	1.42	0.41
1965	4.56	3.65	1.89	0.37
1966	3.00	4.90	2.66	0.35
1967	2.11	4.87	4.23	0.35
1968	1.18	5.57	4.80	0.36
1969	2.17	4.32	4.72	0.39
1970	2.34	4.65	3.57	0.45
1971	2.38	2.97	4.83	0.59
1972	2.00	2.10	4.80	0.85
1973	1.67	1.17	5.49	0.97
1974	1.18	2.16	4.27	1.00

[a] Projected values are for those aged 15–19.
[b] Three-year moving average.

SOURCES AND METHODS

General Note on Base for Rates or Percentages:

Tables D-2, D-7, D-9, D-15, D-17: Total population, including armed forces overseas.
Tables D-3, D-4, D-6, D-8: Civilian noninstitutional population plus members of the armed forces living off post or with their families on military reservations.
Tables D-11 through D-13: Civilian noninstitutional population.
Tables D-5 and D-10: Civilian labor force.
Table D-16: 1920–50, total population excluding armed forces overseas; 1960–85, including armed forces overseas.

Table D-1

[201, p. 9, Table 4] and *Monthly Vital Statistics Report,* Vol. 13, No. 6, p. 5, Table 4. Births adjusted for underregistration, 1940–59, were extrapolated to 1963 by series for registered births.

Table D-2

[58, 1965, p. 209, Table B-16].

Table D-3

1941, median values from unpublished worksheets underlying [22, p. 49, Table A-1] were kindly supplied by Dorothy S. Brady. 1947–60, Bureau of the Census, *Trends in the Income of Families and Persons in the United States: 1947 to 1960,* Technical Paper No. 8, Washington, 1963, Table 12. 1961–63, [180, Nos. 39, 41, and 43]. Medians are based on population of income recipients only, excluding persons without income. For all years, median incomes in current prices have been deflated by the Consumer Price Index shifted to 1959 = 100. (Cf. [58, 1965, p. 244, Table B-45].)

Table D-4

1947–60, Table 3 of 1947–60 source cited for Table D-3; 1961–63, same as for Table D-3. Percentile values were obtained by interpolation. Medians are based on population including families both with and without income. Current value data were adjusted to constant as in Table D-3.

Table D-5

Both sexes, 14 and over, [58, 1965, p. 214, Table B-21]. Males, 14–19, 20–24, 25–34: 1940, [181, No. 19, p. 7]; 1947–64, [202, March 1965, p. 205, Table A-12].

Table D-6

1941, [22, p. 24, Table 7], (figure for males 14 and over supplied by Dorothy S. Brady from unpublished worksheets). 1947–63, [180, Nos. 5–7, 9, 11, 14, 16, 19, 23, 27, 30, 33, 35, 37, 39, 41, 42].

Table D-7

[190].

Table D-8

[182, Nos. 10, 26, 38, 44, 50, 56, 62, 72, 81, 87, 96, 105, 114, 122, 135].

Table D-9

[Nos. 16, 33, 38, 44, 53, 67, 75, 83, 88, 100, 106, 116, 125, 135].

Table D-10

1940, Bureau of the Census, *Current Population Reports: Annual Report on the Labor Force*, Series P-50, No. 19. 1947–64, Department of Labor, *Manpower Report of the President, March 1965*, p. 205.

Table D-11

1940, Bureau of the Census, *Current Population Reports: Annual Report on the Labor Force*, Series P-50, No. 11, p. 10. 1948–64, Department of Labor, *Manpower Report of the President, March 1965*, p. 216.

Table D-12

1940 and 1950 values are an approximation based on data for ever married women with children under five years old given in [12, p. 58]. The 1940 value refers to native white women; that for 1950, to total white. Figures shown as 14 and over are for those aged 15–49. 1948–64, [202, p. 218].

Table D-13

1940 and 1950, same as for Table D-12. 1951, 1959–63, Bureau of Labor Statistics, *Special Labor Force Report*, Nos. 7, 13, 20, 26, and 40.

Table D-14

[202, March 1965, p. 224].

Table D-15

1940–59, 1961, 1963, same source as for Table D-1 (from p. 5, Table 1, and p. 9, Table 4). Values for 1961 and 1963 were adjusted to levels for 1960's shown in next source. 1960, 1962, 1965–75, Bureau of the Census, *Current Population Reports: Population Estimates*, Series P-25, No. 286, p. 63.

Table D-16

1920–40, Bureau of the Census, *1950 Census of Population, U.S. Summary*, p. 1–238. The pre-1940 values were inferred from the values for the appropriate cohorts as reported in 1940, the first date at which data on educational attainment were collected. 1950, *ibid.*, p. 1–236. 1960–85, [183, No. 305].

Table D-17

[183, Nos. 98, 146, 170, 212, 265, 276, 286, 293].

E / APPENDIX FOR CHAPTER 6

TABLE E-1. TOTAL LABOR FORCE,
1870–1965
(thousands)

Date	Census Data	CPS Data
10 Years of Age and Over		
1870	12,925	
1880	17,392	
1890	23,195	
1900	28.838	
1910	36,271	
1920	41,811	
14 Years of Age and Over		
1920	41,433	
1930	48,595	
1940	52,789	56,180
1950	60,326	64,749
1955		68,896
1960		73,081 [a]
1965		78,357 [a]

[a] Includes Alaska and Hawaii. The value for 1960 omitting them = 72,820.

TABLE E-2. AVERAGE ANNUAL RATE OF CHANGE IN UNEMPLOY-
MENT RATE AND AVERAGE LEVEL OF UNEMPLOYMENT RATE, REAL
WAGE RATE, AND IMMIGRATION RATE, NBER REFERENCE CYCLES,
1890–1915

Reference Cycle (calendar years)	Unemployment Rate of Civilian Labor Force		Real Wage Rate, Manu-facturing (1957¢ per hr.) (3)	Reference Cycle (fiscal years) (4)	Gross Immigration Rate (per thousand total population per year) (5)
	Level (per cent) (1)	Rate of Change (percent-age points per year) (2)			
1890–92	4.4	−0.5	46.9	1890–93	8.0
1891–94	8.9	4.3	48.2	1891–94	7.2
1892–95	12.8	3.6	48.6	1893–96	4.5
1894–96	15.0	−2.0	48.5	1894–97	4.0
1895–99	12.8	−1.8	49.3	1896–1900	3.9
1896–1900	10.8	−2.4	50.1	1897–1901	4.5
1899–1903	4.5	−0.6	54.3	1900–03	7.6
1900–04	4.2	0.1	55.3	1901–04	9.0
1903–07	3.7	−0.3	57.4	1903–07	11.9
1904–08	3.9	0.6	58.2	1904–08	12.3
1907–10	5.8	1.0	59.2	1907–10	10.0
1908–11	6.1	−0.4	59.8	1908–11	9.6
1910–13	5.5	−0.5	61.4	1910–13	10.0
1911–14	5.4	0.4	62.1	1911–15	9.9

TABLE E-3. LEVEL AND RATE OF CHANGE OF INDUCED COMPONENT OF LABOR FORCE GROWTH AND UNEMPLOYMENT RATE: ACTUAL, 1870–1965; PROJECTED, 1965–70

Induced Component (contribution to labor force growth of participation-rate change plus net migration)		Unemployment Rate of Civilian Labor Force		Change Since Preceding Period (percentage points per decade [a])	
Period	Percentage Per Decade (1)	Period (2)	Percentage (3)	In Col. 1 (4)	In Col. 3 (5)
1870–80	13.3	1870–79	10 ?	–	–
1880–90	13.3	1880–89	4 ?	0	–6
1890–1900	8.7/7.5	1889–99	10.3	–4.6	6.3
1900–10	.9.7	1899–1909	4.5	2.2	–5.8
1910–20	4.6	1909–19	5.2	–5.1	0.7
1920–30	1.3/1.7	1919–29	4.6	–3.3	–0.6
1930–40	–3.6	1929–39	17.5	–5.3	12.9
1940–50	4.3	1939–49	5.7	+7.9	–11.8
....					
1940–50	6.4	1940–50	4.7	–	–
1950–55	7.0	1950–55	4.0	0.8	–0.9
1955–60	3.6	1955–60	5.2	–6.8	2.4
1960–65	2.4	1960–65	5.7	–2.4	1.0
		Projections: 1965–70			
BLS	5.5	1965–70	4.0	6.2	–3.4
Tella	7.6	1965–70	4.0	10.4	–3.4
Strand-Dernburg	13.5	1965–70	4.0	22.2	–3.4

[a] Changes from 1940–50 on adjusted to decade rate basis.

SOURCES AND METHODS

Table E-1

The sources are the same as those for labor force data in Table A-3.

Table E-2

Wage rate: same source as for Table B-2, series 9. *Immigration rate:* same sources as for Table B-1, series 7. *Unemployment rate:* [110, pp. 512, 522].

Table E-3

Labor force (sum of contributions to total labor force growth of net migration and participation rate change): 1870–1965, Table A-3; 1970, BLS, sources are the same as those for population, labor force, and migration based on 1964 population projections in Tables B-6 and B-7; 1970, [154, February 1965, p. 80]; 1970, [150, p. 389]. *Unemployment:* 1870–79, 1880–89, [110, p. 189] (question mark is in original); 1889–1929, [*ibid.*, pp. 512, 522]; 1929–65, [191, Vol. 12, No. 7 (January 1966), p. 1]; 1965–70, assumed. Unemployment averages for 1889 on are averages of annual estimates with terminal years weighted one-half.

F / APPENDIX FOR CHAPTERS 6 AND 7

THE BEARING OF DEFECTS IN CENSUS LABOR FORCE DATA ON THE LONG-SWINGS PATTERN

The analyst of historical census labor force data is in the unusual position of having the benefit of a number of major studies that have looked intensively into the problem of historical comparability.[1] The nature of the problems has been extensively described in these studies and there is no need to recount them here.[2] For the present purpose, what is especially relevant is that most of these studies attempt not only to identify specific comparability problems but also to adjust the original data, at least for the most serious defects. The analysis of labor force in Chapters 6 and 7 and elsewhere in the volume has been conducted on the basis of such adjusted series, the choice of the particular series depending primarily on the aspect of labor force under study (industry, sex-age, and so on) and the length of the series. The issue of whether the comparability problems seriously impair use of the census data for study of long swings can be reduced to two questions. First, do long swings in aggregate labor force growth appear in the original *unadjusted* data? Second, do long swings appear in the *adjusted* labor force series, and, if so, in those of all the experts, or only in a few?

In Figure F-1, the decade growth rates of total labor force since 1870 implied by the original census returns have been plotted at the top of the upper panel. Since the Census Office itself published a revised 1890 estimate, two series are shown through 1900, one using growth rates based on the original 1890 returns, and the other, on the revised 1890 returns. In the case of the revised series, the sawtooth pattern of long swings appears throughout the entire period. The same is true of the original series except for the first swing. The initial conclusion is therefore that long swings do appear in the original data, though in the case of the first swing (but only the first swing) this conclusion presupposes use of the revision of the 1890 data published by the Census Office itself.

A second way of approaching this question is to confine attention to the data for the nonagricultural sector of labor force. This is suggested by two considerations—first, many of the alleged defects of the data arise in connection with enumeration of the agricultural labor force, particularly unpaid women and child workers, and, second, the analysis in Part I of this study indicates that U.S. long swings after 1870 were predominantly a nonagricultural phenomenon.

Unfortunately, a precise identification of the nonagricultural labor force in the original returns for the censuses from 1870 to 1900 is handicapped

[1] Cf. [31, 52, 110, 111, 116, 173].
[2] For a succinct and excellent recent survey, cf. the Miller-Brainerd discussion in [111, pp. 401–409].

FIGURE F-1

AVERAGE GROWTH RATE OF TOTAL AND NONAGRICULTURAL LABOR FORCE:
COMPARISON OF VARIOUS ESTIMATES, DECENNIALLY, 1870–1950

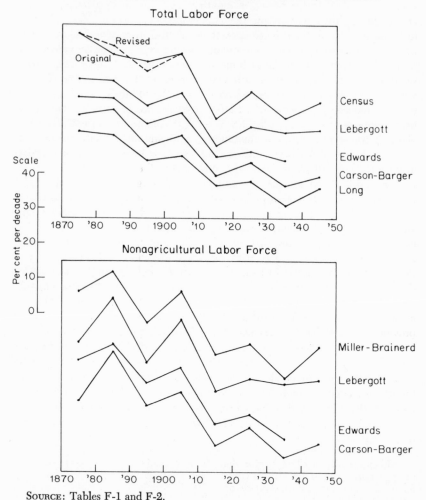

SOURCE: Tables F-1 and F-2.

by the existence of a sizable "laborers, not specified" category. The experts who have studied this problem agree that this category includes both agricultural and nonagricultural laborers and have attempted to estimate the distribution of these workers between the two sectors (cf. [111, p. 384] and the references cited therein). For the present purpose, use is made of the estimates of the nonagricultural labor force derived by Miller and

Brainerd. Preference is given to this series because together with the series for agriculture, it sums to the labor force totals in the original census returns for the entire 1870–1900 period. Thus the Miller-Brainerd series for *total* labor force in this period is identical with the original census series, and consequently fails to show the first swing.[3] The Miller-Brainerd series for nonagricultural labor force growth is plotted at the top of the lower panel of Figure F-1. The sawtooth pattern appears clearly in nonagricultural labor-force growth throughout the entire period even though their series for total labor-force growth does not show the first swing. To test whether this conclusion depended on the specific Miller-Brainerd allocation of the "laborers, not specified" (LNS) category, we constructed two alternate series—one assuming all LNS were agricultural, the other, that they were all nonagricultural. The sawtooth pattern still appeared. It seems reasonable to conclude, therefore, that long swings exist in the original census data on nonagricultural labor force throughout the entire period.

To turn to the second question, whether long swings appear in the adjusted series, and, if so, in all or just a few of the adjusted series, this is readily handled by adding to Figure F-1 the growth rates derived from the adjusted labor force estimates made by the various experts. A glance at the chart is sufficient to reveal that the adjusted series uniformly show the long swings pattern, differing only with regard to amplitude. The first swing in the growth of total labor force is shown more clearly in the adjusted series than in the census series, original or revised. This is because not only do all experts accept the need for adjusting the 1890 data, but they agree too on a similar need with regard to the 1870 data. The Census Office itself provided the justification for this. It not only recognized that the 1870 returns involved a general underenumeration in parts of the South, but actually itself developed a corrected estimate for population. It did not, however, attempt to extend this to labor force or other census magnitudes, though the need for such was clearly indicated. As is clear from the lower panel of the figure, with regard to those series for which separation of the nonagricultural labor force is possible, the sawtooth pattern appears even more markedly.[4]

[3] Miller and Brainerd recognize that there are defects in the total; they did not attempt to adjust for these because their primary interest was in state labor force estimates and an appropriate basis for differential adjustment of the state series was not available.

[4] The Lebergott series for the 1930–50 period shows only a mild movement. This is because Lebergott assumes that the various comparability problems are such that the 1940 CPS estimate may be taken as directly comparable with the 1930 census estimate, whereas all other investigators have linked the 1940 census data to the 1930 census data (though in some cases adjusting one or the other). Since the 1940 CPS level is much higher than the 1940 census level, Lebergott obtained a noticeably higher growth rate than other analysts for 1930–40 and a correspondingly lower rate for 1940–50.

TABLE F-1. COMPARISON OF ESTIMATES OF AVERAGE GROWTH RATE OF TOTAL LABOR FORCE,[a] 1870–1950 (per cent per decade)

	Census (1)	Edwards (2)	Durand (3)	Carson-Barger (4)	Long (5)	Lebergott (6)
1870–80	32.7	29.5	–	29.5	29.7	29.4
1880–90	26.6 (29.1)	29.1	–	30.9	28.6	29.1
1890–1900	24.5 (22.0)	22.0	24.4	20.2	21.7	22.0
1900–10	27.0	25.0	–	23.7	22.8	25.3
1910–20	8.6	12.7	–	12.1	14.2	10.4
1920–30	16.0	14.0	15.8	16.0	15.5	16.0
1930–40	8.3	11.7	11.7	9.2	8.3	14.2
1940–50	12.9	–	–	11.9	13.3	15.1

Col. 1. Census reports. Rates in parentheses are based on revised 1890 value published by the Bureau of the Census in [172, pp. lxvi–lxxiii].
Col. 2. [173, p. 91, except 1930 and 1940, p. 12].
Col. 3. [52, pp. 208–209].
Col. 4. [31, p. 47], except 1950, [13, p. 4].
Col. 5. Unrounded data underlying published estimates in [116, Tables A-1, A-2].
Col. 6. [110, p. 510]. Data for all dates are for those aged 10 and over.
[a] Aged 10 and over, 1870–1930; 14 and over, 1930–50.

TABLE F-2. COMPARISON OF ESTIMATES OF AVERAGE GROWTH RATE OF NONAGRICULTURAL LABOR FORCE,[a] 1870–1950 (per cent per decade)

	Miller-Brainerd (1)	Edwards (2)	Carson-Barger (3)	Lebergott (4)
1870–80	36.8	36.7	30.0	31.9
1880–90	42.1	41.2	44.0	44.8
1890–1900	27.4	30.3	28.8	26.2
1900–10	36.7	34.7	32.7	38.6
1910–20	18.2	18.3	17.7	18.1
1920–30	21.4	21.3	22.8	21.6
1930–40	11.9	14.4	14.2	19.9
1940–50	20.8	–	18.0	20.9

Col. 1. [111, p. 609, except 1940, p. 389]. Data for all dates are for those aged 10 and over.
Col. 2. [173, p. 91, except 1930–40, p. 12].
Col. 3. See preceding table, source for col. 4.
Col. 4. [110, pp. 510–511]. Data for all dates are for those aged 10 and over.
[a] Aged 10 and over, 1870–1930; 14 and over, 1930–50.

To sum up, in the case of nonagricultural labor force, long swings appear in the original census series and each adjusted series throughout the entire period. The same is true for total labor force, except that the original census returns fail to show the first swing. The census itself, however, revised the 1890 data and recognized the need for revision of the 1870 data, though confining its own efforts in the latter case to the population totals. In each case, the corrections lead to the long-swing pattern. It seems reasonable to conclude that the swings are not merely the product either of defects in the data or adjustments made to them. This conclusion is further strengthened by additional technical and analytical considerations mentioned in the text of Chapter 6.

G / APPENDIX FOR CHAPTER 7

TABLE G-1. LABOR FORCE PARTICIPATION RATE BY SEX-AGE GROUP, DECENNIALLY, 1900–60 (per cent)

	1900	1910	1920	1930	1940	1950	1940	1950	1960
	Census Data						CPS Data		
Both Sexes									
10 and over	49.8	50.7	50.5	49.5	52.2	53.7			
14 and over				54.5			55.3	57.3	57.4
Males									
10 and over	79.3	78.6	78.5	76.2	79.0	79.2			
14 and over				84.1			82.6	82.5	80.0
10–13	17.7	9.2	5.9	3.3					
14–19	74.9	72.3	70.1	62.3	57.7	59.9	44.0	53.1	46.3
20–24							95.2	90.9	88.9
25–34	96.3	96.8	98.1	97.6	95.0	93.3	96.6	94.0	96.4
35–44							96.8	93.3	96.4
45–54	93.3	93.8	94.0	94.1	88.7	88.2	93.8	93.7	94.3
55–64							85.4	86.3	85.2
65 and over	68.4	58.3	60.2	58.3	41.5	41.4	44.2	42.2	32.2
Females									
10 and over	18.7	20.8	21.2	22.0	25.4	29.0			
14 and over				24.3			27.9	32.7	36.1
10–13	6.1	3.9	2.9	1.5					
14–19	29.2	31.5	32.9	31.5	30.5	32.3	23.1	31.2	30.1
20–24							49.2	45.8	46.1
25–34	18.0	21.0	22.6	25.4	30.2	33.3	35.0	33.7	35.8
35–44							28.7	38.2	43.1
45–54	14.1	17.2	17.2	18.7	19.8	28.8	24.1	38.1	49.3
55–64							18.3	27.4	36.7
65 and over	9.0	8.6	8.0	8.0	5.9	7.8	7.2	9.0	10.5

TABLE G-2. AGE PROFILE OF CHANGE IN LABOR
FORCE PARTICIPATION RATES BY SEX: AVERAGE
OF DECADES 1900–40 COMPARED WITH THAT OF
DECADES 1940–60
(per cent per decade)

	1900–40 (Census Data)	1940–60 (CPS Data)
Males		
10–13	−4.8 [a]	n.a.
14–19	−4.3	1.2
20–24		−3.2
25–34	−0.4	−0.1
35–44		−0.2
45–54	−1.2	0.3
55–64		−0.1
65 and over	−6.7	−5.9
Females		
10–13	−1.5 [a]	n.a.
14–19	0.3	3.5
20–24		−1.7
25–34	3.1	0.4
35–44		7.2
45–54	1.4	12.7
55–64		9.2
65 and over	−0.8	1.7

Note: n.a. = not applicable.
[a] 1900–30.

TABLE G-3. PREDICTED AND ACTUAL AGE PROFILE OF CHANGE IN LABOR FORCE PARTICIPATION RATES, BY SEX, DECENNIALLY, 1900–60 [a]

(per cent per decade)

	1900–10		1910–20		1920–30		1940–50		1950–60	
	Predicted	Actual	Predicted	Actual	Predicted	Actual	Predicted	Actual	Predicted	Actual
	Census Data						*CPS Data*			
Males										
10–13	−3.0	−8.5	−3.5	−3.0	−4.0	−2.6	−2.9	9.1	−5.3	−6.7
14–19 ⎱	−0.8	−2.6	−0.7	−2.2	−6.4	−7.8	−3.6	−4.3	−3.2	−2.2
20–24 ⎰							0.3	−2.6	0.9	2.4
25–34 ⎱	0.1	0.5	0.2	1.3	0.1	−0.6	0.7	−3.5	1.3	3.2
35–44 ⎰							1.3	−0.1	1.2	0.7
45–54 ⎱	0.3	0.5	0.3	0.2	0.2	0.1	3.0	0.9	2.6	−1.0
55–64 ⎰										
65 and over	0	−10.1	0	1.9	0	−1.8	−3.2	−1.9	−7.6	−9.9
Females										
10–13	−3.1	−2.2	−3.1	−1.0	−2.8	−1.3	2.1	8.1	−2.0	−1.1
14–19 ⎱	0.3	2.3	0.4	1.4	−1.7	−1.4	−6.6	−3.4	−3.4	0.1
20–24 ⎰							−2.5	−1.4	−0.8	2.1
25–34 ⎱	1.1	3.0	1.4	1.7	1.2	2.8	9.1	9.5	5.8	4.9
35–44 ⎰							15.7	14.1	11.9	11.2
45–54 ⎱	3.2	3.0	4.0	0	3.5	1.5	16.9	9.1	13.9	9.3
55–64 ⎰										
65 and over	0	−0.4	0	−0.6	0	0	0	1.8	0	1.5

[a] Except 1930–40.

TABLE G-4. PREDICTED AND PROJECTED
AGE PROFILE OF CHANGE IN LABOR FORCE
PARTICIPATION RATES, BY SEX, 1960–70
(per cent per decade)

	Predicted	Projected
Males		
14–19	−3.1	−1.9
20–24	−4.1	−2.3
25–34	0.4	−0.2
35–44	0.5	0.3
45–54	0.8	0.7
55–64	−3.2	−0.9
65 and over	−2.4	−7.1
Females		
14–19	−0.8	0
20–24	−0.3	4.2
25–34	0.7	2.8
35–44	4.4	4.4
45–54	6.9	6.0
55–64	8.7	7.1
65 and over	0	−0.7

SOURCES AND METHODS

Tables G-1, G-2, G-3 (Actual), and G-4 (Projected)

Rates were computed from the population and labor force data for 1890–1950 and 1940–65 described in sources for Table A-3. 1970 data, from [35, p. 130]. (Data for 1960 and 1970 include Alaska and Hawaii.)

Tables G-3 and G-4 (Predicted)

Sex-age distributions of the "domestic" working-age population (i.e., excluding immigration during the preceding decade) obtained in the components of change analysis were used (cf. sources for Table A-3). For estimates of population and labor force by school-enrollment status, marital, and child-dependency status, use was made of [12, pp. 46, 54, 58], [52, p. 231], [116, Tables A-2, A-6], [174, p. 17], [177, p. 114], [195, pp. A-8, A-13], [196, p. 14], [202, p. 221], and relevant tables in the census summary volumes for 1950 and 1960. Projected population distributions for 1970 by these characteristics based on series B population projections, underlying [35], were kindly supplied by BLS.

BIBLIOGRAPHY

BIBLIOGRAPHY

1. Abramovitz, M., *Evidences of Long Swings in Aggregate Construction since the Civil War*, New York, NBER, 1964.
2. ———, "Growing Up in An Affluent Society," in Eli Ginzberg (ed.), *The Nation's Children*, Vol. I: *The Family and Social Change*, New York, 1960.
3. ———, in National Bureau of Economic Research, 37th, 38th, 39th, and 40th Annual Reports, New York, 1957–60.
4. ———, "The Nature and Significance of Kuznets Cycles," *Economic Development and Cultural Change*, April 1961, pp. 225–248.
5. ———, Statement in Hearings before the Joint Economic Committee, 86th Cong., 1st Sess., Pt. 2, *Historical and Comparative Rates of Production, Productivity, and Prices*, Washington, 1959, pp. 411–466.
6. ———, and David, P. A., "Preliminary Notes on the Postwar and Long-Term Growth Experience of the United States," Research Center in Economic Growth, Stanford University, January 1964, mimeo.
7. Adelman, I., "An Econometric Analysis of Population Growth," *American Economic Review*, June 1963, pp. 314–339.
8. ———, "Business Cycles—Endogenous or Stochastic?," *Economic Journal*, December 1960, pp. 783–796.
9. ———, "Long Cycles—A Simulation Experiment," in F. Balderston and A. C. Hogatt (eds.), *Proceedings of a Conference on Simulation*, Cincinnati, 1964.
10. ———, "Long Cycles—Fact or Artifact?," *American Economic Review*, June 1965, pp. 444–463.
11. Alterman, J., "The Federal Government's Program of Economic Growth Studies," ASA 7th Annual Forecasting Conference, New York, April 23, 1965.
12. Bancroft, G., *The American Labor Force: Its Growth and Changing Composition*, New York, 1958.
13. Barger, H., *Distribution's Place in the American Economy since 1869*, New York, NBER, 1955.
14. Becker, G. S., "An Economic Analysis of Fertility," in *Demographic and Economic Change in Developed Countries*, Princeton University Press for NBER, 1960, pp. 209–231.
15. Beckford, G. L. F., "Secular Fluctuations in the Growth of Tropical Agricultural Trade," *Economic Development and Cultural Change*, October 1964, pp. 80–94.

16. Bernstein, E. M., "The Postwar Trend Cycle in the United States," *Quarterly Review*, First Quarter, 1963, pp. 1–10.
17. Berry, T., *Western Prices before 1861: A Study of the Cincinnati Market*, Cambridge, Mass., 1943.
18. Bird, R. C.; Desai, M. J.; Enzler, J. J.; and Taubman, P., "Kuznets Cycles in Growth Rates: Their Meaning," *International Economic Review*, May 1965, pp. 229–239.
19. Bogue, D. J., *The Population of the United States*, Glencoe, Ill., 1959.
20. Borrie, W. D., "Demographic Cycles and Economic Development: Some Observations Based Upon Australian Experience," *Population Index*, January 1960, pp. 3–15.
21. Bowen, W. G., and Berry, R. A., "Unemployment Conditions and Movements of the Money Wage Level," *Review of Economics and Statistics*, May 1963, pp. 163–172.
22. Brady, D. S., *Age and Income Distribution*, Washington, 1965.
22a. ———, and Friedman, R. O., "Savings and the Income Distribution," Studies in Income and Wealth 10, New York, NBER, 1947.
22b. Bratt, E. C., "Recent Thinking on Economic Growth and Fluctuations," *Annals*, March 1966, pp. 162–163.
23. Bridge, L., "The Financing of Investment by New Firms," in *Conference on Research in Business Finance*, Universities-National Bureau Conference Series 3, New York, NBER, 1952, pp. 65–75.
24. Buckley, K. A. H., *Growth and Housing Requirements: A Report on Economic and Social Aspects of the Housing Problem in Saskatoon*, Saskatoon, Canada, 1958.
25. ———, "The Role of Staple Industries in Canada's Economic Development," *Journal of Economic History*, December 1958, pp. 439–452.
26. ———, "Urban Building and Real Estate Fluctuations in Canada," *Canadian Journal of Economics and Political Science*, February 1952, pp. 41–62.
27. Burns, A. F., *Production Trends in the United States since 1870*, New York, NBER, 1934.
28. Campbell, A. A., "Recent Fertility Trends in the United States and Canada," in *Proceedings of the World Population Conference, 1965*, Vol. II, United Nations, New York, 1967, pp. 200–204.
29. Campbell, B. O., *Population Change and Building Cycles*, Urbana, Illinois, 1966.
30. ———, "Long Swings in Residential Construction: The Postwar Experience," *American Economic Review*, May 1963, pp. 508–518.
31. Carson, D., "Changes in the Industrial Composition of Manpower since the Civil War," in Conference on Research in Income and Wealth, *Studies in Income and Wealth 11*, New York, NBER, 1949, pp. 46–134.

32. Coale, A. J., and Zelnik, M., *New Estimates of Fertility and Population in the United States*, Princeton, 1963.
33. Cole, A. H., "Cyclical and Sectional Variations in the Sale of Public Lands, 1816–60," *Review of Economics and Statistics*, January 1927, pp. 41–53.
34. Conference on Research in Income and Wealth, *Output, Employment, and Productivity in the United States after 1800*, Studies in Income and Wealth 30, New York, NBER, 1966.
35. Cooper, S., and Johnston, D. F., "Labor Force Projections for 1970–1980," *Monthly Labor Review*, February 1965, pp. 129–140.
36. Creamer, D., *Capital Expansion and Capacity in Postwar Manufacturing*, New York, 1961.
37. ———, *Recent Changes in Manufacturing Capacity*, New York, 1962.
38. ———; Dobrovolsky, S. P.; and Borenstein, I., *Capital in Manufacturing and Mining: Its Formation and Financing*, Princeton for NBER, 1962.
39. Daly, D. J., "Kuznets Cycles in Canada," paper presented to the Ottawa Chapter, Canadian Political Science Association, March 1962.
40. ———, "Long Cycles and Recent Canadian Experience," in Royal Commission on Banking and Finance, *Appendix Volume*, Ottawa, 1964, pp. 279–301.
41. ———, "The Scope for Monetary Policy—A Synthesis," unpublished paper, Conference on Stabilization Policy, University of Western Ontario, August 30–September 1, 1965.
42. David, Paul A., "Factories at the Prairies' Edge: A Study of Industrialization in Chicago, 1848–1893," doctoral dissertation in process, Harvard University.
43. Davis, J. S., "Implications of Prospective United States Population Growth in the 1960's," *Milbank Memorial Fund Quarterly*, April 1961, pp. 329–349.
44. ———, "The Population Upsurge and the American Economy, 1945–80," *Journal of Political Economy*, October 1953, pp. 369–388.
45. ———, *The Population Upsurge in the United States*, War-Peace Pamphlet No. 12, Stanford, Calif., 1949.
46. Davis, K., "The Theory of Change and Response in Modern Demographic History," *Population Index*, October 1963, pp. 345–366.
47. Denison, E. F., "Discussion," *American Economic Review*, May 1963, pp. 530–532.
48. Dernburg, T. F., and Strand, K. T., "Hidden Unemployment 1953–62: A Quantitative Analysis by Age and Sex," *American Economic Review*, March 1966, pp. 71–95.
49. ———, "Manpower Gap," *Challenge*, December 1964, pp. 41–43.
50. Douglas, P. H., *Real Wages in the United States, 1890–1926*, New York, 1930.

51. Duesenberry, J. S., *Income, Saving, and the Theory of Consumer Behavior*, Cambridge, Mass., 1949.

51a. Duncan, O. D., "Farm Background and Differential Fertility," *Demography*, 1965, Vol. II.

52. Durand, J. D., *The Labor Force in the United States, 1890–1960*, New York, 1948.

53. Easterlin, R. A., "Discussion," *1964 Proceedings of the Business and Economic Statistic Section of the American Statistical Association*, pp. 387–392.

54. ———, "Influences in European Overseas Emigration before World War I," *Economic Development and Cultural Change*, April 1961, pp. 331–351.

55. ———, "Long Swings in U.S. Demographic and Economic Growth: Some Findings on the Historical Pattern," *Demography*, 1965, Vol. II, pp. 490–507.

56. ———, On the Relation of Economic Factors to Recent and Projected Fertility Changes," *Demography*, 1966, Vol. III, pp. 131–153.

57. Economic Council of Canada, *First Annual Review: Economic Goals for Canada to 1970*, Ottawa, 1964.

58. *Economic Report of the President*, Washington, various dates.

59. Eldridge, H. T., and Thomas, D. S., *Population Redistribution and Economic Growth, United States, 1870–1950*, Vol. III: *Demographic Analyses and Interrelations*, Philadelphia, 1964.

60. Evans, G. H., Jr., *Business Incorporations in the United States, 1800–1943*, New York, NBER, 1948.

61. Evans, W. D., and Hoffenberg, M., "The Interindustry Relations Study for 1947," *Review of Economics and Statistics*, May 1952, pp. 97–142.

62. Eversley, D. E. C., and Jackson, V., "Problems Encountered in Forecasting Housing Demand in an Area of High Economic Activity: Headship Rates in Relation to Age Structure, Fertility, Education, and Socio-Economic Groups," in *World Population Conference, 1965*, Vol. IV, United Nations, New York, 1967, pp. 418–422.

63. Fels, R., "Discussion," *American Economic Review*, May 1963, pp. 533–534.

64. Ferber, R., "Research on Household Behavior," *American Economic Review*, March 1962, pp. 19–63.

65. Ferenczi, I., *International Migrations, I: Statistics*, Walter F. Willcox (ed.), New York, NBER, 1929.

66. Fishlow, A., *American Railroads and the Transformation of the Ante-Bellum Economy*, Cambridge, Mass., 1965.

67. Freedman, R., "Norms for Family Size in Underdeveloped Areas," *Proceedings of the Royal Society*, 1963, B, Vol. 159, pp. 220–245.

68. ———; Goldberg, D.; and Bumpass, L., "Current Fertility Expectations

of Married Couples in the United States: 1963," *Population Index,* January 1965, pp. 3–20.

69. ———; Whelpton, P. K.; and Campbell, A. A., *Family Planning, Sterility, and Population Growth,* New York, 1959.

70. Frickey, E., *Production in the United States, 1890–1914,* Cambridge, Mass., 1947.

71. Fuchs, V. R., "Action Programs to Deal with Unemployment," *1961 Proceedings of the Business and Economic Statistics Section of the American Statistical Association,* pp. 162–166.

72. ———, "Population Growth Concepts and the Economy of Tomorrow," *Commercial and Financial Chronicle,* December 13, 1956.

73. Galbraith, V. L., and Thomas, D. S., "Birth Rates and the Interwar Business Cycles," *Journal of the American Statistical Association,* December 1941, pp. 465–476.

74. Gallaway, L. E., *The Retirement Decision: An Exploratory Essay,* Department of Health, Education, and Welfare, Social Security Administration, Division of Research and Statistics, Research Report No. 9, Washington, 1965.

74a. Gallman, R. E., in *Trends in the American Economy in the Nineteenth Century,* Studies in Income and Wealth 24, Princeton for NBER, 1960.

74b. ———, in *Output, Employment, and Productivity in the United States After 1800,* Studies in Income and Wealth 30, New York, NBER, 1966.

75. Gerschenkron, A., *Economic Backwardness in Historical Perspective,* Cambridge, Mass., 1962.

76. Goodrich, C.; Cranmer, H. J.; and Segal, H. H., *Canals and American Economic Development,* New York, 1961.

77. Gordon, M. S., *Employment Expansion and Population Growth: The California Experience: 1900–1950,* Berkeley, Calif., 1954.

78. Gordon, R. A., "Discussion," *American Economic Review,* May 1963, pp. 537–540.

79. ———, "What Kind of a Business Cycle in the Years Ahead?," *Commercial and Financial Chronicle,* September 5, 1963, pp. 3 ff.

80. ———, and Gordon, M. S. (eds.), *Prosperity and Unemployment,* New York, 1966.

81. Gottlieb, M., "Fluctuations in Marriage and Migration Experience in Long Swings in Economic Growth," abstracted in *World Population Conference, 1965,* Vol. IV, United Nations, New York, 1967, pp. 464–465.

82. Grabill, W. H.; Kiser, C. V.; and Whelpton, P. K., *The Fertility of American Women,* New York, 1958.

83. Gutman, R., "The Birth Statistics of Massachusetts during the Nineteenth Century," *Population Studies,* July 1956, pp. 69–94.

84. Hagen, E. E., "Population and Economic Growth," *American Economic Review,* June 1959, pp. 310–327.

85. Hall, A. R., "Some Long Period Effects of the Kinked Age Distribution of the Population of Australia 1861–1961," *Economic Record*, March 1963, pp. 43–52.

86. Hansen, A. H., "Economic Progress and Declining Population Growth," *American Economic Review*, March 1939, pp. 1–15.

87. ———, *Fiscal Policy and Business Cycles*, New York, 1941.

88. Hickman, B. G., *Growth and Stability in the Postwar Economy*, Washington, 1960.

89. ———, "The Long Cycle: Hidden Force in the Economy," *Dun's Review and Modern Industry*, December 1963, pp. 48 ff.

90. ———, "The Postwar Retardation: Another Long Swing in the Rate of Growth?," *American Economic Review*, May 1963, pp. 490–507.

91. "Housing of Nonfarm Families," *Federal Reserve Bulletin*, September 1959, pp. 1097–1113.

92. Isard, W., "A Neglected Cycle: The Transport-Building Cycle," *Review of Economics and Statistics*, November 1942, pp. 149–158.

93. ———, "Transport Development and Building Cycles," *Quarterly Journal of Economics*, November 1942, pp. 90–110.

94. Jaffe, A. J., and Carleton, R. O., *Occupational Mobility in the United States, 1930–1960*, New York, 1954.

95. ———, and Stewart, C. D., *Manpower Resources and Utilization*, New York, 1951.

96. Jerome, H., *Migration and Business Cycles*, New York, NBER, 1926.

97. Jones, E. B., "New Estimates of Hours of Work Per Week and Hourly Earnings," *Review of Economics and Statistics*, November 1963, pp. 374–385.

97a. Kaplan, D. L., and Casey, M. C., *Occupational Trends in the United States, 1900 to 1950*, Bureau of the Census Working Paper No. 5, Washington, 1958.

98. Kelley, A. C., "International Migration and Economic Growth: Australia, 1865–1935," *Journal of Economic History*, September 1965, pp. 333–354.

99. Kendrick, J. W., *Productivity Trends in the United States*, Princeton for NBER, 1961.

100. Keynes, J. M., "Some Economic Consequences of a Declining Population," *Eugenics Review*, April 1937, pp. 13–17.

101. Kramm, E. R., and Thomas, D. S., "Rural and Urban Marriage in Relation to the Sex Ratio," *Rural Sociology*, March 1942, pp. 33–39.

102. Kuznets, S., *Capital in the American Economy: Its Formation and Financing*, Princeton for NBER, 1961.

103. ———, "Long Swings in the Growth of Population and in Related Economic Variables," *Proceedings of the American Philosophical Society*, February 1958, pp. 25–52.

104. ———, "Quantitative Aspects of Economic Growth of Nations, I:

Levels and Variability of Rates of Growth," *Economic Development and Cultural Change,* October 1956, pp. 1–94.

105. ———, *Secular Movements in Production and Prices,* New York, 1930.

106. ———; Miller, A. R.; and Easterlin, R. A., *Population Redistribution and Economic Growth, United States, 1870–1950,* II: *Analyses of Economic Change,* Philadelphia, 1960.

107. ———, and Rubin, E., *Immigration and the Foreign Born,* New York, NBER, 1954.

108. Lansing, J. B., and Morgan, J. N., "Consumer Finances over the Life Cycle," in L. H. Clark (ed.), *Consumer Behavior,* Vol. II: *The Life Cycle and Consumer Behavior,* New York, 1955, pp. 36–51.

109. Lebergott, S., "Annual Estimates of Unemployment in the United States, 1900–1954," in *The Measurement and Behavior of Unemployment,* Universities-National Bureau Conference Series 8, Princeton for NBER, 1957.

110. ———, *Manpower in Economic Growth: The American Record since 1800,* New York, 1964.

111. Lee, E. S.; Miller, A. R.; Brainerd, C.; and Easterlin, R. A., *Population Redistribution and Economic Growth, United States, 1870–1950,* I: *Methodological Considerations and Reference Tables,* Philadelphia, 1957.

112. Leibenstein, H., *Economic Backwardness and Economic Growth,* New York, 1957.

113. Lewis, J. P., *Building Cycles and Britain's Growth,* New York, 1965.

114. ———, "Growth and Inverse Cycles: A Two-Country Model," *Economic Journal,* March 1964, pp. 109–118.

115. Long, C. D., "The Illusion of Wage Rigidity: Long and Short Cycles in Wages and Labor Costs," *Review of Economics and Statistics,* May 1960, pp. 140–151.

116. ———, *The Labor Force under Changing Income and Employment,* Princeton for NBER, 1958.

117. Losch, A., *Bevolkerungswellen und Wechsellagen. Beitrage zur Ertorschung der wirtshaftlichen Wechsellagen. Autschwung, Krise, Stockung,* Vol. XIII, Jena, 1936.

118. ———, "Population Cycles as a Cause of Business Cycles," *Quarterly Journal of Economics,* 1937, pp. 649–662.

119. Madden, C. H., "On Some Indications of Stability in the Growth of Cities in the United States," *Economic Development and Cultural Change,* April 1956, pp. 236–252.

120. ———, "Some Spatial Aspects of Urban Growth in the United States," *Economic Development and Cultural Change,* July 1956, pp. 371–387.

121. ———, "Some Temporal Aspects of the Growth of Cities in the United States," *Economic Development and Cultural Change,* January 1958, pp. 143–170.

122. Marker, Gordon, "Internal Migration and Economic Opportunity, France, 1872–1911," unpublished doctoral dissertation, University of Pennsylvania, 1964.
123. Matthews, R. C. O., *The Business Cycle*, Chicago, 1959.
124. Mayer, K., "Diminishing Class Differentials in the United States," *Kyklos*, XII, 1959, Fasc. 4, pp. 605–628.
125. McDougall, D. M., "Immigration into Canada, 1851–1920," *Canadian Journal of Economics and Political Science*, May 1961, pp. 162–175.
126. Miller, A. R., "Components of Labor Force Growth," *Journal of Economic History*, March 1962.
127. Mincer, J., "Labor Force Participation and Unemployment: A Review of Recent Evidence," in R. A. Gordon and M. S. Gordon (eds.), *Prosperity and Unemployment*, New York, 1966, pp. 73–112.
128. ———, "Labor Force Participation of Married Women," in *Aspects of Labor Economics*, Universities-National Bureau Conference Series 14, Princeton for NBER, 1962, pp. 63–105.
128a. Minsky, H. P., "Longer Waves in Financial Relations: Financial Factors in the More Severe Depressions," *American Economic Review*, May 1964, pp. 324–335.
129. Mintz, I., "Discussion," *American Economic Review*, May 1963, pp. 534–537.
130. Modigliani, F., "Fluctuations in the Saving-Income Ratio: A Problem in Economic Forecasting," *Studies in Income and Wealth* 11, New York, NBER, 1949, pp. 371–443.
131. North, D. C., *The Economic Growth of the United States, 1790–1860*, Englewood Cliffs, N.J., 1961.
132. Okun, B., *Trends in Birth Rates in the United States since 1870*, Baltimore, 1958.
133. O'Leary, P. J., and Lewis, W. A., "Secular Swings in Production and Trade, 1870–1913," *Manchester School of Economic and Social Studies*, May 1955, pp. 113–152.
134. Orcutt, G. H., et al., *Microanalysis of Socioeconomic Systems: A Simulation Study*, New York, 1961.
135. Palmore, E., "Retirement Patterns Among Aged Men: Findings of the 1963 Survey of the Aged," *Social Security Bulletin*, August 1964, pp. 3–10.
136. President's Committee to Appraise Employment and Unemployment Statistics, *Measuring Employment and Unemployment*, Washington, 1962.
137. Rosovsky, H., and Ohkawa, K., "Economic Fluctuations in Pre-War Japan: A Preliminary Analysis of Cycles and Long Swings," *Hitotsubashi Journal of Economics*, October 1962, pp. 10–33.
138. Ross, A. M. (ed.), *Unemployment and the American Economy*, New York, 1964.

139. Rostow, W. W., *The Stages of Economic Growth,* Cambridge, England, 1961.
140. Schmookler, J., "Economic Sources of Inventive Activity," *Journal of Economic History,* March 1962, pp. 1–20.
141. Schumpeter, J. A., *Business Cycles,* New York, 1939.
142. Shinohara, M., "Growth and the Long Swing in the Japanese Economy," *Hitotsubashi Journal of Economics,* October 1960, pp. 59–83.
143. Siegel, J. S., and Akers, D. S., "Outlook for Population at Mid-Decade," *American Statistical Association: 1964 Proceedings of the Business and Economic Section,* pp. 358–366.
144. ———; Zitter, M.; and Akers, D. S., *Projections of the Population of the United States, by Age and Sex: 1964 to 1985,* July 1964.
145. Silberling, N. J., *The Dynamics of Business,* New York, 1943.
145a. Silver, M., "Births, Marriages, and Business Cycles in the United States," *Journal of Political Economy,* June 1965, pp. 237–255.
146. ———, "Births, Marriages, and Income Fluctuations in the United Kingdom and Japan," *Economic Development and Cultural Change,* April 1966, pp. 302–315.
146a. Simon, M., "The Pattern of New British Portfolio Investment, 1865–1914," mimeo., 1965.
147. Smith, W. B., "Wage Rates on the Erie Canal, 1828–1881," *Journal of Economic History,* September 1963, pp. 298–311.
147a. Smolensky, E., and Ratajczak, D., "The Conception of Cities," *Explorations in Entrepreneurial History,* II (1965), pp. 90–131.
148. Somers, A. T., "The Economic Environment of the Middle Sixties," *Conference Board Record,* September 1964.
149. Spengler, J. J., *The Fecundity of Native and Foreign-Born Women in New England,* Washington, 1930.
150. Strand, K., and Dernburg, T., "Cyclical Variation in Civilian Labor Force Participation," *Review of Economics and Statistics,* November 1964, pp. 378–391.
151. Strauss, F., and Bean, L. H., *Gross Farm Income and Indices of Farm Production and Prices in the United States, 1869–1937,* Washington, 1940.
152. Swerling, B. C., *Agriculture and Recent Economic Conditions,* San Francisco, 1959.
153. Taeuber, C. and I. B., *The Changing Population of the United States,* New York, 1958.
154. Tella, A., "Labor Force Sensitivity to Employment by Age, Sex," *Industrial Relations,* February 1965, pp. 69–83.
155. ———, "The Relation of Labor Force to Employment," *Industrial and Labor Relations Review,* April 1964, pp. 454–469.
156. Thomas, B., *Migration and Economic Growth,* Cambridge, Eng., 1954.

157. ———, "Wales and the Atlantic Economy," *Scottish Journal of Political Economy,* November 1959, pp. 169–192.

158. Thomas, D. S., "Age and Economic Differentials in Interstate Migration," *Population Index,* October 1958, pp. 313–324.

159. ———, "International Migration," in Philip M. Hauser (ed.), *Population and World Politics,* Glencoe, Ill., 1958, pp. 137–161.

160. ———, "Some Aspects of a Study of Population Redistribution in the United States, 1870–1950," *Proceedings of the World Population Conference,* 1954, Rome, 31 August-10 September, United Nations, New York, 1956–57, Vol. II, pp. 667–713.

161. ———, *Social Aspects of the Business Cycle,* New York, 1925.

162. ———, *Social and Economic Aspects of Swedish Population Movements, 1750–1933,* New York, 1941.

163. ———, and Zachariah, K. C., "Some Temporal Variations in Internal Migration and Economic Activity, United States, 1880–1950," International Union for the Scientific Study of Population, *International Population Conference, New York, 1961,* London, 1963, Vol. I, pp. 525–532.

164. Thompson, W. S., and Whelpton, P. K., *Population Trends in the United States,* New York, 1933.

164a. Thorp, W. L., *Business Annals,* New York, NBER, 1926, p. 105.

165. Tiebout, C. M., *The Community Economic Base Study,* New York, 1962.

166. T'ien, H. Y., "A Demographic Aspect of Interstate Variations in American Fertility, 1800–1860," *Milbank Memorial Fund Quarterly,* January 1959, pp. 49–59.

167. Tostlebe, A., *Capital in Agriculture: Its Formation and Financing since 1870,* Princeton, 1957.

168. Ulmer, M. J., *Capital in Transportation, Communication, and Public Utilities: Its Formation and Financing,* Princeton, 1960.

169. United Nations Department of Social Affairs, *The Determinants and Consequences of Population Trends,* New York, 1953.

170. Universities-National Bureau Committee for Economic Research, *Demographic and Economic Change in Developed Countries,* Princeton for NBER, 1960.

171. ———, *The Measurement and Behavior of Unemployment,* Princeton for NBER, 1957.

172. U.S. Bureau of the Census, *Census of Population: 1900, Special Report: Occupations,* Washington, 1904.

173. ———, *Census of Population: 1940, Comparative Occupation Statistics for the United States, 1870 to 1940,* Washington, 1943.

174. ———, *Census of Population: 1940, Population Characteristics of Persons Not in the Labor Force,* Washington, 1943.

175. ———, *Census of Population: 1940*, Vol. II: *Characteristics of the Population, United States Summary*, Washington, 1943.
176. ———, *Census of Population: 1950, United States Summary*, Washington, 1953.
177. ———, *Census of Population: 1950, Special Report P-E No. 1A: Employment and Personal Characteristics*, Washington, 1953.
178. ———, *Census of Population: 1950, Special Report P-E No. 3A: Nativity and Parentage*, Washington, 1953.
179. ———, *Census of Population: 1960, United States Summary*, Washington, 1963.
180. ———, *Current Population Reports: Consumer Income*, Ser. P-60.
181. ———, *Current Population Reports: Labor Force Bulletin*, Ser. P-50.
182. ———, *Current Population Reports: Population Characteristics*, Ser. P-20.
183. ———, *Current Population Reports: Population Estimates*, Ser. P-25.
184. ———, *Farm Population: 1880 to 1950*, Technical Paper No. 3, Washington, 1960.
185. ———, *Forecasts of the Population of the United States 1945–1975*, Washington, 1947.
186. ———, *Historical Statistics of the United States, Colonial Times to 1957*, Washington, 1960.
187. ———, *Historical Statistics of the United States, Colonial Times to 1957; Continuation to 1962 and Revisions*, Washington, 1965.
188. ———, *Immigrants and Their Children, 1920*, Washington, 1927.
189. ———, *Ratio of Children to Women, 1920*, Washington, 1931.
190. ———, *Statistical Abstract of the United States, 1960*, Washington, 1960.
191. U.S. Bureau of Labor Statistics, *Employment and Earnings*, Washington, 1961.
192. ———, *Population and Labor Force Projections for the United States, 1960 to 1975*, Bulletin No. 1242, Washington, 1959.
193. ———, Special Labor Force Report No. 24, *Interim Revised Projections of United States Labor Force, 1965–75*, Washington, 1962.
194. ———, Special Labor Force Report No. 49, *Labor Force Projections for 1970–80*, Washington, 1965.
195. ———, Special Labor Force Report No. 13, *Marital and Family Characteristics of Workers, March 1960*, reprint from *Monthly Labor Review*, April 1961.
196. ———, Special Labor Force Report No. 20, *Marital and Family Characteristics of Workers, March 1961*, reprint from *Monthly Labor Review*, January 1962.
197. U.S. Department of Agriculture, *Agricultural Statistics 1960*, Washington, 1961.
198. ———, Agricultural Marketing Service, *Farm Population: Effect of*

Definition Changes in Size and Composition of the Rural Farm Population, April 1960 and 1959, Series Census-AMS (P-27), Washington, April 17, 1961.

199. ———, Agricultural Marketing Service, *Farm Population Estimates for 1950–1959*, AMS-80 (1959), Washington, February 1960.

200. ———, Agricultural Marketing Service, *Farm Population: Migration to and from Farms, 1920–54*, AMS-10, Washington, December 1954.

201. U.S. Department of Health, Education, and Welfare, Public Health Service, National Center for Health Statistics, *Natality Statistics Analysis: United States—1962*, Series 21, No. 1, Washington, 1964.

202. U.S. Department of Labor, *Manpower Report of the President*, Washington, 1963, 1964, 1965.

203. U.S. Housing and Home Finance Agency, *Population Growth in Standard Metropolitan Areas, 1900–1950*, Washington, 1953.

204. U.S. National Resources Committee, *Population Statistics, 1: National Data*, Washington, 1937.

205. ———, *The Problems of a Changing Population*, Washington, 1938.

206. U.S. National Resources Planning Board, *Estimates of the Future Population of the United States 1940–2000*, Washington, 1943.

207. U.S. Office of Business Economics, *U.S. Income and Output*, Washington, 1958.

208. U.S. Office of Manpower, Automation and Training, "Manpower and Immigration," *Manpower Report*, November 20, 1962.

209. U.S. Public Health Service, *Vital Statistics of the United States 1958*, Vol. I, Washington, 1960.

210. ———, *Monthly Vital Statistics Report*, May 31, 1961.

211. U.S. Senate, 61st Congress, 3rd Sess., Doc. No. 747, Reports of the Immigration Commission, *Abstracts of Reports of the Immigration Commission*, Washington, 1911, Vol. I; Vol. II, pp. 451–500.

212. Walker, F. A., "Immigration and Degradation," *Forum*, August 1891, pp. 634–644.

213. ———, "Restriction of Immigration," *Atlantic Monthly*, June 1896, pp. 822–829.

214. Weintraub, R., "The Birth Rate and Economic Development: An Empirical Study," *Econometrica*, October 1962.

215. Wilkinson, M., "Evidences of Long Swings in the Growth of Swedish Population and Related Economic Variables," *Journal of Economic History*, March 1967, pp. 17–38.

216. Williamson, J. G., *American Growth and the Balance of Payments, 1820–1913*, Chapel Hill, N.C., 1964.

217. ———, "Dollar Scarcity and Surplus in Historical Perspective," *American Economic Review*, May 1963, pp. 519–529.

218. Wolfbein, S. L., *Employment and Unemployment in the United States*, Chicago, 1964.

219. Zarnowitz, V., "Cyclical Aspects of Incorporations and the Formation of New Business Enterprises," in G. H. Moore (ed.), *Business Cycle Indicators*, Princeton for NBER, 1961, Vol. I, pp. 386–419.
220. Zelnik, M., "Estimates of Annual Births and Birth Rates for the White Population of the United States from 1855 to 1934," unpublished doctoral dissertation, Princeton University, October 1958.

INDEX